VIEW OF THE CITY OF DUNFERMLINE FROM THE S.E.

REMINISCENCES

OF

DUNFERMLINE

AND NEIGHBOURHOOD,

*ILLUSTRATIVE OF DUNFERMLINE
LIFE, SIXTY YEARS AGO.*

BY

ALEXANDER STEWART.

WITH CHRONOLOGICAL APPENDIX,
1064-1880.

EDINBURGH:
SCOTT & FERGUSON, AND J. MENZIES & CO.
LONDON: SIMPKIN, MARSHALL, & CO.
1886.

" *Like the odour of brine from the ocean,*
  Comes the thought of other years."—LONGFELLOW.

" *Tell me the tales that to me were so dear,*
  Long, long ago—long, long ago."—BAYLY.

EDINBURGH: PRINTED BY SCOTT AND FERGUSON.

PREFATORY NOTE.

A considerable portion of the following *Reminiscences* of the Author's native city, Dunfermline, Fifeshire, appeared from time to time in the columns of the *Dunfermline Saturday Press*, but many important and additional incidents and sketches of life and character have since been added.

They treat of the Dunfermline and its neighbourhood of modern times, and they date back, for the most part, fifty-five or sixty years; but several of the incidents referring to an earlier period have been told to the writer by friends who have long since passed away.

The particular field he has attempted to occupy is a wide one, for perhaps no town in Britain excelled Dunfermline fifty or sixty years ago for the number of its intelligent, thrifty, shrewd, good-living people, many of whom were quaint in their ways, and out of the common run.

These *Reminiscences* are now gathered together in book form, at the request of various friends, who have expressed a desire to see them in this shape, and they are the writer's first attempt at sustained literary work.

The book is made up of numerous homely shreds and patches, but if it is found capable of yielding a gleam of sunshine, or giving pleasure to any human heart for a passing hour or so of life's brief journey, the thought of this will be to him a sufficient reward.

ALEXANDER STEWART.

FALKLAND ROAD, EGREMONT,
        CHESHIRE.

CONTENTS.

LIST OF ILLUSTRATIONS.

ERRATUM.

Page 3, line 23, *for* "July" *read* "June."

Dunfermline in the Olden Time.

◆◆

DUNFERMLINE! thy ruins grim and old
Could many a wondrous tale unfold
Of monarch and monk and gallant knight,
Vanished and gone as a dream of night!

Thy stately chambers welcome no more
The royal guest and the priest of yore;
Nor the weary pilgrim from distant clime,
Who sought thy shade in the olden time.

Gone are the men who at eventide,
In thy festive halls sat side by side;
No more thine altars and cloisters dim
Echo the morning and evening hymn.

The solemn chant and the fervent prayer,
Not weekly, but daily, ascended there;
Nor grudged they an hour from worldly strife
To breathe the air of the better life.

Ignorance all, and blindness indeed!—
Screams he of the dark and narrow creed;
Forgetting that darkness, vice, and crime,
Rage rampant now as in olden time.

In our feverish day of toil and strife,
With scarce a thought for the other life,
With quenchless thirst for perishing gold,
Say—Where do we rival our sires of old?

In ages hence, when our days shall be
The days of a past antiquity,
What if it be that our boasted light
Is reckoned as naught but the gloom of night;

Or, at best, as but the glimmering ray
Of morning dawn preceding the day;
Of better times the herald and birth,
The hope of a glorious age to earth?

Then revered be the men of the olden day,
Who have shed some gleams o'er life's highway;
Withhold from them not the gen'rous meed
That belongs to the high and the noble deed.

DUNFERMLINE! to thee in sacred trust
Is given the keeping of royal dust;
Nor deem that thy charge scant honour brings,
To treasure the dust of Scottish kings!

A noble and honoured name is thine,
Thou ancient city—Dunfermline;
Oh! may thy sons, where'er they be,
Remember, cherish, and honour thee!

(In the *Scotsman*, March 8th, 1866.)

Before giving the following reminiscences, it may perhaps not be out of place to refer the general reader very briefly to what the city of Dunfermline has been in former ages.

Some centuries before the time when Malcolm Canmore and Queen Margaret reigned here, there appears to have been a Culdee settlement in this place. The Culdees, whose founder was Columba, the Abbot of Iona in the sixth century, and whose doctrines and discipline differed in some respects from the Church of Rome, were amongst the first teachers of Christianity in Scotland. The name Culdee, which is Celtic, means a "*servant*" or "*attendant of God.*"

After that period, and upwards of eight hundred years ago, Dunfermline figured very prominently in Scottish history. It was then the royal residence of Malcolm III., or Canmore (who was the contemporary of William the Conqueror), and of his saintly consort, Margaret, a most beautiful and affectionate woman, for whom Malcolm cherished unbounded love and reverence. Here it was that they founded in 1075 a magnificent Abbey or Metropolitan Church, "the largest and fairest in the land" at that time. Here it was that they reared their large family. It was in Dunfermline where David II., James I. of Scotland, Charles I., and his sister, afterwards the Queen of Bohemia (from whom her present Gracious Majesty, Queen Victoria, is descended), were born. Here also (although, alas! with only one exception, there is nothing visible to indicate the fact) were interred within the old Abbey walls Malcolm III. and his beloved Queen Margaret, also King Edgar, their son, and his brother Edward, Alexander I., and David I., and likewise Malcolm IV. Here, too, Alexander III., and Margaret, his consort, and their sons, found an honoured resting-place, and also the mother of Scotland's greatest and noblest patriot, Sir William Wallace.

Beneath the pulpit of the present Church lie the remains of King Robert Bruce, the hero of that eventful day for Scotland, the 24th of July 1314; he who that day at Bannockburn, along with his small but devoted band of 30,000 Scottish patriots, pledged to death or victory, successfully overthrew 100,000 English troops under Edward II., and gained the freedom and the independence of their native land. Probably all the details connected with that most eventful and decisive battle were arranged in Dunfermline after much anxious thought and care. King Robert Bruce lies here, because no place of greater honour could then be found in Scotland ; likewise his heroic Queen Elizabeth and their daughter. Here, too, lie the remains of Annabella Drummond, Queen of Robert III., and mother of James I., and also those of several other noble and distinguished persons in Church and State. It appears that, in all, there were interred within Dunfermline Abbey eight Kings, five Queens, eight Princes and Princesses, likewise several Abbots, warriors and patriots, "men of light and leading" in their day and generation, who had fought and bled in defence of fatherland, and whose names would be household words in Scotland in the olden time. Three of the above personages were canonised as Saints, viz., St. Malcolm, St. Margaret, and St. David.

Dr. Samuel Johnson, on visiting the Island of Iona, says,—"*That man is little to be envied whose patriotism would not gain force upon the plain of Marathon, or whose piety would not grow warmer among the ruins of Iona.*" The same may well be said of the ancient city of Dunfermline, which, after Iona, was by Malcolm Canmore constituted the *Locum Sepulturæ Regium*, the *Campo Sancto* or Holy Field, where the greatest in the land were interred for centuries.

Above all, here it was that in olden times the light of Christianity shone when all around was dark. Dunfermline is said to have been "a centre of civilising

RUINS OF THE ABBEY CHOIR, AULD KIRK, &c., DUNFERMLINE

CIRCA A.D. 1670.

(From Old Sketches and Plans.)

and Christian influence when Edinburgh was a rude fortress looking down upon woods and marshes." It was in fact after this period that Edinburgh rose into any importance, and its strong Castle was selected as the only proper place of security for the Royal household, and for Government offices, such as the Mint, &c. It was not until the year 1436 that Edinburgh became the recognised Capital of Scotland.

Dunfermline, with its ancient Abbey and its old associations, its stately Palace ruins, and the crumbling remains of its once magnificent Fraters' Hall, where many a kingly banquet was held, and its vast and hospitable Monastery, carry us back to a period when distinguished persons of this and other lands assembled there, and when great numbers of pilgrims flocked from foreign shores to worship at the shrine of Saint Margaret, and neath the venerable shade of our city's highly distinguished and far-famed sanctuary.

> Here pilgrims flocked from many a shore,
> To seek thy shade, renowned of yore,
> The patriot prince, and lady fair,
> And mitred abbot, and priest were there.
>
> 'Neath the vaulted dome were heard to rise
> The morning and evening sacrifice,
> The wailing dirge for a spirit gone,
> Or the chimes of joy as the years rolled on.
>
> But ne'er shall the outcast in want or pain
> At thy monastery find a welcome again ;
> Where never a suppliant was denied,
> At morning, or noon, or eventide.

All gone to their doom the men of old ;
O ! life's sad tale, thou art briefly told ;
A name writ on sand, or a fleet moonbeam,
A passing ripple on time's swift stream !

All gone are they from our praise or blame,
From the tongue of hate or the blaze of fame ;
Each passing hour we, too, are borne
On to the dawn of "the coming morn."

REMINISCENCES OF DUNFERMLINE.

SOCIAL LIFE.

WHAT a wonderful distance have we not travelled since
the days when Malcolm Canmore and his beloved consort,
the saintly Queen Margaret, reigned in Dunfermline, eight
hundred years ago! What amazing changes have taken
place since then, not only in the aspect of the entire
country, but also more especially in the social condition
and material circumstances of the people of Scotland, and
throughout Europe!

Formerly the royal and honoured abode of the kings,
princes, and patriots of Scotland, this ancient city is
known in these modern days for its extensive linen manu-
factures and damask weaving. It has always, however,
had the great honour of standing in the very front rank,
and been distinguished for taking a leading part in all the
ecclesiastical, social, and political movements of the day.

Few manufacturing towns present such a thriving, well-
to-do aspect as this city now does. May it long continue to
prosper in the future as it has done in the past!

Between fifty and sixty years ago the bulk of the
dwelling-houses in Dunfermline were of one storey, and
had red-tiled roofs; very few were slated, and many of
them in the outskirts of the town were thatched. The
streets then had a quaint and old-fashioned look about
them, compared to what they have now. Outside stairs
were very common all over the town. At a somewhat
earlier period, those outside stairs were so common, that in
the Cross Wynd there was only about six feet left in the
centre of the street for pedestrians and street traffic.
Instead of the causeway and footpaths being nicely and

evenly paved and kept clean, they were laid with large
whinstone boulders ("petrified kidneys," as they were sometimes called), which made locomotion difficult, and the
roads uncomfortable for man and beast to pass over. In
consequence of the deep ruts everywhere, holding in solution in numerous pools fluid garbage of every kind, there
was great difficulty in keeping the highways and byways
clean. Street drainage was then unknown. The supply
of water was also very scarce in summer time, and in dry
seasons there was often quite a dearth of this inestimable
blessing.

The ordinary every-day aspect of the streets was very
different from what it is now. At present large crowds
of workers, the bulk of them young women, may be
observed at stated times during the day going in large
groups to and returning from the various factories (the
most of them fresh and healthy looking and comfortably
dressed), the sound of the factory steam whistles warning
them that time is up. Nothing of this kind was seen sixty
years ago, for the hand-looms were then spread over almost
every street in the town. At that period heads enveloped
in striped or scarlet woollen nightcaps, or broad blue
bonnets, or women with their *sow-back mutches*, short-gowns
and wincey dresses, might be observed peering out of doors
at different times of the day; and here and there, at street
corners, especially at the meal hours, groups of men would
be seen leisurely smoking, and sometimes discussing with
great vigour and intelligence the political affairs of the
nation. On all hands there were to be found men going
to the different warehouses with their cuts of cloth on
their shoulders, or returning therefrom carrying warps or
weft, or women laden with bobbins or yarn.

There was one special feature in which the aspect of the
streets differed greatly from those of the present day, viz.,
the large number of women and young persons that used
to be seen going at all hours to the public pipes and wells
for water. Women carrying wooden "stoups" and pitchers
were continually seen going for their daily supplies. Neither
can we see now the hosts of little children called *pirn*

cadgers, going "a tentie errand" to some neighbour's shop, carrying in an old "pirn hat" the supplies to keep the looms going. All this is changed!

Hand-loom weaving was the almost universal industry pursued, and when trade was prosperous, Dunfermline then possessed as contented, as intellectual, and as prudent and careful a class of working-men as could be found anywhere in Great Britain. In passing up or down the streets, by day or night, the "swish" of the weaver's shuttle, and the heavy thud of the "lay" were constantly heard; and also the sound of the bobbining and pirn-wheels on all sides. Those who were "eident" at their work were in course of time rewarded by becoming the owners of a loom or two, and in many instances they afterwards became possessors of their own dwellings. The knowledge that in course of time, by thrift and industry, they had a good chance of owning their looms and dwelling-house, was a very great incentive to exertion and self-denial. They generally lived in a but-an'-ben, while the loom shop was adjoining. This was a homely and comfortable arrangement, for in many cases the wives and daughters were as industrious as the men, in filling pirns, bobbining, &c.; and they were thus within hail if the supply of pirns ran short. In passing up or down the streets it was a common thing to hear the weavers singing at work, and now and again impatiently shout with all their might the word "*pir-rans*" from the shop to their wives in the kitchen or upstairs. If this did not do, they had an opportunity and a pretext, if they wished it, of having a "crack" with the wife, a "quiet reek o' the pipe," and a little breathing time with her and the children at the fireside now and again during the day. Sometimes they would pay a visit to their little gardens, to see and to smell their beds of pretty flowers. There was then, as there is now, great competition amongst them as to who could rear the most perfect specimens of vegetables and flowers. Some of the tulip and dahlia beds were unmatched anywhere. This was a very pleasant variety to the otherwise monotonous round of labour of the hand-loom weavers. In those days

they enjoyed far greater freedom of action, and far greater
independence, when trade was good, than what the factory
workmen can now enjoy. They could take half a day or
a whole day for recreation, or for public or private business,
whenever it suited them to do so. For this indulgence
they could prepare beforehand by extra exertions, and if
necessary, by working longer time.

In contrasting former days with the present, it must be
borne in mind that Dunfermline was bound to go forward as
a manufacturing town, in the direction indicated by the
times. The days of hand-loom weaving are for ever past;
but still there is no doubt that the weavers of a past generation enjoyed life as well as, if not infinitely better than,
those cooped up in factories can now lay claim to, notwithstanding the higher wages of the latter, and the other
material comforts they possess. The average rate of wages
was small, but the tastes and habits of the people were simple
and plain, and their wants few. Many of them were patterns of industry and good sense, and it was the constant
aim of most of them to keep out of debt, and to make a
respectable appearance at kirk or market on the little
they had. In their humble mode of living, with its poor
surroundings, there was nothing approaching the squalor
seen in some of our modern cities and towns, or anything
in their habits of a degrading tendency. Unlike many
highly paid English mechanics, with their one suit of
moleskin, the most of those men had a respectable suit of
clothes for Sabbath wear, which was most carefully
brushed and laid past in the "kist" or drawer till the next
"day of rest" came round. The solemn injunction to
young folks often was, "*Don't wear your Sabbath day claes
on your ilka day's back.*" Spinning-wheels might be seen
in many dwellings, and webs of home-made linen and
harn were often provided in advance of what was required,
and were then bleached at some burn side. Many of them
had abundance of vegetables from their ain "kail-yaird," and
a "Sandy Campbell" (pig) for "kitchen" about Hairst Fair
or Martinmas time. There was also, in almost every household, the kebbock of cheese, and some meal in the awmrie

or girnel. In the matter of eggs, they were plentiful, cheap, and "new born." They did not need to go to France and other places for eggs and vegetables, as we do now-a-days. Bannocks of whole flour or barley meal, scones of pease meal, "farrels" and cakes of oat meal,—these formed the common fare, and more wholesome or nutritious food could not be found. The fine, healthy, sound teeth of the old people generally proved this. They had also fresh, honest, unadulterated butter; butterine and oleomargarine, and such chemical abominations, were then unheard of. Luxury in eating and drinking was almost unknown : the produce of their own country was the almost universal fare. Tea was not greatly used, for the price forbade its use. It cost 6s. to 7s. per pound, and sugar 8d. and 10d., and both were often of a coarse and inferior description. The style of living when trade was good was plain, substantial, and healthful : "They seasoned meat wi' health instead o' spice."

A great many worthy and intelligent workmen were, like some of the brilliant luminaries of the *Edinburgh Review,* under the necessity of "cultivating literature," and doing other work, "on a little oatmeal" in those days. One of the greatest and deepest thinkers, and also one of the most powerful writers the present age has produced, whose name is a household word in Europe and America (Thomas Carlyle), has left it on record that in his father's house the family, when by themselves, "lived for months on porridge and potatoes, with no other condiment than what our own cow yielded ;" and he adds, "Thus are we not now all beggars, as the most like us have become." Sowens were then also occasionally used as an article of diet. This dish was made from the bran of oatmeal. It was steeped in tepid water, and allowed to stand till it became slightly sour. When afterwards well boiled, it took the consistency and appearance of blanc-mange, and when eaten with fresh good milk was of easy digestion, and most suitable for those suffering from dyspepsia, and so it was that—

"Buirdly chiels and clever hizzies,
Were reared in sic a way as this is."

Oatmeal was then the staple article of food for old and young. They were well off who had always a good supply of this food, and hence the old proverb, "*May the moose ne'er leave your awmrie wi' the tear in its e'e!*"

Some of the weavers, but more especially the country weavers, went for four or five weeks to the harvest-field in autumn, and engaged in shearing and binding. Very few of them ever went to sea as "winter weavers and summer sailors." The harvest-field was an enjoyable and healthful change from the sedentary life they led. Reaping, mowing, and binding machines were then unknown; all was done by the sickle and by hand labour. In the autumn mornings and evenings large bands of men and women might be seen going to and returning from the harvest fields, carrying their sickles over their arms, gay and light-hearted, singing lively songs on their way; the women dressed in their shearer's garb, most of them barefooted, and some with huggers on, and having on their heads gaily striped and ample cotton caps to protect them from the blazing sun. The toil was great, but the most of the shearers were young and light-hearted, and the prospect of their hard-won, substantial "hairst fee" was cheering to look forward to. To the most of them the fee was of signal benefit, for £2 or so in those days was a sum far greater in reality than what the same amount would be regarded now. This field labour was to some rather severe, but on the whole it was healthful and invigorating to most of them. In the wake of the shearers came bands of boys and girls to gather, as it was called. Those gleaners were generously allowed by the farmers to pick up what they could honourably glean off the stubble fields. In many cases large bundles of "singles" used to be carried home every evening to many a fireside, to be afterwards ground into meal. This healthful industry has now ceased, for by the aid of machinery crops are now expeditiously cut down and carefully gathered in. The farmers, I suppose, acted on the injunction given in Leviticus, chapter 19th—"Thou shalt not wholly reap the corners of thy field, neither shalt thou gather the gleaning of thy harvest; thou shalt leave them for the poor and stranger."

KIRSTY'S FIRST HAIRST.

" Come awa', Kirsty,
    Keep up your rig,
Hungry or thirsty,
    Care nae a fig :
Push in the sickle,
    An' dinna be slack
At crookin' your elbow
    An' bendin' your back.

" Haud laigh wi' the stubble,
    Cut canny and clean,
There's nought withoot trouble,—
    Ye mauna compleen :
Keep up your credit,
    You're somebody noo ;
In wi' the sickle,
    An' let us get through."

G. Webster.

There was at that period a number of weavers who did " customer " work. They lived principally in the country places in the neighbourhood, and worked for private families. The produce of the spinning-wheels was given to the " customer " weaver to make into sheets, bed ticking, &c. &c., and some of the cloth then made would often last for two or three generations. There was also a good deal of flax cultivated about seventy or eighty years ago. It was the custom in some parts of the country to allow every married farm-servant or hind a tenth part of an acre of ground to be sown with flax for home use. In those days there were a large number of hecklers, or flax-dressers, as they were called, who dressed the flax and prepared it for spinning. After it was spun into yarn it was bought up by yarn merchants. The produce of the spinning-wheels long ago was in many cases the only means of subsistence to a large number of women. There were also tambouring-frames to be seen in many houses, which gave employment to many unmarried females in the town. This work was for a long time pretty well remunerated, but the introduction of steam power and the changing fashions gradually extinguished the domestic spinning-wheel and the tambouring-frame.

GREAT STAGNATION IN TRADE.

UNFORTUNATELY the people of Dunfermline were then subjected to periodical and great depressions of trade, and much suffering was the result, especially to those who did not succeed in laying past anything for a "rainy day." Thanks to our Free Trade policy, our swift steamers, our railways, new markets are being continually opened up in our numerous colonies and in all parts of the world, and those periodical calamities have been for many years of less frequent occurrence.

One of the severest trade depressions that ever visited Dunfermline occurred in the winter of 1837-38. The weaving population suffered greatly. But although this was the case, and a large sum of money was charitably raised by subscription, in order to give them work in repairing and improving the streets and roads about the town, comparatively few availed themselves of the work or of the supply of provisions offered. Although about 800 persons were reported as out of their usual employment, strange to say, there were found only about forty men and sixty boys who applied for work on the roads! The outdoor work was no doubt somewhat unsuited for men accustomed to an indoor occupation, but still the above speaks much for the independence of spirit that prevailed, and showed their abhorrence of anything like the acceptance of public charity, and also the thrifty, saving, self-denying habits of the working-classes. Many of them must have suffered great privations during that dark period, and their daily bill of fare must have been poor indeed. As for looking to a poorhouse or living on charity, as their natural inheritance at the end of life's journey (as many now-a-days do), that was a humiliation never for a moment to be thought of. The Rev. Charles Marshall expresses correctly the universal feeling that prevailed—

> " Our mither a pauper !—she brought us a' up,
>   Behauden to no one, except to her God ;
> Sae lang as God spares her, my awmrie, my cup,
>   Are hers, till her auld head sleeps under the sod."

With regard to the appearance of the shops of the grocers, cloth merchants, &c., they were small, close, and stuffy places as a rule, with small windows, totally unlike what they are now. There was very little attempt made to attract customers by a show of business, or by anything in the way of advertising or puffing. The only temptation was a *greybeard*, which the drapers in those days kept in their back shops to treat customers, especially those from the country, and to stimulate the purchasing powers. This questionable practice was given up by mutual consent. All was comparative quiet and monotonous from day to day, except on a fair or market day, when the Nethertown was full of roaring cattle for sale, and the Maygate crowded from end to end with shoe-stalls and shoemakers from all parts of the country. On such days the High Street was filled with carts having all kinds of produce, stalls with gingerbread, sweeties, and toys in great variety, and with water-stoups, tubs, and bickers, and all kinds of crockery. Great crowds were moving about in holiday garb; the noise made by "Cheap Johns," and men rubbing earthenware bowls together in order to attract customers to their wares, was something deafening to listen to.

At night the aspect of the streets during the winter months was very gloomy. On the counters of the shops, or in the windows, one tallow candle, or perhaps two at most, glimmered sickly in the darkness.

GOD-FEARING MEN.

THE New Road (now known as Moodie Street, and so named after Provost Moodie), as well as many other streets in the town, had within them the abodes of many excellent working-people, many of them quaint in their ways and appearance, and many who were known and honoured as God-fearing men. Although they earned their bread by the sweat of their brow, many of them possessed a quiet and dignified appearance and manner, and were truthful and sincere in their ways. Some of the old patriarchs were most consistent, good-living men, and their presence at a sick or dying bed was often sought after and welcomed. Never a meal was partaken of in their humble dwellings without first a blessing being asked upon it, and afterwards thanks returned, as was the usual custom of the time. This was often done with great reverence, unction, and power, and there was sometimes a peculiar and beautiful quaintness in their utterances, such as—"Early were we *cuissen* (cast) upon Thy care, yet hitherto hast Thou cared for us." To the young they readily offered a word of warning, and they were free with such advices as the following:—" *Ye're a fine callant, the Lord gie ye grace;*" "*Ever pray for an honest through-bearing;*" "*Haud forrit*" (hold forward); "*Dinna read novells,*" &c., &c. To those young people who were leaving the parent roof in order to push their way in the world, they were ever ready with their sage and fatherly counsels. Those counsels were embraced in the words of our townsman, the Rev. Charles Marshall:—

> " Be carefu' o' thy master's gear,
>   Beneath thy hand let naething tyne,
> Betimes repair the tear an' wear,
>   Mind this—' *A steek in time saves nine.*' "

> " To mak' thee blythe 's the mornin' lark,
>   To keep baith head and heart in tune,
> In God's great name begin thy wark,
>   An' thank God when thy wark is dune."

The older men usually wore on their heads red or striped Kilmarnock nightcaps, and many of the women had a pride in their clean, snow-white " sow-back mutches." Many of the men wore knee-breeches, and on Sundays had long-tailed blue coats with gilt buttons. Some of those coats were of fine quality, and of durable, honest materials, and had often to do duty for a generation or so. In many cases

> " Granny was drest in her best Sunday gown,
>   That very same gown at her wedding she wore."

Married women were all known by their maiden names, as Tibby Henderson, Betty Black, &c.

In Moodie Street several of the Trades' Deacons resided, and several elders belonging to different churches in the town. It was a very common thing to hear rising from many of the humble dwellings all over the town the strains of family worship, when one passed up or down the streets between nine and ten o'clock, morning or evening :—

> " Oh, little Bethle'm ! poor in walls,
>   But rich in furniture."

In some of those small abodes, with their clean-washed, uncarpeted floors, and bright cheery hearths,

> " Nearness to God, with its untold power,"

was the pervading desire of many of the inmates. It is told that London merchants coming to make purchases from the manufacturers were occasionally to be seen pacing up and down the streets of a morning, waiting till the family worship was over, and an opportunity given them to make purchases. How the times have altered, how the tables are turned now, and how the American and other buyers are waited upon, welcomed, and caressed !

It was then an extraordinary event when a manufacturer ventured to go to London on business. It was not unusual for him to have the prayers of the congregation to which he belonged for a safe and prosperous voyage amidst the perils of the deep, even although that voyage was only betwixt Leith and London in a sailing smack—"God willing," and "Wind and weather permitting." Even on the River Clyde, before steamers were introduced, there was no way of getting down to Rothesay or Greenock except by boats with sails. Sometimes passengers would have to wait day after day for a week until the wind changed! A voyage to London would sometimes occupy four or even five weeks, if the winds were stormy and contrary. Contrast the ease, comfort, and expedition of a voyage or a railway journey to London now, compared to what they were then! It was a common thing for those who had such a long journey before them to make their Wills previous to venturing on their undertakings. The following extract is given as a specimen of what was recorded in the Will of a gentleman who was about to embark from Leith to London in the beginning of the last century, viz. :—

"Be it kend till all men be thir present letters, me, Thomas D——, forasmeikle as I am, God willing, presentlie boun furth of this Realme towards Londone, for doing of my necessary affairs and business, and being for the present haill in bodie and spirit, praisit be God, and that knowand nothing mair certain than death, and nothing mair incertane than the hour, tyme, and plaice thairof, I now mek my testament, legacie, and lattre will, as efter follows. In the first, I recommend my saull to the protection of Almichtie God, my Creator, and hopes to be saweid throw the merits of Jesus Chryst, my blessed Saviour and Redeemer. And as for my worldlie affairs, I declair hereby that I nominate and ordain, &c. &c. &c.

STYLE OF LIVING.

As regarded the usual style of living, the manufacturers, as a rule, lived in a manner noway superior to that of many of our mechanics of the present day. One of the smaller manufacturers was asked one day if he had got his dinner. "*Oo ay, I've haen baith roasted an' biled the day.*" He meant that he had roasted herrings and boiled potatoes! In many respects, they did not enjoy the material comforts that modern well-paid mechanics can now boast of. The exceptions to this were very few. When times were prosperous, the hand-loom weavers, and not the manufacturers, were in point of fact masters of the situation, and the services of a good weaver were often eagerly sought after and much appreciated by the employers.

To show the primitive customs of the times, it may be mentioned that one of the Dunfermline manufacturers named Mr. Wilson took a quantity of oatmeal with him to make his own brose on the voyage to London! Those were the days when the Glasgow carrier intimated to his customers that he would "go to Glasgow, God willing and weather permitting, on Monday, but on Tuesday whether or no!" None but the most opulent citizens with cultivated and aspiring tastes had such a rarity as a piano in their houses. As regarded watches, for example, there are now perhaps more gold watches worn in Dunfermline than were in the whole of Scotland sixty or seventy years ago! Many persons could well afford the expense, but it was looked upon as almost a crime to throw "guid siller awa'" in this reckless manner. They had the town clock, and so they were satisfied with what are usually termed "turnips" or old verges, good sonsy watches of silver or pinchbeck, though unfortunately they were often in the hands of such as Henry Ogg or Peter Penman for repairs. To the watches were attached metal chains, coins, shells, &c., which hung from the fob in a stylish manner. Some

of the people I remember could sometimes tell the time
of day with considerable exactness by noting the passing
shadows made by the sun on their door-steps.

MASTER AND SERVANT.

There was then not a single factory in Dunfermline
worthy of the name, and the manufacturers stood in
a more primitive position towards their employees than
the same class do now—more on a footing of equality
with them. As an example of this, it may be mentioned
that Mr. Spence went one day into the shop of one of his
weavers who happened to be a deacon. He made some
remark to the deacon about the "spring" on his web, and
expressed an opinion that it was not quite suitable. The
deacon did not like the remark, and his dignity was
touched, so he told his employer that he was wrong, and
that he (the deacon) "kent about 'springs' lang afore he
(Mr. Spence) was able to dicht his ain neb!" Another case
was that of a man who took his web to the warehouse. At
that time birds were much in vogue in damask patterns,
and the manufacturer who examined the web, and who
himself had a squint in his eyes, found fault with the
cloth, and said that the eyes of the birds could scarcely be
seen. To this he replied that, " There's some folks has a
waur squint in their e'en than my birds hae!"

DUNFERMLINE POST-OFFICE.

THE following lines appeared in the Dunfermline newspaper of the time, and they are worthy of being preserved :—

> " There's Sandy M'Phail has carried the post
>   In winter and summer, in rain, snaw, and frost,
>   Through the streets o' Dumfarlin' for twenty long years,
>   A herald o' happiness, sadness, and tears !
>
> " Ah ! little kens Sandy, as *he* sallies forth,
>   Wi' his bundle o' letters frae south an' frae north,
>   The hearts that are beatin', depressed or elate,
>   For the news that maybe determine their fate.
>
> " How aft has a puir mither run to the door
>   For the long looked-for letter, wi' hope brimmin' o'er,
>   An' started wi' horror to see the black seal
>   On the letter that's brocht her by Sandy M'Phail.
>
> " An' mony a maid feels her heart beatin' fast,
>   An' the tear fills her e'e when Sandy gangs past ;
>   Or if there's a letter, her blushes reveal
>   The dear treasured secret she fain wad conceal.
>
> " An' puir working folk, fashed wi' trouble an' debt
>   To grocer or baker that canna be met,
>   Would far rather taickle a ghost or a deil
>   Than a lawyer's epistle frae Sandy M'Phail !
>
> " Sae lang may auld Sandy trot o'er the plainstanes,
>   Lang may a kind Providence guard his auld banes ;
>   When able nae langer to earn maut or meal,
>   May Rowland Hill pension auld Sandy M'Phail !"

Between fifty and sixty years ago the Post-Office was a
very primitive establishment as compared to the one now
in the High Street. Letters were carried to and from
Dunfermline in large canvas wallets slung on horseback,
and the post-boy carried a long tin horn to herald the
approach and departure of the Royal Mail. For some
years Mr. Andrew Angus, printer, was postmaster, and
after he died in 1833 he was succeeded in that office by
his daughter, who had been his assistant. The Post-Office
was then in the Kirkgate, and it was a place of small
dimensions. Miss Angus was postmistress till 1851, when
she was succeeded by Mr. Steedman, who for thirty years
faithfully filled the office of postmaster. She was a most

anxious and painstaking public servant. She was very sharp, and a most intelligent woman, and what one would call quite a lady in her ways. Perhaps she might be considered too particular and too exacting, but she was highly conscientious, and had the best interests both of H.M. Service and also the public at heart. During her tenure of office the service was a slow-going affair compared to what it is now. She was for a number of years assisted by her brother George, a very worthy man; but he ultimately got so infirm with rheumatism that he had to relinquish his post. For some years he had to rise from his bed at midnight to receive the mails, and despatch them by the young lad who had come on horseback from Queensferry, and who then galloped, booted and spurred, with his bags for the west.

Let the present young and rising generation mark and consider well the following:—There was then no penny post, and the postage was so high that thousands of letters, invoices, &c. were sent in parcels and by private favour. There were no money or postal orders issued, no Post-Office savings banks, no registered letters, no parcel post, and no postage stamps or post cards issued. That marvellous and inestimable blessing, telegraphic and telephonic communication, was unknown and utterly undreamt of. The letters of soldiers and men-o'-war's men were *franked* by some nobleman or high official, and this was a boon which saved the expense of postage at home or abroad. This was abolished in 1840. Through the agency of the telegraph, news from all ends of the earth is now brought, silent as thought, while we are quietly taking our night's rest! Letters to or from Edinburgh cost from 5d. to 7d. each, to or from London 1s. 3d. if single, but if double letters the cost was greater. One sheet of either pott or foolscap was considered a single letter; if a half-sheet were enclosed, the rate of postage was doubled. I remember well of seeing the Post-Office officials looking through the letters by means of an ivory folder, to see if they were single or double, in order to charge them accordingly. Sixty years ago there was only one letter-carrier for the town ; her name was Peacock, and I remember she carried her letters in a small black silk hand-bag. Annie Couper, Miss Angus' domestic servant, succeeded Peacock as letter-carrier.

A lady friend of the writer's lately told him that she remembered seeing the letter-carrier, while delivering letters from house to house, sit down at the people's firesides and have a quiet chat as she leisurely went along on her onerous duties. And yet the folks used to say, when they saw any one in a hurry, "they were going *post haste !*"

There were then no swift steamers defying wind and tide, no network of railways such as we have now on all hands, and there was no special haste in the transmission of mails or in the delivery of them ; a few hours sooner or later did not matter so much as in these go-a-head times of ours. Wind and tide were matters of vital consideration, and it was an event of frequent occurrence for mails to be detained for hours in consequence of the stormy state of the Firth of Forth.

It was a very common thing for people to address their letters, " *With care,*" sometimes " *With haste,*" and in some instances " *With haste and care.*" Envelopes were never used, because then unknown. Letters sealed with wax usually bore the impression of the watch seals which used to hang imposingly from gentlemen's watch-fobs. Some ladies were content to use their thimbles or a sixpence. The writer remembers well the case of a man in Limekilns who had lost his child, and had sent out funeral letters inviting friends to the funeral. The large black wax was sealed, inadvertently and unthinkingly no doubt, with his watch seal, which bore upon it the figure of a cock, and the startling motto, " *While I live I'll crow !*"

Up till about the year 1840, when Rowland Hill's uniform rate of postage was fully inaugurated, and postage stamps were introduced, the business of the Post-Office was carried on in a quiet and easy-going fashion ; but after that period this department of the public service awoke up with amazing energy, and other nations followed in our wake. The rapid extension of the railway system and the great increase of steam ships, combined with the introduction of the telegraph, have given enormous facilities for the transmission of correspondence and of news to all parts of the world. The book-post branch was established in 1848; the money order department was in existence many years before that. In 1839 the total amount transmitted throughout the three kingdoms by Post-Office orders from all the various Post-Offices was only £313,000; in 1863 it was £16,494,000! It is very large now, being £24,223,295 in 1885. As regards postal orders, £646,989 was transmitted in 1881; and in 1885 £18,831,104! At the time Mr. Steedman was appointed postmaster the postal department of this country was just beginning to develop, and has gone on increasing ever since. The small premises in the Kirkgate were soon found quite inadequate for the transaction of the ever-increasing business, and the department was moved to Guildhall Street, where it was carried on for some years, till that place also became unsuited for the purpose. It seems that even now, in the larger premises in the High Street, they are greatly hampered for want of room, and no doubt some other place may by and by have to be provided.

Through the kindness of the late and the present post-masters, I am enabled to give the following statistics of the Dunfermline Post-Office :—

Officials Employed.

1826.		1845.		1885.	
Postmaster,	1	Postmistress,	1	Postmaster,	1
Assistant,	1	Assistant,	1	Clerks, telegraphists,	
Letter - carrier (the		Letter-carriers,	2	letter-carriers, and	
domestic servant),	1	Rural do.	3	messengers,	28
Total,	3	Total,	7	Total,	29

Business.

1851.		1875.		1885.	
Number of letters delivered weekly,	4700	Letters, &c. per week,	16,112	Letters, papers, cards, &c. per last return, 29,218 in the week.	

The annual amount of revenue has also correspondingly increased.

LIGHTING OF THE STREETS, DWELLINGS, &c.

FIFTY-FIVE years ago there was no gas in the town.
The streets were lit up with lamps here and there, placed
at wide intervals, and they were furnished with train oil
and cotton wick. The feeble glimmer they struggled to
send forth only served to make the darkness visible. After
burning for a few hours in a sickly way, the lamp-
lighter, with his ladder over his shoulder, went his rounds
and *blew* them out. In dwelling-houses and shops,
candles, called long sixes or short sixes, long or short eights,
tens, &c., also oil lamps, or the ancient cruisie, were used at
night. The cruisie was a very primitive lamp, having one
or perhaps sometimes two wicks ; it was fed with train oil,
and it gave a dim light and a disagreeable odour to the
house.

Churches, when used in the winter evenings, and places
for public meetings, were lit up with tallow candles, placed
in large uncouth-looking candelabra, which hung from the
ceiling by cords attached to pulleys, to enable them to be
drawn up or down. The aspect of a congregation or public
meeting was dull and gloomy in the extreme. On a Sabbath
evening the candles in the churches had to be snuffed
during the service ; and it happened sometimes, when the
beadle was an awkward hand at the business, he would
snuff out one, or sometimes two by mistake, or even occasionally knock a burning candle down upon a lady's
bonnet ! This would cause a quiet titter in the congregation, and disturb the equanimity of the minister. In other
cases, if the candles were not of good quality, or if they
were burning where there was a draught, serious damage
was often done to those sitting below the candelabra, by
the falling of grease over their heads and shoulders. An
elderly lady recently told the writer that a very handsome shawl, which had been presented to her, was found
one Sabbath morning when she was going to dress for
church to be badly stained with grease. As she was not

in the habit of going to church at night, it was discovered
that one of the servants in the house where she was staying on a visit had actually gone to the lady's trunk, taken
out the shawl, and worn it at an evening's service.
"Murder will out!"

"Oh, for the good days of old, the dip and the mould,
With the tinder-box, spunks, and the snuffers!"

There were then no fine lucifer matches, vestas, and
other similarly useful conveniences. Tinder-boxes, containing tinder made of burnt linen, along with a steel and flint,
were used to light the sulphur "spunks" with which the
fires were kindled. The tinder-box was flat, and usually
made of tin. With the steel and flint a spark was struck,
which, alighting amongst the tinder, caused it to light the
sulphur "spunk." It was a tedious way of making a fire, and
bellows were then rarely used. Numerous spunk-vendors
used to go from door to door with bundles of "spunks"
slung over their shoulders, calling out, "Are ye needin' ony
spunks the day?" This was a great industry even
then, requiring little capital and yielding good profits;
but as a class of artisans, the spunk makers, like the
makers of heather besoms, stood on a very low platform in
the community. Mostly every household had a hand
lantern for the dark nights of winter, and when those
lanterns were seen in the dark flitting along in the dim
distance in all directions, they gave the streets a weird-like
appearance. The youngsters of the present day will not
know what a "save-all" was, but the working-men of those
times, who were anxious to economise every inch of their
tallow-candles, knew well the use and the value of this
little contrivance for saving.

With all their want of artificial light, the worthy people
of those days did not break their hearts over the circumstance, for the simple reason that they neither felt the loss
nor knew the benefit of our modern improvements and comforts, and were happy with what they had. A day may likely
come when future generations will look back with pity and
amazement upon us, for having been able to exist without

the benefits of electricity as a light in our dwelling-houses, and more especially as a motive power to drive sewing-machines and washing-machines, and perform many other domestic duties. It has been remarked that "the moderns of that day are the ancients of ours, and we speculate upon *them* in this present year of grace as our children's children, a hundred years hence, will give their judgment about us." If our forefathers had no sewing-machines, garments were made simpler and plainer than at present ; and if news did not come so quickly, there was far more leisure to consider and ponder the information that was received. If there were no railway trains and tram-cars, there was in general the ability to walk long distances, and a journey of ten or twenty miles was then thought nothing of. For many of the inconveniences they suffered they were compensated in other ways, and their lives were not quite so dreary as young people of the present day would suppose.

There was then little or nothing done in Dunfermline in the way of newspaper advertising. No one was in any special haste, and people took things easy. At the same time, while they were never in a hurry, they were never idle, but always industrious. Competition was almost *nil*, and there was no need for crowing cocks and other startling newspaper illustrations and devices to attract public attention. Public intimations were universally made by the town's drummer and the bellman. The cost of the drum giving a certain fixed round was, I think, one shilling, and the bell threepence. Bell Mary flourished about sixty years ago, and Sandy Finlayson and other quaint characters succeeded her. The style of intimation differed very much, as did the different criers themselves. There was often a touch of humour and sometimes pathos in their advertisements. It might be that a lady's black silk bag had gone amissing between the "fit o' the Geelies Wynd and the Rotten Raw," or about "a wee bit bairnie that was lost this mornin', at the back o' the dam ; it had a white curly headie, an' wore a blue chacket daidlie. It is supposed that the aforesaid little bairnie had wandered after its faither when he gaed till's wark aboot the aforesaid

time.   Whoever has found the same, by returnin' it to me,
or to its *distractit pawrents*, will be weel rewardit an' paid
for their pains."   Or it might be that "there had arrived
at the Tron twa cartload o' caller haddies and green skate,
twal' pund for saxpence,—noo's the time for your bargains;"
or "there can noo be obtained every nicht, between sax an'
aucht o'clock, het penny pies an' tippenny anes, at the pie-
office, next door to Jenny Barclay's in the Kirkgate," &c. &c.

POLICE, CRIME, &c.

THERE was surely less tendency to crime half a century ago than there is now, for only one man was "town-keeper" at that time. He had, I suppose, the town drummer, or some such assistant in time of need, and also some untrained, undisciplined special constables to fall back upon in the case of a riot or extraordinary emergency. One would naturally suppose that with all the social advantages and comforts now enjoyed, our intellectual culture, our great progress in science and art, and our system of national education, the number of policemen would not require to be periodically augmented, as of late years it has been, but rather be diminished. It appears to be otherwise, for as civilisation and outward improvement, along with physical comfort and wealth, increase, so in proportion does our police force increase. Why is this? Is crime on the increase, and are thefts and burglaries more frequent? I would respectfully venture to call the attention of our School Boards to this point; also to a fact stated by a well-known politician lately, that there is now spent in this country on drink £1 per head *more* than was spent forty years ago. Some of the members of our School Boards imagine that education can do everything. I am of opinion that unless this is accompanied by wisdom, common sense, and moral training, it will be of small avail. A reverend doctor has well said that "a boy may pass every Oxford and Cambridge Local Examination, and yet be entirely deficient in those elements of character which will make him a good citizen and a useful man." We see this in every newspaper we open. The swindling by corporations, joint stock companies, banks, building societies, and the other scandals now so rife, are all perpetrated by educated men. It is not for a moment to be insinuated that education is the cause of this—nothing of the kind. Knowledge acquired in school and otherwise is calculated to have a different tendency, and to make *a good man better.* But there is a great gulf between wisdom and knowledge. "With all thy getting get understanding." Wisdom and common sense are not to be bought. Like sleep, they are not in the market.

"*To be true*—to be genuine. No education is worth anything that does not include this. A man had better not know how to read—he had better never learn a letter in the alphabet, and be true and genuine in intention and in action, rather than, being learned in all sciences and in all languages, to be at the same time false in heart and counterfeit in life."

In the old days, when the streets were so dark in the long winter nights, and while there was a population of 10,000 in the town and suburbs, including nearly 3000 hand-loom weavers, the "town-keeper" went comfortably to his bed, and neither disturbed himself or any one else, unless when occasion demanded. There was not such a regard for door and window fastenings as now. It is a fact that, eighty or a hundred years ago, in many districts of this country, houses were neither bolted nor barred. Hugh Miller mentions that the door of his uncle's house in the north was not even furnished with a lock or a bar. Chubb's locks, Milner's safes, and other contrivances, the outcome of modern civilisation, were also unknown. There are, I believe, at present *fourteen men* employed in watching and guarding the bounds of the old and venerable city, with its population of about 17,000, according to census of 1881, at a cost of about £1028 annually to the city and the imperial exchequer, which latter means the public purse, to which all are contributing daily.

NEWSPAPER AND MAGAZINE CLUBS.

ALTHOUGH there was nothing like the same extensive field of literature and knowledge opened up to the people that there is now, still the working-men were very shrewd and well read on many subjects. They were keenly observant of the progress of current events, social and political, often intensely bent on theological questions, and were severe critics of the ministers' sermons every Sabbath. When *Chambers' Journal* commenced in 1832 there were many clubs formed for reading it. It was published first on large-sized sheets, and in no other place in Scotland did it become so great a favourite and so popular as in Dunfermline.

With regard to newspapers, the *Scotsman* (which was originally published at tenpence, and appeared once a week), fifty-five years ago, cost fourpence, and was published twice a week. There were then no daily newspapers out of London. The taxes on knowledge were in full swing, and a Government red stamp, costing one penny, adorned the foot of every news-sheet. Scores of newspaper clubs abounded in the town, as very few working-men could afford to get a paper or magazine for their own separate use. Those clubs had a tendency to make the people more neighbourly in their ways than they are now. Eight or ten persons would club together to get the *Scotsman*, the *Caledonian Mercury*, or the *Courant*. Each person kept it for a couple of hours, and the entire family would arrange to hear the news read aloud while sitting round the fireside, and the paper was then passed on to the reader next in turn. The last reader in the club got the paper to keep by paying a little extra. Sometimes the papers were retained in the custody of the last reader, and at the end of the quarter were divided equally. Just fancy any one now taking the trouble of reading a newspaper two or perhaps three months old!

It has been already stated that the working-men were,

as a rule, very shrewd and intelligent. Many of them would not look at most of the books which are perused by the same class of men now. Something more substantial was desired, something to engage the thinking powers, something "to make the man a better mechanic, and the mechanic a better man." Much of the literary sponge-cake food now indulged in, and the vast amount of desultory reading, may, it is to be feared, in course of time tend to lower the mental powers, and to have a result the opposite of that which built up the characters of our forefathers, and made them a permanent power for good. Like the celebrated naturalist Thomas Edwards of Banff, and Robert Dick, geologist, of Thurso, both of them poor men, many of the old Dunfermline people had special hobbies of their own in which they excelled. Some were botanists, some ornithologists, some bee-doctors, and the most of them were great readers. The bulk of the books they read consisted of works on divinity, political economy, biography, science, voyages and travels, and there was nothing like the demand for works of fiction that now exists. All of them were keen politicians.

THRIFTY HABITS AND HEROISM.

THE working-people who lived half a century ago knew better than we do the real meaning, the desirability, and the necessity of "thrift." Those who wished to do well, and were desirous to bring up their families in an honourable and creditable manner, had, with their small wages and means, to study the art of thrift in every direction. One of the greatest compliments that could be paid to a young woman was, "She is a thrifty lassie." As already mentioned, there were many households where the spinning wheels were kept going for the purpose of making homespun garments, blankets, &c. The old well-known song in those days will be almost incomprehensible to the young of the present generation—

> " Tarry 'oo, oh tarry 'oo,
> Tarry 'oo is ill to spin ;
> Card it weel, oh card it weel,
> Card it weel ere ye begin."

It was the ambition of the young women to lay past perhaps £20 or so, which was a large sum in those times, the savings of years ; and this, with the accumulation of linen, sheeting, &c., made them more eligible for marriage, if this offered itself, or for the " garret," if such were to be their destiny.

Many people of the present day imagine that thrift consists in the mere saving up of money, and putting it into the Savings Bank or other investment. This is a mistake ; for true thrift has as much to do with the judicious *spending* of money as it has with the saving thereof. In short, it consists as much in the careful management of what one has, as in anything else. On the statue of a former M.P. for Manchester, there is the following noble inscription :—

> " My wealth consists not in the largeness of my possessions,
> But in the fewness of my wants."

True it is that while one man is rich on little, another is poor on much.

The great value and advantage of making the most of daylight was then very much appreciated. If anything could be done to save the cost of candle or oil, it was taken advantage of. Hence daylight, with its attendant blessings, was often spoken of in the following terms:—" Daylight has mony een ;" or " An hour in the mornin's worth twa at nicht ;" or " He that would thrive must rise at five ; he who has thriven may lie till seven," &c. &c.

As showing the *couthie* way in which the working-people lived when trade was good, it may suffice to say that the more thrifty of them would attend a potato roup, and purchase a few drills of potatoes, which, when taken up in October, kept the families well supplied till far on in the following spring. The " 'tattie howkin'" in October, followed by the " 'tattie maiden," or harvest home, was a great occasion to old and young. It was also a common thing for neighbours to club together and purchase amongst them a " *mairt*," and have it divided and salted about Martinmas time. The " mairt " consisted of a fat cow or ox, and when cut up each person received the share he bargained for. This served them so far with butcher meat, or " kitchen," during the winter; and those of them who had kail-yards and a sonsy pig could look forward to the approach of the long, cold winter with serenity. The " puddin' fair " in November or December was so named on account of many pigs being killed about that time of the year, when there were many puddings made and used in the households in town and country. The following lines were written by a townsman on an occasion of this kind, showing how one's friends and neighbours were all interested in the " killin' o' the soo." Presents of pudding, haggises, &c. were then freely distributed amongst each other.

> " On the twenty-third December,
>   Eighteen hunder and thirty-two,
> If my mind I do not alter,
>   Sandy Luive will kill my soo.

> " If my wife an' little bairnie
>   Should till then be keepin' well,
> Every friend an' every neighbour
>   Mark the tidings which I tell !"

On looking back upon the last half century and more, there is one circumstance which is rather striking in its way, and that is the great number of labourers who during that time have been gradually divorced from the cultivation of the soil. It is deplorable to think that while we have millions of acres of good arable land lying waste, and while our cities and towns are so congested with dense populations, and our streets and workhouses teeming with half-starved idle men, we have to go to France, Belgium, &c. for a large portion of the vegetables we consume ! Not only that, but we must also go abroad for much of the butter and cheese we require, and for the inferior and high-priced eggs we get at our breakfast tables. The tempting *fresh eggs* that used to be so plentiful are now rarely to be met with in our large cities and towns now. A very great number of the smaller cultivators of the soil have been gradually absorbed into our populous towns, and their small allotments have been taken from them and added to large sheep and other farms and deer forests. History repeats itself, and now we hear an outcry raised for "three acres and a cow." In course of time it is to be hoped that many of our unemployed town labourers may again find their way from the congested, unwholesome slums to the healthful country; but it will take a generation or two to qualify them properly for agricultural work.

Many instances of genuine thrift could be recorded in connection with the cultivation of many of those small land-patches around the neighbourhood of Dunfermline, where husband and wife, and also the children as they grew up, managed by thrift and industry to make a comfortable living, and were indebted to no one for assistance in their struggles. We have often seen them during the proper season bravely working upon their little land plots from morning till evening, carefully manuring, planting, and keeping the ground in proper order; and in consequence, the soil, ever grateful for labour bestowed upon it, repaid them well for all their care and attention. With their cow and a pig or two, and poultry, their lot—hard

though it might occasionally be—was infinitely preferable
to that of many of the ordinary town labourers. To them
their children were a real help and a blessing, as the
Almighty intended children to be; while to the labouring
classes living in the dense city slums they are not unfre-
quently regarded as "*encumbrances*," and many of them are
sent forth as recruits to swell the ranks of the city *Arabs*,
as they are called.

There is one case amongst many that might be mentioned, showing not only thrift, but true heroism. A
worthy couple, who lived not very far from Dunfermline,
brought up a large family of eight or ten children
respectably and honourably. The income of the head of
house from his loom did not exceed ten shillings per week
on an average. This, with the produce of the small croft
of land, their cow, a pig, and some poultry, formed the
entire source of their income. They were blessed with
good health, and did not sit down and whine under their
burdens and frequent difficulties, but had an earnest determination to do well, believing that "where there's a will
there's a way;" and, above all, they had a firm depen-
dence on a Higher Power than their own to help them.
One of that family was educated for the ministry, two or
three of the sons are now in excellent positions as business men, and every member of that family, male and
female, is doing well. It is not on the battlefield alone
where true heroism is to be found, for here is a case in
point, and it is not an isolated one; and I know that
similar cases are still to be met with in the neighbourhood.

The stipends of many Scottish clergymen sixty or seventy
years ago were very small; many of them did not exceed
£60 to £100 a year, with in some cases a manse and
glebe. Yet some of those manses were noted for their
hospitality. In many districts the parishioners were very
kind to their ministers, and presented them frequently
with fowls and farm and garden produce. From many of
those humble manses young lads were sent forth to college
and university with the invariable bag of oatmeal in a

corner of their boxes, and after years of brave struggle many became very distinguished men. In order to illustrate the struggles which some of the ministers in Dunfermline and neighbourhood (whom I could name) had to endure then, one or two cases, taken from other parts of the country, may be given.

The Rev. Dr. Paul of Aberdeen mentions the case of an Aberdeenshire clergyman who had a stipend of £50, with manse and glebe. On his slender means he was able to bring up respectably a family of *seventeen children.* The most of them, he informs us, "reached the age of man and woman-hood, and bore the marks of the good upbringing at the manse; and all of them prospered in the world. Some of them I knew intimately. Two of the sons, who were wood merchants and contractors for wood for the Navy, amassed very large fortunes." Such cases were frequent, and while many persons would now hold up their hands in amazement at the bare recital of such instances of true heroism, such feats of generalship and brave management were far from being uncommon in Scotland. This was rather the rule than otherwise in those old days, for Scotland was very poor. The father of the late Rev. Dr. Russell of Yarrow, who was for many years minister of Ettrick, and a man of sterling worth and ability, had only £45 a year of stipend. Out of this slender sum the "minister's man" was paid £5, and the housekeeper not much less. There was also his annual subscription to the Widows' Fund, and the upkeep of a horse, to enable him to overtake the duties of his extensive district; and he says—"*How the minister managed to keep the house above his head, and the wolf from the door, would require a conjuror to tell.*"

The style of living was then of course different from what it is now, and while there were many trying hardships to be endured by many who were not very well prepared to meet them, their lives were not without frequent gleams of sunshine, for this poverty, as we may call it, was just the normal state of things at that time.

We are reminded of the lines contrasting the years 1798
and 1874, which we have met with somewhere:—

YEAR 1798.

" Farmer at the plough,
   Wife milking cow,
   Sons thrashing in the barn,
   Daughters spinning yarn,—
       All happy to a charm."

YEAR 1874.

" Farmer gone to see the show,
   His lady at the piano,
   Sons at college learning Latin,
   Daughters gaily dressed in satin,—
       With a mortgage on the farm."

WATER SUPPLY.

THERE is one thing that Dunfermline now stands pre-eminently favoured in, compared with what it was long ago, and that is, its very fine supply of pure wholesome water. The grateful thanks of the community are ever due to Mr. Lauder, ex-Provost Mathieson, and others, who unceasingly advocated and fought for the great Devon Water scheme. If the men who fought in season, and sometimes out of season, for that great boon had done nothing else in their lifetime, they accomplished a task worth living for, and one worthy of being ever gratefully remembered by the inhabitants of the old city. How different the supply is now, compared with the old intermittent supply! There were many private wells in those days, but the quality was very hard. There was no fine Glensherup water to be thankful for; such a thing as a supply from a locality so far distant was never dreamt of as being possible. The loss and inconvenience arising from the want of water were very great. This was continually felt, day and night, and was an unceasing cause of trouble and anxiety both to rich and poor. What a deal of precious time was lost in going to and from the "pipes" and the public wells in those days! Just imagine a row of twenty or thirty pairs of wooden stoups, belonging to as many persons, standing around the "pipes" early of a summer morning, each pair placed so as to keep their regular turn when the water came on. A colloquy something like the following might sometimes have been heard.

Tibby.—" Whaur hae ye been this mornin', Betty ?"

Betty.—" I've been at the 'pipes,' waitin' my turn aff an' on since five o'clock. I was feared that Kirsty Nettlekail would shift my stoups, and pit me oot o' my turn. So there's been nae parritch made nor pirns filled this mornin', an' oor gudeman wull be naether to haud nor to bind when I gang hame. Oor bit laddie Willie, ye ken, is no weel i' the noo, ill wi' an income in his tae, and likewise has gotten a glisk o' cauld, and is no able to carry a gang o' water in the noo, puir man !"

Many were the squabbles that arose at the public "pipes;" many the violent exhibitions of " tongue fence" shown by those of a quarrelsome disposition over their " turn ;" but now this is all past, and almost forgotten. A bountiful supply of pure, wholesome water flows into every household, bringing with it untold blessings to old and young. Such a thing as public baths would have been unattainable then, but now that water is so abundant, the people have also had conferred upon them, through the kindness of a generous-hearted friend and native of Dunfermline, the commodious and handsome " Carnegie " Baths.

OLD CUSTOMS AND SUPERSTITIONS.

ABOUT sixty years ago, the belief in ghosts, fairies, warnings, &c. existed to a considerable extent amongst a certain class, but was gradually dying out. Remnants of such superstitious feeling lingered amongst the aged, and the writer has often listened to stories told in the long winter nights at the firesides by old people, who were firm believers in ghosts, warnings, and unlucky persons, till the hair of the listener's head stood on end, and he was afraid to venture into a dark room by himself. He remembers very well the case of an elderly woman who had a cow, the condition of which gave her much concern. A neighbour asked her one day—"Whaur are ye gaun wi' your coo the day, Janet?" To which she replied, "*I'm gaun to sell her; she'll dae nae mair guid wi' me, for auld Meg —— has cuissen an ill e'e (an evil eye) on her!*" It was a common thing to throw salt on the fire if one's house had been visited by any one who was reported to be "*no canny.*" Some persons also carried with them a spray of rowan-tree (mountain ash) in their pockets to keep away any malevolent influence!

The superstitious feeling regarding the unluckiness of Friday continued to abide in the minds of many, especially of those in the seafaring trade. While Friday was considered an unlucky day, Sunday was thought to be the very reverse, hence the old maxim, "Sunday sail, never fail." This feeling has now almost vanished, but at that time some ship captains stoutly objected to sail on that day, or even on any other week day, if they happened to meet on the morning of sailing with any one who was considered an unlucky person. An old, experienced, and efficient boatman at Limekilns and Charlestown, named John Knox, who will be still remembered by many in connection with the Stirling and Granton steamers, was in his younger days a sailor in a small sloop. The said vessel had got her cargo of lime all on board, but unfortunately had lain at Charlestown windbound for a fortnight. One fine morning a fair wind sprang up, and John and the mate got the vessel all ready for proceeding to sea. They were now only waiting the arrival of the skipper, who soon made his appearance. He at once told the men that it was of no use going to sea that day, for he had just met on his way to the ship that auld body Lizzie C——! This captain and others, when they passed "Auld Lizzie" on the road always put themselves between her and the sun! They thought she was endowed with the gift of second sight. This gift of second sicht, as it was called, was possessed chiefly by the aged,—those in "the sunset of life,"—hence the well-known words of the wizard in *Lochiel's Warning*—

> "'Tis the *sunset of life gives me mystical lore*,
> And coming events cast their shadows before."

If a captain on his way to set sail, or if a marriage party passed on their road three black crows, or a magpie sitting on a dyke or by the roadside, it was considered an evil omen. It was thought unlucky if two knives happened to be crossed on the table, or if thirteen persons sat down together to a meal. Even now, the virtue of a horse-shoe nailed on the door of the stable, byre, or kitchen is still in many quarters believed in, and is considered a panacea against witchcraft. To present a knife or sharp-cutting implement to any one, without first getting a penny or other small coin in exchange, was deemed an unlucky gift, as it was sure to cut or sever love! Some would not put on the left shoe first of a morning. It was also believed to be uncanny to weigh an infant before it was a year old, or to let the moon shine on its face whilst it was asleep. It was also very desirable to cut an infant's nails for the first time over an open Bible. Even now many people open the pages of that sacred book at random, as it were, to ascertain thereby what they consider the Divine will concerning them. It was sometimes usual to refer to the thirty-first chapter of Proverbs in order to ascertain one's fortune. This chapter contains thirty-one verses, and if persons referred to the verse corresponding with the day of the month on which they were born, there they would be told their fortune. When an infant was being carried to the church on Sunday to be baptised, the *"bairn's piece"* was sent along with it, and it was given by the nurse who carried the child to the very first person she met on the way thither. No one, however exalted his station, whether on horseback or on foot, was so unkind or ungallant as to refuse the interesting gift. If two or three small bits of tea stems were found floating in a cup of tea, it was an omen that one or more strangers or visitors were to call soon ; the same thing was to happen if a string of soot were found hanging to the bars of the grate. A dog howling loudly during the night was a sure sign that a neighbour or some near friend was approaching the gates of death.

Amongst the poorer and less educated classes in Scotland and England, even at the present day, remnants of such superstitions still abound. In England, you may yet see hawkers of fish in the large towns spit on the first coin they get of a morning, in order, as they say, to bring them good luck that day. It was accounted unlucky for one to turn back for anything after commencing a journey ; and whilst it was deemed unlucky to break a looking-glass, it was thought very lucky to have crickets chirping at one's fireside, or a cat entirely of a black colour. The spider, which was of such momentous value to King Robert the Bruce, and to Scotland, when he was a fugitive, and whose perseverance he is said to have watched with such intense interest till it finally triumphed, was held to be an insect which it was unlucky to kill. In some of the rural districts of England a few of the people still look with terror through a glass window on the first new moon of a new year ! It is right enough to see it first out of doors, but thought to be a sad calamity if seen for the first time through a window of glass ! Now and again we observe in the English newspapers, " A *child's caul* for sale ; the notice of ship captains is directed to this." It is considered lucky for captains to have one of these on board ship.

It was considered an ill omen for a person to give another a pin for any purpose when they were about to part or to go away any distance from one another,—for it was said that "*preens pairt love !*" The writer remembers the case of a friend who was a ship captain. On his way to his ship, accompanied by his wife, by some accident or other, in going through a gate or stile, he happened to get some part of his dress torn. He asked her for a pin, to pin the garment in a temporary way; this she gave, but she laughingly remarked, "Do ye no ken that preens pairt love ?" And it was a very strange coincidence that in this case husband and wife never again met; he being unfortunately drowned on that voyage. Of course no one is so ignorant as to believe in a theory of this kind, but the above incident is known to the writer as perfectly authentic.

Reading the tea-cups often caused much diversion. The grounds and tea-leaves left in the tea-cup were shaken round the sides of it, and some young folks were very expert in the way of discovering and tracing the figures of men, women, ships, horses, &c. on the sides of it, and telling the future fortunes of those who had "tried their luck" in this way.

On the occasion of a death happening in a household there were several superstitious customs carried out, such as covering the looking-glass up with a cloth, or turning the front of it to the wall; and all domestic animals, especially cats, were not permitted in a house where there was a corpse.

To this day the custom of throwing a bottle of wine after a ship while she is being launched is still continued, and I fear that even amongst many intelligent, strong-minded, and well-informed people, great disappointment would be felt, especially by those who were the owners of the vessel, if it unfortunately happened that the bottle escaped breakage on that interesting occasion. This would be regarded as an evil omen.

I remember the time when it was considered not desirable to have a clergyman on board of a vessel, as they were sometimes thought to bring "ill-luck" with them. Whistling at sea was also looked upon as uncanny, and likely to raise a gale or storm.

There was an old *freit* attended to at the time of the baptism of infants in the church, and it is still carried out in some quarters. That was for the male infants to have the ordinance administered to them first, if there happened to be both males and females presented. It was thought that if a girl were baptised before a boy the girl would be likely to have a beard, and the boy to be of a feminine disposition.

The month of May has somehow or other been regarded as an unlucky month, and hence there is a disinclination on the part of those who wish to get married to choose that month. The last day of the year—Hogmanay—was considered an especially lucky day for this purpose, and hence very many marriages in Scotland take place on that day.

OLD-FASHIONED PHARMACY.

" Calces o' fossils, earths and trees ;
　True salmarinum o' the seas ;
　The farina of beans and pease,
　　　He has't in plenty ;
　Aquafortis, what you please,
　　　He can content ye.

" Forbye some new, uncommon weapons,
　Urinus spiritus of capons ;
　Or mite-horn shavings, filings, scrapings,
　　　Distill'd *per se ;*
　Salalkali o' midge-tail clippings,
　　　And mony mae."

　　　　　　　　　　　　　　Burns.

AMONG old people many varieties of roots, herbs, and
simples for the relief of the different kinds of diseases
were used, and it was surprising to find how many persons
there were who gave themselves to the study of this
important subject. Culpepper's *Family Herbal,* Buchan's
Domestic Medicine, and John Wesley's *Primitive Physic*
were then in full swing; and the docken, dandelion,
yarrow, horehound, and agrimony were held to be possessed of sovereign virtue.

" Kirn milk and agrimony,
　Mak the lasses fair and bonny."

Let us recall the names of some of the medicines, &c.,
that used to be prescribed, and the ailments and diseases
for which they were considered specifics.　For pleurisy,
take half a drachm of soot ; for nettlerush, rub the parts
with parsley ; for gout, apply lean raw beef; for a cut,
bind on it toasted cheese or pounded grass; for asthma,
live for a fortnight on boiled carrots only ; for dropsy, use
a tea made from broom.　When young infants cried,
apparently from some inward spasms, we have seen
anxious mothers take out of the fire one or two redhot
cinders and put them into a cup of water, and give
the child a teaspoonful or two of that.　For dysentery,
a lump of alum to be carried in the pocket ; bronchitis.
goose grease and treacle ; smallpox, sheep's tongue boiled

in milk; cramp, the knuckle bone of a leg of mutton to be carried in the pocket; rheumatism, the garters to be worn filled with sulphur. It was not from a superstitious feeling that an old and respected friend-of the writer's carried about with him in his pocket a raw potato; he was firmly convinced that it relieved him from rheumatism, with which he was sometimes afflicted. "*Flannel* and *patience*" were also considered of great service in the case of those suffering under this severe ailment. Rubbing with swine's seam, and also with ointments of fresh butter and soot, was very often recommended.

Some old people, who made pharmacy a specialty or a hobby, were reputed to be what was termed very skilly in the art of curing diseases, and in almost every town and village such persons were to be found. Some of them became noted for their skill and the cures they performed, and patients would sometimes travel long distances to consult them. Dunfermline had its quota of such amateur professionals—its Mrs. M'Gorams and its Sarah Wilsons, with their healing herbs, celebrated " saws " or ointments, to whom many resorted for advice. The pharmacopœia of those days differed entirely from that of our highly scientific times. Even the most enlightened and the best educated medical men of only sixty years ago used to bleed or blister their patients for almost every ailment! If they did not blister or bleed, they were neglecting their duty, and were considered unsafe and unworthy of confidence—in short, unfit for their work. Some country people were in the regular habit of going to some apothecary or other twice a year to be " blooded," as it was called, in order to *prevent trouble coming upon them.* They were often bled till they fainted: the usual charge for this was one shilling. If patients escaped this mode of treatment, they were well dosed with drastic medicines. Epsom and Glauber salts, aloes, calomel, senna, jalap, Castille soap, magnesia, and cream of tartar, were held in high repute and universally recommended. Old and young had to be coaxed to swallow the nauseous powders and mixtures that were then prescribed;

and in the case of refractory children, a tin filler or funnel, and physical force, had often to be resorted to in order to get them to swallow their doses of repulsive physic! Some kindly, well-meaning mothers gave their children a dose consisting of salts and senna every Sabbath morning, to take the ill humours out of their system, and to cool their blood, and all for their good! In some well-conducted families, if one of the youngsters expressed an earnest desire to stay at home from church on Sabbath, the request was generally granted, but frequently on the express condition that he would take a dose of salts or senna. Pharmacy was a regular course of depletion, and, as Darwin would say, only the fittest survived!

Those who usurped the domain of the college bred medical man (and their name was legion) invariably prescribed very homely remedies. Some prescribed the application of "moose wabs" (cobwebs) for sores, and also pills of the same to be taken internally. There were also decoctions of herbs and poultices of horse and cow dung. Marigold tea was usually given to children suffering from the "nirles" (measles); and the holding of a child over the mouth of a coal-pit was resorted to as a change of air for relieving "kingkost" (hooping-cough). For those who were troubled with warts, the rubbing of those excrescences with the fasting spittle—the first thing in the morning—was prescribed; or, what was considered better and more highly recommended, was to steal a piece of butcher meat, rub the warts with it, then bury the meat in the ground, all without the knowledge of any one, and as the meat decayed so would the warts. The writer has frequently seen boys anointing their warts with the white milky juice exuding from the stems of dandelion flowers. No doubt there is *acid* in this, as well as in the fasting spittle.

The druggists of those days, such as Charles Macara on the Bridge, and Dr. Cameron, did an extensive business in the way of giving medical advice and in practising surgery in their back shops in cases of illness. It was the practice all over the country for those who kept apothecary shops to do a good deal in simple cases requiring medical and surgical treatment. At a former period the barbers did the bleeding business. There is a story told about one of those druggists in the west country. A poor woman had a sick child, which she took to him for advice. She was recommended by him to put the child into a black sheepskin newly taken from the animal, and let it remain in that all night! This was faithfully attended to, but the child died before morning. She afterwards told the druggist her sorrowful tale with all minuteness; but he told her she had "used the best means in her power," and to "go home and get the child buried," and he would not charge her anything for the cure he gave!

In cases of fever the putting of a patient into a sheepskin, while the feet were well saturated with new milk, to draw the fever down, was very frequently adopted.

Pharmacy has made wonderful progress during the last fifty or sixty years. Like all other sciences, it is still making extraordinary advances, which all tend to the alleviation of human suffering. In old times we had no chloroform, with its soothing and blessed influence, in cases of severe surgical operations. We had no infinitesimal, tasteless, homœopathic doses of medicine, but the very reverse; nor had we the stately hydropathic palaces we see on all hands. There were no public analysts to test our food and our drink, such as we have now in our towns and cities. Water in many towns and villages was often very impure and most unwholesome, and was the cause of diseases of which we now hear almost nothing. But then our ears were not dinned, as they are now, about the deadly germs which are floating in the air around us, in the food we eat, and in the water we drink. It appears that we cannot possibly go where germs are not. They abound everywhere, and much to our discomfort. Little did we know that the milk which had got "blinket," or turned, was in consequence of the pranks of those germs we now hear so much about; but of all this we then lived in blissful ignorance.

THE DUNFERMLINE BONE-SETTER.

ALTHOUGH Dunfermline could never boast of having a College or University, the little neighbouring village or hamlet of Pattiesmuir could boast of that honour. Not only was there a so-called "College," *sui generis*, but there was also a veritable professor. The most of the "collegians" belonged to Dunfermline, and a very lively set they were. The introduction or installation of new "collegians" was observed with all due decorum, yet with much genuine humour. In Pattiesmuir they adhered more to the French and the German ideas of what the functions of a "college" really are than those attached to it in England. It was in reality *Collegium*, merely a collection or assemblage of persons; and the one at Pattiesmuir was intended for recreation and amusement. Those who figured at these gatherings have mostly all passed away, "as a tale that is told," and the archives belonging to the Pattiesmuir *Collegium* are now out of existence. From what can be gathered regarding the past of that amusing assembly, it would appear that there was much harmless diversion carried on at their meetings—amusement and recreation, and not education or instruction, being the principal objects they had in view. I sometimes think that the bulk of the people of those days enjoyed life with much real zest, notwithstanding the fewer advantages they had, compared with those we now enjoy. Men were not so driven and harassed with the cares and the bustle and anxieties of business as they now are.

There is a story told about one of the leading members of the "College," who lived in Pattiesmuir, and it is worth recording. A younger brother of his had unfortunately got his ankle dislocated one Sunday morning. It caused the young lad great pain, and there was no other course left but for him to be taken up to Dunfermline on his brother's back to Provost Low, who was a celebrated bone-setter, in order to get the swollen and painful joint put into its place. A journey of this kind did not appear so formidable an undertaking as it would do now, so, with his disabled brother on his back, the young man set out on his journey of two and a half miles, Sabbath though it was, arriving with his burden at the Provost's shortly before church time. The old domestic admitted them into the kitchen with no good grace—gave them "a bit of her mind," telling them it was a shame "to disturb the Provost on the Lord's mornin', an' him a' ready for to gang till the kirk." The elder one pleaded as an excuse the great pain that his brother was suffering, and said they were sorry to trouble him at such an inconvenient time. Soon after, his worship, the stately Provost, came into the kitchen where they were. He was dressed in full official costume—knee breeches and silk stockings, laced coat, fine frilled shirt, powdered hair, silver buckles on his shoes, and his cocked hat in his hand; arrayed, in short, in all the glory and state of the first magistrate of one of the most venerable and renowned cities of the kingdom. He was a very kind-hearted man, but he felt just a little annoyed at being disturbed at that untimeous hour. Laying his cocked hat carefully on a chair, he took out his silk pocket handkerchief, which he spread on the floor to protect his knee-breeches. After this he proceeded to examine the boy's ankle to find out the extent of the damage. During the manipulation the boy winced several times, owing to the pain induced through the severe nibbling to which the joint was subjected; but when it came to the grand finale the pain was so unexpected and intense as to cause the lad, unintentionally, to kick the Provost right in the chest with his other foot with all his might, sending that worthy gentleman sprawling all his length on the floor! O ye limners with a clever pencil, here was a fine subject for such as you to portray! Behold the Provost of the ancient city of Dunfermline, clad in all the habiliments of official glory, lying flat on his back, and on his own kitchen floor on the Sabbath morning!

This good, worthy Provost died in 1817, full of age and honours. To many of his suffering fellow-creatures far and

near he had proved a great blessing. In the avocation
which he took upon himself in his later years as bone-
setter, &c., for which he took no fees, he displayed great
skill and judgment, and his services were eagerly sought
after. He used to say that he obtained his knowledge of
the human bones "at the grave's mouth." His fellow-
townsmen and friends at a distance, to show their great
regard for him, subscribed for his portrait, which was
painted by the celebrated Sir Henry Raeburn, R.A., Limner
for Scotland, the attached friend of Sir Joshua Reynolds.
This fine work of art now adorns the Council Chamber of
Dunfermline.

THE RESURRECTION TRADE.

" Be honours which to kings we give,
    To doctors also paid ;
  We're the king's *subjects* while we live,
    The doctors' when we're dead."

LONG ago the medical schools in this country had not the
same facilities they have now for getting subjects for dissection. The dreaded names of Burke and Hare were
spoken with bated breath, and with universal execration,
while the expert deeds of the "resurrectionists" spread un-
easiness and dismay everywhere. Youngsters were
frightened to venture out of doors after nightfall, for fear
of being "Burked," and carried off in a sack to the
doctors. They were afraid that some doctor's emissary
would come behind them and put a plaster on their
mouths and choke them. Others were afraid to enter into a
tavern in our large cities, for fear of being drugged and
their bodies sold for dissection. Frightful and exaggerated
stories were told about people who were inveigled into
houses where there were trap-doors, and where the victims
were precipitated headlong into boiling cauldrons below
the floor ! It is a fact that Burke and his associate Hare
were the murderers of sixteen persons. High prices were
then given for bodies by the medical schools, and the temptation given by Dr. Knox and others was very great. An
Act was passed in 1832, 2d and 3d William IV., which
put a stop to this infamous traffic. I remember of
seeing small parties of volunteer watchers taking their
turn in going to the Dunfermline Churchyard for the purpose of keeping watch there during the long, cold nights
of winter. When they sallied out on these expeditions
they were well muffled up, had large woollen "comforters"
round their necks, and extra clothing on. They carried
good strong "rungs" in their hands, also a lantern or two,
and an old flint gun or "Brown Bess" among them. They
were looked upon with much interest when they left their
own warm firesides and ventured upon those nocturnal
watchings. They took with them a good supply of bread
and cheese, and the unfailing bottle of mountain dew, to
cheer them and keep their courage up during their long

vigils. They sat in a sort of watch-house by the Fraters' Hall, had a good blazing fire, and, after all, had a very pleasant time of it. They would go out in pairs, and make their rounds during the eerie hours of midnight, gun in hand and at full-cock, to see if any body-snatchers were plying their ghostly vocation. About that period many bodies were exhumed in different parts of the country, especially the bodies of those who had died from mysterious or complicated diseases which had baffled the skill of the doctors. So expert were they, that in Glasgow bodies were known to have been cleverly exhumed between the times the watchers were taking their periodic rounds! In that city a lantern would be placed over a newly covered-in grave, like a beacon light, that the watchers might observe from a distance during the night. Strange to say, the lantern would be removed from its place, inch by inch, and so stealthily that it could not be noticed, and it was in this way taken some yards distant, so as to enable the robbers to get the booty they were in search of! Lonely churchyards, away from human habitations, such as that belonging to Limekilns and neighbourhood, were most convenient for the resurrectionists. This industry of body-snatching is now over, the large hospitals, workhouses, &c. amply supplying the demands of the surgical schools. Our own Dunfermline *"Blue Beddel"* was sometimes blamed for doing a little in aiding and abetting the "resurrection" business, but he always said he would "far rather bury ten persons than rob the grave of one!" Be this as it may, it is a fact nevertheless that his house was attacked and wrecked by a mob one Handsel Monday morning, as there was a suspicion that he had dealings with those interested in the grave-snatching trade. When his ghastly trade was dull, he used to complain that he had not *"buried a livin' flesh for a week!"* His dismal occupation did not in the least affect his genial flow of spirits; he was fond of a dram, and many a funny story he could tell when his boon companions were assembled around him. With a pawky smile he used to say, "'Deed man, I'm feared to speer at ony body hoo they are, in case they micht think that I was wearyin' on them, or even o'er a dram to say to them 'My services to ye!'"

FAIRS AND PUBLIC AMUSEMENTS.

" ' Mither, I'm gaun to Laurence Fair ; '
   ' Lassie, what are ye gaun to dae there ? '
   ' I'm gaun to buy baith ribbons an' lawn,
     To wear on my head when I get the gudeman.' "

A PASSING reference has already been made to the fairs
that were held, and it may be here observed that
such occasions often did duty not only for transacting
business of all kinds, but also for public amusements. The
" Hairst," the " Puddin'," and Martinmas, and one or two
other principal fairs, were eventful and stirring times. They
hove in sight not only as seasons for extensive buying and
selling, but also for social merry-making and good-fellow-
ship, and they interrupted the dull level and monotony of
country life. In some districts, where the hiring of agricultural labourers and servants yet prevails, there is a deal
of life and excitement to be seen. In Dunfermline the
fairs were the principal marts for the purchase of farm
and domestic furniture and utensils of all descriptions,
and were most convenient; but the introduction of railway
communication over the country has changed all this,
for the remotest districts are now brought within easy
range of good markets. What tempting wares of all
kinds were to be seen at those lively gatherings, and
happy were the youngsters who could then boast of a
few coppers in their pockets ! What cart-loads of ripe
apples, pears, cherries, and gooseberries were there in their
season. After the lapse of many long years, we almost
fancy yet that we feel the strong odour of the apple carts
of early days. On their arrival from the fairs, youngsters
besieged the old folks for their "fair." The great question
with them was, " What ' fair ' hae ye brocht to me ?" The
answer might be a braw new gown, a wooden luggie or a
bicker, a cake of Roby Salmond's gingerbread, a rattle, a
whistle, or some such toy to baby, reminding us of the lines—

> " I've a drum an' a trumpet for Dick ;
> I've some yards o' blue ribbon for Sal ;
> I've a book fu' o' babs, and a stick,
> An' some 'baccy and pipes for mysel'.''

At those fairs hawkers, pedlars, and travelling packmen, who then abounded, were to be seen everywhere. As the gloaming came on, great bands of the "Chapman billies" and visitors from a distance began to "tak the gate" homewards—some with heavy hearts, lamenting over a poor stroke of business done, and others "fou, and unco happy." The apple carts and stands began then to show their lights in all directions, and those consisted generally of a candle burning dimly inside of a *paper pock,* and the fun and noise went on till nine or ten o'clock.

On all the principal fair occasions there were "shows" in temporary wooden and canvas booths, and sometimes caravans. For many years the Nethertown (on the ground now occupied by Mr. Mathewson's factory) used to be the great resort for such, and for circuses, menageries, and "penny keeks." The most of them were adorned, as such exhibitions still are, with great canvas pictures in front, to tempt the old and the young to "walk up." The usual charge was, for ladies and gentlemen sixpence each, for the working-classes threepence, children half-price. The arrival of those shows was a source of great pleasure and excitement, especially to the young, and broke pleasantly on the monotony of every-day life. How eagerly the erection of those poor, fragile specimens of carpentry was watched and admired by the crowd of youths from all quarters! About the first show I ever remember seeing erected was one which contained a big woman who had been born without arms, and she exhibited feats of writing by holding the quill between her toes! There were no steel pens used then. Bits of paper containing specimens of her *foot*-writing were readily bought up for two or three coppers. I had not the pleasure of seeing her, but I remember well of seeing her full-length portrait in front of the booth, representing her in the act of writing. One of the most popular shows that then came at intervals to the town, and the first I ever entered, was Steven's Exhibition of Marionettes, or little mechanical figures. The *tableau* of the " Babes in the Wood," accompanied by the small flying birds cleverly covering over with leaves the hapless pair; also that of " Willie brewed a peck o' maut," together with the " Laird o' Cockpen;" and all these, accompanied by a fiddle or two and several excellent voices, were things to be remembered. Then at intervals came menageries of wild beasts, and also—most attractive of all—came the veteran Ord, with his famous equestrian exhibition. Memory yet recalls him to view,—the old man of sixty years and upwards, so agile and so perfectly formed, bestriding the bare backs of four or five galloping horses, working out his little day and generation, leaping and vaulting with marvellous grace and agility for a bit of bread; his exploits giving to many a poor, weary, heavy-laden onlooker a blink of sunshine for the time being! All those bits of play-acting were, I am sure, considered by some far more impressive, and were far better relished, than some of the higher class of theatrical displays seen in after years.

THE PENNY CRUSH.

THE honour of first introducing what are now popularly known throughout the country as "Penny Readings" has been claimed by different towns in England. A few years ago such public readings were greatly in vogue in every city, town, and village throughout Great Britain. When they were well conducted they were conducive of good, affording a source of instruction to old and young. It should be known, however, that Dunfermline has the honour of being the first place to introduce those pleasant entertainments. About forty-six years ago a series of Saturday evening entertainments were got up there. The originators of those most attractive and useful meetings, which are now universally known and appreciated throughout the entire kingdom, were Mr. Robert Anderson, in conjunction with the late Mr. Robert Hay, both of them well-known and respected townsmen of Dunfermline. They were held in the Maygate Masons' Lodge—admission one penny. They were under the auspices of the Dunfermline Temperance Society, which was instituted in 1830, and the crowds attracted were so great that those gatherings got the title of the " Penny Crush."

The entertainments, consisting of a short address, songs, recitations, and readings by amateurs and untried young men principally, had a most beneficial tendency, and were carried on with much spirit for a good while. On many occasions hundreds of persons could not get into the hall for want of room. The mind's eye can yet conjure up some of the leading spirits who figured on the boards at these lively gatherings. Memory calls up one after another, after the lapse of between forty and fifty years. Alas, "life's fitful fever" is over with the most of them ; and of those who are left it may be said that they are scattered far and wide,

" By mount, and stream, and sea !"

Amongst some of the more prominent of those who officiated were Alexander Younger, Robert Kilpatrick; Robert Walls, with his "Donald and his Dog" and "Margaret and the Minister;" James Russell, with his popular recitation of "The Auld Sark Sleeve;" and foremost among them all, and the leading spirit in this popular and most beneficial movement, was Robert Anderson, then in the full glow of youth and vigour. The recital of "Wallace's Address to his Army," "Mary, the Maid of the Inn," "Tell's Speech on Liberty," "Soda Water," &c., evoked rounds of applause. Where are the crowds who then cheered him and the others so vociferously? The most of them have passed the boundaries of time, and have vanished

"Like a ghost at cock-crowing!"

We have listened to famed elocutionists and accomplished public singers since then, but never have we seen surpassed the genuine enthusiasm and hearty, intelligent appreciation that were called forth at the Dunfermline "Penny Crush" in the days of langsyne!

In connection with those crowded and popular entertainments some curious episodes occurred. There was one in connection with a harmless character in the town who was lame, and who used to officiate as public bellman, and proclaim, "Haddies at the Tron, twal pund for saxpence!" and was generally a kind of public hanger-on, ready for any job that turned up. He felt himself aggrieved by something said or sung regarding him at the "Penny Crush." Halliday the singer had introduced Sandy, and mimicked him to the life on the platform, thus bringing him into public contempt, as he thought. He sought the advice of some one connected with the meetings as to how he should act in the circumstances, in order to get the offender punished. This gentleman was a bit of a wag himself, so he advised Sandy that, as the case was evidently a serious one, approaching to defamation of character, he should by all means try to obtain an interview with the Provost on the matter. So to the Provost he went limping along. In addition to his having a limp in his gait, he had also the misfortune to have an impediment in his speech. He was ushered into the presence of the first magistrate, and told his story in a broken, disjointed manner, to the effect that "a f-f-fellow named Ha-a-liday, at the p-p-p-penny crush, had been making a f-f-fool of him," and he came to see about redress. The Provost very good-naturedly listened to the poor fellow's story, painfully told, patted him kindly on the back, and advised him to go home, and when Saturday night came, to go to the platform and mimic the man who had dared to do him such a serious injury, and thus pay him back in his own coin. Sandy thanked the Provost for his advice, which he considered as wise as that of any judgment of Solomon's, and he promised to act upon it next Saturday night! Whether he did so, deponent sayeth not. No one had any idea that so many persons could be found in the town capable of acquitting themselves at those meetings so well as they did. The amount of latent talent evoked was extraordinary.

Theatrical amusements were by no means greatly patronised fifty years ago. Occasionally a small company of actors—Johnston the tragedian and others—would come to the town for a brief space. There was then a strong prejudice against theatres and theatricals, and as a rule good concerts were far better supported and appreciated. The bulk of the music sung and played in those days was of course Scottish. The Misses Smith, the Fraser Family, J. Harrison, John Wilson—the greatest of Scottish vocalists—and others, visited Dunfermline periodically, and were always heartily welcomed and well patronised. The foremost of our local vocalists was James Rankine; and for many years Messrs. Air, Halliday, and Shields took a prominent position in the town as glee singers, and wherever they appeared they acquitted themselves well and were very popular. With regard to Mr. Rankine, it may be said that the present generation in Dunfermline will, it is feared, have to wait a very long while before they can ever hear the songs and lyrics of Scotland sung and accompanied with such exquisite taste and masterly skill as they were when he was in his palmy days, and when he was in deed and in truth the "master of song,"

THE KING'S BIRTHDAY.

THIS used to be a great occasion when holidays were few and far between, and it was looked forward to with great interest, especially by the youngsters of the town. As the day approached, every spare copper was put aside in order to purchase gunpowder, or a small brass cannon, or a second-hand pistol. Samuel Doherty the gunsmith, and Dougald Kirk, had their hands filled with work, repairing and altering guns, flint-locks, and old pistols, in anticipation of the great coming event. The boy who was the happy possesser of a pistol on that day was greatly to be envied, even although it might have a rusty flint lock, and might be dangerous to all who came near it. As a substitute for a pistol, some lads would often tie their small brass cannons to a piece of wood, hold them up like a musket, and fire away, regardless of consequences. Bonfires were kindled in various parts of the town, without being interfered with, and without leave being asked or obtained of the policeman, or town-keeper, as he was usually called. The Abbey bells pealed a merry chorus, the Town-Council met and had cake and wine, and drank long life to his Most Gracious Majesty. Cannons and pistols were brought out, and firing a *feu de joie* was the order of the day. Those householders who lived in the neighbourhood of a bon-fire, or biel-fire as it was familiarly called, liberally contributed pieces of coal and wood to keep it going. Boys went round the neighbourhood collecting coal in baskets and buckets to keep it blazing. The roots of large trees, called " clogs," gathered by young lads weeks beforehand in the plantations and the country around the town, were now brought from their hiding-places, and were heaped upon it. Any well-dressed persons going up or down the streets on that day were besieged "for a bawbee or a penny to the biel-fire." The money got in this way was usually spent in gunpowder, squibs, &c.

There were about a dozen places over the town selected for the biel-fires. In the course of the morning or fore-noon the fires were set ablaze. Cannons of all kinds were fired during the day; even old keys, in which by means of a file touch-holes were made, did duty as cannons. Some of them were charged with gunpowder and *chuckie stanes*, and a slow match, made of common brown paper saturated with saltpetre, and prepared days beforehand, was then applied, while the boys kept at a little distance to watch the explosion. *Pee-o-ies*, made of wet gunpowder kneaded into a paste in the hand, were now and again set fire to; and while they sent up their thousand brilliant sparks, like a miniature burning volcano, they gave the youngsters an uncommon degree of pleasure. In the evening, a great gathering took place in the west end of Bridge Street (which was at that period beyond the bounds of the burgh), and there pistols, muskets, and cannon were fired, and rockets, Roman candles, and squibs by the hundred were set off, and much rough horse-play and fun were carried on. Accidents from gunpowder were of frequent occurrence, and during the time when the fun and frolic were at their height, it must be confessed that sometimes it was unsafe for a person wearing a fine silk hat to go along Bridge Street. It was like a red rag in front of a bull; the hat became a target for those who were charging each other with squibs, and by the time its wearer reached the Cannon, he would find to his sorrow that much of the glory and gloss of his head-gear had suddenly departed. The fun went on fast and furious for two hours or so, the poor "town-keeper," meanwhile, being safe at his own fire-side; but soon the streets wore their usual quiet and solemn aspect, and the disturbance and excitement passed away.

SCHOOLS AND SCHOOLMASTERS.

" Up four timmer stairs, in a garret fu' clean,
  In awful authority Madie was seen ;
  Her close luggit mutch tower'd aloft in its pride,
  Her long winsey apron flowed down by her side ;
  The taws on her lap like some dreaded snake lay,
  Aye watchin' an' ready to spring on its prey ;
  The wheel at her foot, an' the cat on her knee,
  Nae Queen on her throne mair majestic than she."

" To the whirr o' the wheel auld baudrons wad sing,
  On stools wee an' muckle, a' ranged in a ring,
  Ilk idle bit urchin, wha glower'd aff his book,
  Was caught in a twinklin' by Madie's dread look.
  She ne'er spak a word, but the taws she wad fling,
  The sad leather whang up the culprit must bring,
  While his sair bluther'd face, as the palmies wad fa',
  Proclaimed through the schule an example to a'."

Alex. Smart.

WHAT crowds of "sunny memories" spring up as we ponder over our school-days, and think of

"The years that are no more,
  And never shall return !"

When we think of those who then sat beside us on the same form, who carved their names on the same school desks, and swopped their knives, bools, and peeries with each other, of those who were under the same terror of the master as we were when our lessons were imperfectly learned, of those who had the same leathern "taws" applied to them, who played the same games with us, and vowed a deathless friendship, but who are now absorbed

"In the roaring loom of time !"

Between fifty and sixty years ago, the schools in the town were very differently conducted from what they are now. The teachers did not then require to pass any special examination as to their fitness for that most important work. Any one who considered he or she had a call to that vocation had it freely in their power to enter upon it, and at once commence teaching. The fees and emoluments received by the most of the teachers in both town and country were very small, and hence there was little inducement to undertake that laborious and responsible work, except in cases of necessity, when perhaps all other trades failed, or from pure love of the work. In those days our nobility and gentry would willingly give two or three hundred pounds a year for a French cook, and grudge fifty or sixty pounds for a tutor to their children! It happened in some instances that those who aspired to that important but ill-paid profession had failed as preachers in the church, and were unfortunately in the position of what was known as "stickit ministers." Yet, notwithstanding the small pecuniary inducements held out, there were then many teachers of great ability,—painstaking, worthy men, whose hearts were in their work, and who were a blessing to Scotland. They were then unhampered with Education Codes, and unmolested by School Boards—they were indeed, "monarchs of all they surveyed." Every village dominie looked upon himself as "master" of the village, inasmuch as he ruled the children, who ruled their mothers, who, of course, in their turn ruled the fathers! At that period it was "every one for his own hand" in the teaching line, and it must now be confessed that the system which then prevailed was sadly deficient. In fact, there was the entire absence of the system and the method pursued in all our modern well-regulated schools. Exception must, however, be taken to much of the over-pressure at present adopted at many of our schools, public and private, which may have an injurious tendency upon the coming generations.

I well remember Mr. William Meldrum's school. For many years he was known as a public teacher, and he strove to do his work faithfully. He kept school in what was known as the "Tup's Hoose," an old rickety place, up an outside stair in the Nethertown. Here it may be remarked that the ordinary school-houses in Scotland at that period were as unlike the modern educational palaces now being reared on all hands as could possibly be. The room occupied by Mr. Meldrum and his pupils was not very large, and the ceiling was so low, that an ordinary sized person could on tiptoe touch it with his hand. Here were assembled about sixty or seventy youngsters, male and female. There was a large fireplace in the school, where in the summer time dunces were often put, and sometimes adorned with a paper hat, having the word "Dunce" printed on it in large letters. At other times, for a greater punishment, a boy would be put there to sit between two girls, who had also been transgressing. The culprit would thus sit between the girls with a woe-begone face, for to him this was a very different punishment from what it might be in after years. What was then deemed a punishment, might in after years be considered an honour and a privilege! The noise in the school was sometimes deafening, while ever and anon would be heard the word "*si-lence*" shouted by the master, which would still the tumult only for a moment or two. From the great difficulty the master experienced in hearing the classes properly, the boys or girls who "said their lessons" in a loud shrill voice were considered promising pupils. At an annual examination of the school, where two clergymen were present, one of the boys, who happened to be the present writer, shouted his lesson in a very loud tone, which caused one of the ministers to remark to his brother clergyman, "That young fellow has got a fine voice for a tent!" Tent-preaching was then very common in Scotland, and the preacher gifted with the loudest voice was often deemed the most popular at such gatherings. If it happened that the master was called out of the school and was absent for a time, the gabble of lesson reading was stopped, and a scene of riot and confusion occurred. If he returned upon us unawares, there was promiscuous thrashing all round!

The master was generous and kind-hearted, but sometimes very fiery, and given to losing his temper. I remember well one occasion, when the riot and noise were at the worst, he completely lost command of himself, and, fiercely looking around, he espied one Betsy Browne giggling and laughing at a great rate. He started up from his desk, seized her by the shoulders, and then laid her flat on her back on the floor of the school. There was instant and awful silence, she herself, and every one present, thought that surely her last hour had come. The master then stamped his foot on the floor, in a manner fearful to behold, and with clenched fist held within an inch or two of her nose, shouted in a voice of thunder that "if she stirred one inch, he would grind her to powder!" The silence for a few minutes was solemn and affecting; in truth, a pin might have been heard to drop; but soon she was relieved from her perilous and most humiliating position, and the clamour, alas, was shortly afterwards as bad as ever. Although this incident is as fresh in my recollection as on the day it happened, I have withal a kindly remembrance of William Meldrum. Peace to his dear old memory! I remember well the sand-glass that stood on the little desk beside which he sat, to mark the time for calling up the different classes, and how we small boys used to watch with great interest the grains silently falling, and telling us that the time for the dismissal of our class had come.

> "The sand falls in the glass,
>   And to the dread eternity
> The dying moments pass."

Sand-glasses were common long ago in schools and in churches, and it would appear strange to modern ears if they heard the minister in his sermon say to his hearers— "*Now, my friends, let's have another glass!*"

In the afternoons, if the scholars had behaved extra well that day, he would treat them to a tune on his German flute just before dismissal, first telling his daughter to give his flute a drink. He had a warm heart, and as a teacher, and elder in the old Abbey Church, and as a member of society, he served his day and generation well. With regard to the school curriculum, nothing but the commonest branches were taught. His stronghold was the three R's—*Reading, 'Riting,* and *'Rithmetic.* We had also Spelling, English Grammar, and Catechisms, Longer and Shorter. The scholars were sadly perplexed with their Catechism lessons. Those about "Effectual calling," "Adoption," &c., which they had to learn by heart, also the "Reasons annexed," gave them great concern, and were in fact a mystery to most of them. In many cases the full meaning of much in that venerable school-book would only dawn in after years upon the minds of many of those who committed it to memory. Mr. Meldrum kept a small printing-press, and occasionally did sundry jobs in the printing line. As an incentive to the more advanced and well-behaved scholars, he on Saturday forenoons gave them rough woodcuts of his own printing to colour. They consisted of Highland chiefs, birds, &c., and he kindly gave the use of his colours and brushes, thus affording every encouragement.

As time wore on, some of the more advanced scholars were sent to the principal school in Dunfermline—the Grammar School, taught by Mr. Haxton. He was Rector of that school for many years, and his usher in the English and elementary departments was Mr. Scott. Mr. Haxton succeeded in sending forth into the world many excellent scholars, who afterwards did him credit. He was considered a good linguist, and taught French and Latin well. He was also proficient in mathematics, and he frequently had under his tuition young men from neighbouring places, such as Limekilns, learning navigation. He was, on the whole, well liked by those under his charge, and he took a great interest in their advancement. He would now and again take parties of the senior scholars out into the country on Saturdays, and explain to them many things in their perambulations by the highways and byways—such as the art of land-measuring and surveying, &c. He was a most perfect disciplinarian in school, and although the taws were very seldom brought out and used, he kept excellent order. He had quite a military look about him, was tall and straight, and had a commanding appearance. When necessity arose, and when he did appear on the floor of the school with his huge pair of leathern taws in his hand, it was a caution to all and sundry. In the event of any very serious depredation having been committed, when the culprit or culprits could not be found out, or would not own their transgression, a "court-martial," as he called it, was held in presence of the whole school, and the work of education was suspended. And yet it was not quite suspended, for was not the hearing of witnesses on both sides, and the careful and just sifting of evidence, a most essential part of education—fitting many of those boys and girls for the great business of public as well as family life as effectually as the study of Latin, French, or mathematics could do?

While Mr. Haxton was kind-hearted, he was at the same time strict in his ideas of discipline, without being harsh or severe, and offenders when punished knew that they well deserved the punishment they got. His goodness of disposition was, I am sorry to say, sometimes taken advantage of, and his weak points were by instinct known to some of his far-seeing, scheming pupils, of which an illustration will presently be given. The Rector had a military turn of mind, and was well acquainted with all kinds of military movements and tactics, and nothing gave him greater delight than explaining and illustrating to his listening pupils various modes of conducting warfare, ancient and modern. When he got upon that theme, everything else for the time being was in a measure forgotten. The following will illustrate how this peculiarity of his was taken advantage of on one or two occasions. One of the Latin classes was studying Cæsar, or the Wars of the Gauls, and, as in every other class, there came to school some who were quite unprepared with their lessons, so in this particular class one day two or three of the scholars, who had perhaps been bird-nesting till late the previous night, came with their Latin lesson unlearned. Before the time came for Mr. Haxton to hear them, something like the following observations might be heard from the scholars:—

Bob Henderson.—" I say, Jamie, I canna say a word o' my Latin lesson the day."

Jamie M'Laren.—" Neither can I, but leave it to me; we'll get oot o' the scrape some way."

Bob Henderson.—" Man, I'll be real glad, for I've been in the maister's black books for a day or twa past."

This Latin class was then called up, and a number of those at the top of it went swimmingly along with their lessons, and the master that day was in very good trim. When more than the half of the class had repeated their lessons well, and the turn of the dunces was drawing perilously near, one of the scholars would call the attention of the master to some particular piece of military strategy pursued by the Gauls, and ask for some explanation regarding it. This had the desired effect; it set Mr. Haxton off at a tangent, and he would now proceed to enlarge upon and illustrate at length the points referred to, sometimes suiting the action to the word, as I have seen. He would get so engrossed with the matter in hand, having a most attentive audience listening to his well-told illustrations, that he lost count of time, and the class would thereafter be abruptly dismissed with his usual word, "*Allons.*" The scheming youngsters would in consequence get their fears and anxieties allayed for that day at least.

The mode of teaching being then very unlike the present high-pressure system adopted now at the Board and other schools, the lessons done at school and at home sat very lightly upon us school-boys. The home lessons especially were got over without any great trouble or anxiety—"Sufficient unto the day is the evil thereof" being, alas, the maxim too generally acted upon! It must also be told that many of the boys had a far greater admiration for those of their fellows who knew of the greatest number of birds' nests, who could climb the highest trees, and who were the happy owners of the most bools or peeries, or could fly the highest kite or dragon, rather than for those who had the most book learning.

One of the very many of Mr. Haxton's maxims was to "Do, do; what you do, do!"—that was, to do well whatever you attempted; but unfortunately it was not so often acted upon by his scholars as he desired it should be. To stimulate his pupils to diligence, Mr. Haxton had a large black board, or wooden tablet, fastened to the wall above the fireplace, on the top of which were the words "*Semper Assiduus*" (always diligent). Below this were the names of pupils deserving of being recorded, and there was space left for those who should come after. Two of the names that figured on that board were Ebenezer Henderson, afterwards LL.D., and author of the "Life of Ferguson the Astronomer," "Annals of Dunfermline," &c. &c.; and John Miller, afterwards printer and publisher, and proprietor of the *Dunfermline Advertiser*. Precious little of the midnight oil was burnt in those days over the home tasks. May it not be that the defective sight which is beginning to appear amongst the young of the present generation, as seen in the large number in our towns and cities wearing spectacles, like the students of Germany, is attributable in some measure to the heavy home tasks given to those of tender years in the present day? It is, I think, a great mistake to force mental powers too much, and make boys men before they are boys.

To show the kindly disposition of the Rector of the Grammar School, he had all our exercise or home lesson books spread out on a large table each day, which he examined carefully, and those boys or girls whose work was considered worthy of sixty marks and upwards, were rewarded with a piece of "blackman" (treacle toffy). This blackman was made up in long sticks and covered with paper. A boy was sent out daily to a neighbouring confectioner's shop for the day's supply, and the master cut with his knife small pieces about two inches long, and placed them on the open pages of the books of the deserving scholars. This was kindly meant, but the inconvenience of the thing was that some of our copy books were smeared daily with treacle, and the leaves would consequently stick together, and present a most extraordinary spectacle by the time the book was finished. Such a course as this, if pursued now-a-days, would throw our modern School Boards into fits. When it neared four o'clock, and before the solemn evening prayer or benediction was pronounced, and when the scholars got settled down into their seats, and another day's work almost over, the master, sitting in his square box or desk, the very picture of contentment, his spectacles resting on his forehead, would unbend, and ask and encourage any boy to stand up and tell a story, repeat an anecdote, or recount any incident that had happened during the day. He told them that if any of them would tell a story he would tell another. Some of the boys did so, and some did it well. This, although it may now be deemed a trivial matter by some, was in reality a most excellent piece of training. It gave to boys, by practice, a degree of confidence that not only enabled them to stand up and address their fellow-scholars, but prepared them for some of the great duties of public and private life. If it happened that no one would volunteer, then the master himself, who was a most admirable story-teller, would sometimes entertain us with one, long or short, as the time permitted. His well-told stories and anecdotes were always directed to the main end—the higher education and the moral improvement of the young minds, leading them to the abhorrence of all that was untruthful, dishonest, cowardly, or mean. His aim was to make his pupils manly and true. In many parts of the country his influence is yet felt for good. Every week the scholars were expected to write a piece of original composition in the shape of an essay, or a letter to a friend, &c. Those compositions were read every Friday afternoon in presence of the whole school, and were often most instructive and amusing.

In all the schools of that period the opening and closing of each day's work partook of a religious character. The morning and evening prayers were never long, and were ever solemn and impressive. The Bible (which Sir Walter Scott on his deathbed remarked to his friend Lockhart was the only *one book* after all) was read and explained daily, and its awfully-in-earnest precepts were strongly inculcated on the young of that generation. It might be treated lightly, and even irreverently, by many at the time, as words of wisdom and of warning often are; but in many cases a day would come when the grandeur of its Divine and precious precepts would dawn upon their minds, and when it would be seen by them that "wisdom is the principal thing" after all.

While some of those reminiscences were appearing in the *Dunfermline Press*, the following letter, written by an M.D. practising in Glasgow, who was a pupil of Mr. Haxton's, was published in that paper, and we think it should be inserted here, as it supplies information which is worthy of being preserved:—

"Sir—I have no idea who the writer may be of those quiet and charming Dunfermline reminiscences, but am reading them with much interest. The memorial portrait of Mr. Haxton, the respected Rector of the High School, is true to life. How well I remember his flushed, weather-beaten, solemn countenance; his polished, bald head, with silvery side-locks brushed vigorously upwards; his military bearing and swinging gait. How he used to encourage us in the solution of a problem by feigning to be the learner, and in the end exclaiming, "Oh, I see it now my boy! I see it now!" How scrupulous he was with us about slovenliness in person or dress, and how specially severe in any meanness, prevarication, or untruthfulness. How he encouraged us in our outdoor sports and excursions, and listened with real delight to our weekly narration of them in the form of letters addressed either to himself or some companion. So much did the prevention of cruelty to any of the lower animals, or to a child, interest him, that it was considered a fortunate circumstance if such an incident on the road to Rossyth, or Limekilns, or Charlestown, or Loch Glow, or Loch Fitty, could without fiction be introduced into these weekly effusions. The Latin declensions he used to intone or chaunt in order to impress them on our memories, and when the cane became necessary, as for utter neglect of Cæsar's Commentaries, or Mair's Introduction to Latin Syntax, it was brought down solemnly, diagonally, and repeatedly across the back, with these words musically rendered, *crescendo*—"It is two bad! It is three bad!! It is thirty bad!!! It is a hundred bad!!!!" There was latent humour here, but we did not see it, or at least enjoy it, at the time. Such correction was borne well, however, for, unlike other punishments I have experienced elsewhere, we knew there was no personal bitterness in it. Far less was there any on those great occasions when "Big Peter," the greater taws, was brought out from a recess of the large, oblong, elevated, mysterious compartment at one corner of the room, which was the Rector's sanctum. Indeed, the whole discipline of the school, like that of Rugby under the famous Dr. Arnold, was directed to the formation of a manly character—special severity being exercised against all laziness, meanness, cruelty, and duplicity, and so as not to lower in any way self-respect, or to excite revenge. Many Hansel Mondays have come and gone since then, but, like your contributor of advancing years, I cherish most kindly memories of Archibald Haxton.—I am, &c.

"GLASGOW, 20th October 1884."

The occasion of the annual examination of the school, and the commencement of the vacation, were looked forward to eagerly for weeks, and when the day came it was a most eventful one. In many of the schools the vacation was usually given about harvest time, to accommodate those whose parents were engaged in harvest work, and also to enable the youngsters to go with the shearers to glean, or "gather singles." The scholars were on the vacation day dressed in their Sunday garb; prizes of books were distributed to those who were deserving, in presence of the clergymen of the town, the parents, and others. There was a ringing cheer given when it was announced that a vacation of five weeks or so would be granted; and then, to finish up the day's proceedings, the master put on a very large white apron, which he filled with "sweeties," giving each scholar a handful on retiring, along with a cordial shake of the hand, and an affectionate farewell. My old and esteemed teacher, Mr. Haxton, has long ago gone the way of all the earth, but I almost feel yet, after the lapse of about fifty years, the kindly pressure of his hand, and hear his last "Farewell," as I passed out to enter his school no more.

I have mentioned that on the vacation day we were all treated with a large handful of sweeties on retiring. This was usual at most of the schools then, but at one of the Dunfermline schools, at least, the scholars on the examination day were treated differently from this, they were regaled with a glass of whisky-toddy, as a sort of *doch-an-dorris,* or stirrup-cup, prior to the breaking-up! There were no teetotal societies, or blue ribbon associations, to interfere with the literal "flow of spirits" in those days; and this proceeding, performed, no doubt, in mistaken kindness, was at that period deemed of no serious consequence. A friend of the writer who attended this particular school informed him that after the examination was over, and the school was about to break up, a large kettleful of water was put on the fire, and in front of this fire " a table was placed, on which were set bottles of whisky, basins of sugar, and some biscuits. A large toddy bowl was then kept going, and served as the toddy brewery, until the scholars, to the number of about one hundred and fifty or so, had all got one and some of them even a second round ! I remember quite well of that being the first time I ever felt drink in my head, and when we got out to the fresh air a number of the scholars felt light-headed, or what might be called elevated !"

I only hope that the pupils who attended that school have since their school-days lived as abstemiously and temperately as my friend who supplied me with the above information has done during his long, honourable, and prosperous career.

SCHOOL PUNISHMENTS.

THE mode of punishing delinquents at the ordinary schools differed very much. Some teachers were very severe, and even cruel; others were the reverse; but as a rule there was far greater severity practised then than would be tolerated now. Those thrashings and palmies with canes and whalebone ribs of umbrellas, and with leathern taws, sometimes burnt at the tips, were so common, that they were looked upon as things in the ordinary course of nature. Severe as punishments were in some of the Dunfermline schools, they were nothing compared to those inflicted in other parts of the country. The Rev. Dr. Paul mentions that at the Grammar School of Aberdeen it was a common spectacle to see a number of boys called to "leave their seats and stand up in a line on the floor to be flogged. The master gave them the word of command *to adjust their garments for the operation,* which they did without the master putting a finger upon them. He then walked up and down the floor, and administered the castigation to his heart's content." At the same school the services of the school porter were sometimes called in, and he took the delinquent on his back, and held him firmly there while the punishment was administered by the master. In some schools in the North they kept "cooling stones," smooth and flat, upon which culprits were sent to cool after a good whipping.

The Aberdonians have long been famed for their great shrewdness, or "long-headedness," as it is called; has this had anything to do with the rather severe school punishments inflicted on them in early life! It is a fact, I believe, that two Aberdonian dominies, some generations since, were bewailing the circumstance that boys could not then be taught to learn Latin, and the two wise-acres agreed that it was on account of their pupils not being able to stand the drubbings that used to be freely

administered in the young days of those two worthy
schoolmasters!

Punishments formed a part of the regular school curriculum, which had to be carried out at all costs. Many good,
thoughtful parents, whilst sympathising keenly with their
children when they came home from the school black and
blue, concealed any resentment for the sake of keeping up
what they considered salutary and necessary discipline,
and for the purpose of supporting the authority of the
master; for was it not written, "He that spareth the rod,"
&c.? If one-half of the punishment were now inflicted
that used formerly to be freely administered, a hue-and-
cry would be got up from one end of the country to
the other, and the Home Secretary would be apprised of
the outrage immediately. It was only recently that a
paragraph went the round of the English newspapers,
headed "Great Cruelty in a School." The school referred
to was in the village of Lochgoilhead, Scotland, and the
teacher was most severely brought to task for having considered it his duty to compel delinquents to swallow castor
oil in lieu of applying the cane or the taws. The case
was actually brought under the notice of the House of
Commons. This treatment of his was, after all, nothing
new. History often repeats itself. About eighty years ago
there might have been seen standing by the side of the
school fire, in a village near Dunfermline, an earthenware
pot, filled either with a decoction of wormwood, or with aloes
or senna. It was only the other day that the author met
a very intimate friend of his, who told him that sixty
years ago he attended a school in Lanark. At that school
the master kept a *greybeard*, or jar, behind the school-door,
and that jar contained a mixture of Glauber salts and
water. Youngsters who were obstreperous, or were con-
firmed dunces, got a glass of this nauseous medicine now
and again, as the master considered it in the light both of
a punishment and a cure for his scholars! This dominie
had a theory of his own that the spirit of insubordination,
or "*devilishness*," as he called it, proceeded from bad humours
in the bodily system, and that lashes and stripes were of

no avail; it was labour in vain; the only perfect punishment and cure were doses of cooling salts!

"Hard is the scholar's lot unpatronised;"

for, in addition to the terrors held over the scholars' heads by the masters, there was often the dread of being beset by pupils belonging to other schools.

In those days there were bitter feuds carried on between the boys of one school and those of another. This was the case all over the country, and I believe this kind of warlike rivalry still exists to some extent. There were often great fights between the Lancasterian School (Mr. Robertson's) and Mr. Meldrum's, and, in the north side of the town, between Mr. Thomas Johnstone's and Mr. Craig's. All kinds of missiles were used—stones, sticks, and grass divots were freely showered upon each other; and in many cases the younger scholars had to be escorted home by the older and stronger ones, in order to prevent assaults being committed.

The practice of nick-naming teachers was then universal; each one was spoken of and known by his particular *soubriquet*. One of them having the misfortune to be deformed, he was known accordingly by that peculiarity. Another was in the habit of eating "baps" and treacle to his lunch, and inadvertently praising this article of diet very much, the nick-name of "Baps and Treacle" fell to his lot. The boys of the different schools were constantly at loggerheads, and frequently called in at the school windows the nick-names of the different schoolmasters. With such a state of things existing, it is easy to see that the solemn and important work of school education was carried on under the greatest impediments.

At that period Mr. Macdonald was the teacher of the English department in the Commercial Academy, and was famed far and near for his excellent mode of teaching English reading. The beautiful style of pronunciation acquired by his pupils was the subject of remark everywhere. Mr. Rodger was the teacher of mathematics, &c. at that Academy.

There were a number of Sunday schools in the town, but for the most part they were not connected with the different churches and denominations, as they are now. They were conducted by various individuals, the most of whom were members and office-bearers of churches, who thought themselves called on and qualified to open a school in their own dwelling-houses, or in any public room suitable for the purpose. Many worthy, earnest, God-fearing men entered upon that work—men well qualified and desirous to do good, and who no doubt did good service. It must at the same time be admitted that there were instances where men quite unfit for this responsible and difficult task undertook to perform it.

> " The gulf of seven-and-fifty years
>   We stretch our welcoming hands across ;
>   The distance but a pebble's toss
> Between us and our youth appears.
>
> " Soul touches soul,—the muster-roll
>   Of life eternal has no gaps ;
>   And after half a century's lapse,
> Our school-day ranks are closed and whole !
>
> " Hail and farewell ! We go our way,
>   Where shadows end, we trust, in light ;
>   The star that ushers in the night
> Is herald also of the day !"
>   *J. G. Whittier.*

MATTERS ECCLESIASTICAL.

THE AULD KIRK BELLS.

At eventide, when in the west
   The gates of night are glowing,
When wearied labour seeks for rest,
And when the young moon's rising crest
   Her softest beams are showing ;

And when through midnight's gloom profound,
   Dark ghostly shades are looming,
O'er slumbering homesteads all around,
And o'er each silent graveyard mound,
   Break forth thine echoes booming !

By day and night, through sun and shower,
   Thy warning voice is falling,
Touching the heart with solemn power,
And telling that each passing hour,
   Is one that's past recalling !

In varying moods thine echoes seem
   Like night-winds dark communing,
Now like the rolling of a stream,
Or strains of music in a dream,
   While choirs their songs are tuning.

And bygone days again appear,
   Bright, vanished scenes revealing,
When broke on childhood's wondering ear
Thy startling music, deep and clear,
   And distant echoes pealing.

From thy grey tower, long may'st thou toll,
   In tones harmonious blending.
Swelling like ocean's solemn roll,
A spirit-song to fire the soul,
   While men are churchward wending.

Ages have come and gone since thou
   First pealed in Sabbath chorus,
Inviting men the knee to bow :
The refrain of thy song is " *now,*"
   In tones deep and sonorous.

Ring, Sabbath bells ! with rousing chime,
   Thy deep and solemn greeting,
Call with thy thrilling notes sublime
The living to "*redeem*" the "*time,*"
   For life is short and fleeting !

The following are the names of the clergymen who officiated in Dunfermline sixty years ago :

Rev. ALLAN MACLEAN, Abbey Church, First Charge.
Rev. PETER CHALMERS, Abbey Church, Second Charge.
Rev. GEORGE BELL BRAND, Chapel Kirk.
Rev. WILLIAM DALZIEL, "Auld Licht" Kirk.
Rev. GEORGE BARLAS, Anti-Burgher.
Rev. HENRY FERGUS, Relief Church.
Rev. ROBERT BROWN, Maygate Chapel, and afterwards
    St. Margaret's Church.
Rev. ALEXANDER FISHER, Queen Anne Street.

Those were the men who in their day and generation were amongst the leading lights of the town. Verily, "One generation passeth away, and another generation cometh." Towards them a feeling of deep reverence prevailed amongst all classes, and they were esteemed and honoured for their Master's sake. If any one, especially a young person, presumed to speak lightly of them, they were instantly rebuked, and solemnly warned that " *the clergy are no craws to shoot at.*"

Much reverence was also shown towards the Day of Rest by the great bulk of the people. In well-ordered houses, preparations were made on the Saturday for the advent of that sacred day. No shoes were brushed, no water was carried from the wells, no beards were shaved on that day, and very little in the shape of cooking was done. The late Dr. Guthrie once mentioned, that on his going to preach for a brother minister in the north, he asked his friend on the Saturday evening, before retiring to rest, if he could get some warm water in the morning, whereupon the minister held up a warning hand, saying, " Whisht, whisht ! speak of shaving on the Lord's Day, and you need never preach here any more !" It was just the same in Dunfermline fifty-five years ago. On Sabbath evenings, when families with their domestics were assembled at the fireside, the head of the household usually put questions from the Shorter Catechism to all round, and to each one in his or her proper turn. No one escaped who was old enough and capable of " *saying their questions.*" Those who answered correctly were commended, and those who failed were faithfully admonished. This "catecheesin'," as it was called, was not confined to the members of the family alone, but to those visitors or "strangers" that might be within their gates. On an occasion of this kind, a family living near Dunfermline was assembled one Sabbath evening. They had a young stranger staying with them that night, and his turn came to say his questions, but he appeared to be sadly deficient of a knowledge of the "single book," as it was called. So, in this awkward predicament, one of the family relieved him from his difficulty by slyly handing him the book in question, from which he read the answers as his turn came. The head of the household (who was an old and much-esteemed friend of the writer) was quite blind, and did not observe the young man quietly glancing under the table for his answers, but, by and by, when the stranger's turn again came round, he by mistake turned over two leaves of the book instead of one, and gave the wrong answer. My old friend in a moment detected the fraud that was being committed; he said little about it, but what he did say would be more in love than in anger, and such as the young folks would never forget while they lived. The young were strictly enjoined "not to think their ain thochts or do their ain deeds" on that day; and the awful fate that befell "the man in the moon," who broke the Sabbath by gathering sticks, used to be freely held over their heads as a terrible warning. It was then looked upon, not merely as a day of rest, but also a day for religious meditation. Family worship was performed in almost every dwelling. The door was seldom opened, and travelling in the country, or from place to place, was rarely indulged in. This was the "public opinion" of those days. No fun or levity was allowed, and it was deemed then, as it is still, especially sinful to whistle on the Sabbath-day.

The Sabbath in Dunfermline at the present day seems to be observed with an amount of decorum that is unsurpassed by the most of towns in this country, but certainly there is not the rigidness abounding now that existed fifty or sixty years ago. Perhaps there was too much of the strict and rigid element on all hands before and about that period. Long ago there were watchers employed to go round the town, and apprehend any one who was considered guilty of Sabbath desecration, such as carrying water from the wells, or loitering about the streets during the hours of Divine Service.

The same severe and rigid regard for the sanctity of the day of rest lingers in some parts of Scotland even at the present day. Let us take the island of St. Kilda as an example. Over this island a most terrific tempest passed only a few months ago, causing the total destruction of the crops, and rendering the poor islanders almost entirely destitute. For several months in the year this little island, far from the mainland and surrounded by a tempestuous sea, is rarely approached by any vessel. Through their clergyman, the Rev. Mr. M'Kay, a small piece of wood was launched from the island, and a bottle with a letter enclosed was attached to it, which, after much tossing about, at last found its way to our own hospitable shores; and soon the steamship *Hebridean* was generously fitted out with a good supply of stores and provisions, and also seed for their little crofts. The steamer, on her urgent errand of mercy, arrived off St. Kilda on a Sunday afternoon, and the island appeared to those on board to be quite deserted, —not a living person was to be seen. The steam whistle was blown, and by and by many persons were seen emerging from the church; but none of them thought of going down to the shore or of sending a boat off to the ship. The *Hebridean* then lowered a boat, and Captain M'Callum and some friends went on shore, and they were received by the minister of the island and the people with suppressed feelings of joy and gratitude—suppressed on account of the sanctity of the day. The Captain then briefly intimated the object of his visit to the island, and asked the minister, the Rev. Mr. M'Kay, as the head of the community, when they would send ashore the supplies to them. "*Not to-day*," said the minister, sternly. Then the Captain asked if Mr. M'Kay could assure him of quiet, favourable weather in the morning. The minister of course could make no such promise; all he could do was to promise that, as soon as the Sabbath was out, *and not one minute before that time*, the islanders would be ready, and would do their very best to assist in landing the supplies so generously sent to them. He also added, that the same kind Providence which had enabled the islanders to let their wants become known, and put it into men's hearts to send them relief in the shape of corn, meal, and potatoes, would keep the wind steady in the north-east till the provisions were landed! We give this as an example of the respect which the people in many parts of Scotland sixty years ago considered due to the day of rest.

It has been well remarked by a great preacher that "it is better to lean to the side of scrupulousness than laxity, and that Scotland and her children owe much to the manner in which they were taught to remember the Sabbath-day." It was perhaps unfortunate for them, however, that they had so few attractive books provided, such as we have at the present time. Bunyan's *Pilgrim's Progress*, Boston's *Fourfold State*, *The Crook in the Lot*, and the *Cloud of Witnesses*, &c., were amongst the only books that young persons could lay their hands on, and were allowed to peruse. We are perhaps going to the other extreme now-a-days, for shoals of all kinds of religious books are constantly issuing from the great seething press. There is now a boundless field of attractive Sunday literature opened up, and at small cost, to suit the wants and tastes of old and young in these wonderful times of ours. It is at the same time very questionable whether much of this Sunday literature is fitted to edify and improve. I fear it has an opposite tendency; and it is in many instances very trivial.

It is well known to all, that Dunfermline has long taken an active part not only in political but also in ecclesiastical movements. After the suspension of the four members of the Church by the Assembly in 1733, they first met at Gairney Bridge, near Kinross, and formed themselves into the first Associate Presbytery, and after that, Dunfermline went into the movement heart and soul. Here the Secession Church was founded in 1739 by the Rev. Ralph Erskine; and here, too, the "Relief" body commenced its career, having been founded by the Rev. Thomas Gillespie in 1752. Dunfermline was thus the birthplace of both branches of the United Presbyterian Church, whose great influence now extends far beyond the bounds of the land where it first took its rise. Dunfermline is therefore highly honoured, and her sons are the citizens of no mean city. But Dunfermline has also been the arena where a good deal of heated discussion over the subject of church government and other religious controversies have taken place. Coming down from the times of the founders of those two religious denominations to a much later date— a date which will be in the memory of some still living in Dunfermline—there was the great controversy regarding the case of the Rev. Mr. Whyte and Queen Anne Street Church. The present generation cannot realise the intensity of feeling that was then evoked and that subsisted between the two parties interested in this case. Members of the same family took opposite sides on the question, and were thus much divided. The climax was reached when the Rev. Mr Hay, of Kinross, a member of the Presbytery, imprudently said, no doubt in his haste, that he did not care although Queen Anne Street Church were blown to the moon! The formation of St. Margaret's Congregation, a branch from Queen Anne Street, followed this great ecclesiastical disturbance.

About that time there was also an intense dislike shown by the Burghers (or "Auld Licht" Kirk) towards the Anti-Burghers (or "New Lichts"). This feeling was frequently expressed by both parties and openly shown. Illustrative of this, a story is told about two boys who had broken into a large garden. While they were in the act of filling their pockets with forbidden fruit, the owner suddenly pounced upon them, and managed to catch one of the culprits, but the other escaped. The one who had been so fortunate as to scramble to the top of a high wall, where he was fairly out of harm's reach, shouted to the owner of the garden, who was holding the other boy in his clutches—"*Leather him weel, for his faither's an Anti-Burgher!*" "As the old cock crows the young one learns!" Another illustration of the somewhat unsatisfactory state of feeling that subsisted between some of the older members of those two bodies may also be mentioned. During the time that some repairs were being made on the Burgher Kirk, the Anti-Burgher folks gave them the use of their place of worship for a portion of each Sunday, which was accepted. On coming out on the first Sunday, one woman was heard to say to another, "*Wasna that a grand sermon the day, Janet?*" to which the other replied, "*Ou aye, the sermon was guid enough; but, oh, it cam oot o' a dirty dish!*"

Country people thought nothing of walking long journeys to hear their usual or favourite minister. In those days, places of worship were not warmed up in winter time; and in most cases they were cold, damp, and comfortless, unless there were fire and fervour (which there often were) in the pulpit. The people would sit for hours together, listening to the old-fashioned, earnest, and usually vigorous orators of the day; and it was not considered a penance, but a duty and a privilege, to do so. There is a story told about an old woman, who was one morning walking on her way to church, which was some miles distant. The country roads were often very bad in winter, and over such for some miles old Tibby had to travel. There was thawing snow on the ground, and her fellow-traveller, seeing her tramp, tramping through the worst part of the road, advised her to come to her side of the way, which was not so wet; but old Tibby's reply was —"'*Deed no, the ordinances o' grace canna be bought owre dear!*"

An American phrenologist—Dr. Fowler, I think, was his name—when lecturing on phrenology, mentioned the case of a man who lived near Kinross, who would worship nowhere else than in the Abbey Church of the old city of Dunfermline. He thus walked about fourteen miles each way, twenty-eight miles in all every Sabbath day, to worship in the temple of the old and hoary city of Dunfermline.   Dr. Fowler afterwards found that this man's organ of *veneration* was exceedingly prominent, and this it was, he thought, which prompted the man to undergo the inconvenience, and sometimes the hardship, of a long pilgrimage every Sunday.

In those old times people were often seen going to church carrying in their hands bits of either spearmint or balm, *apple-ringie* or thyme, which they had taken that morning from their little gardens.   On taking their seats, these fragrant herbs were reverently laid on the bookboard, and during the service were often had recourse to, if a dreary preacher were holding forth, or a fit of drowsiness came over them.   It was no uncommon sight to see old people passing their snuff-mulls from one pew to another during the service, and to see them taking a pinch with a snuff-spoon, and with considerable gusto.   Even in the pulpits we have seen ministers having recourse to their snuff-boxes while preaching, perhaps to stimulate their flagging eloquence and their energy, and in some cases we have observed them dip their fingers into their vest pockets, and from this receptacle adroitly take a pinch.   This was not so conspicuous as the box or snuff-mull.

TENT-PREACHING.

BETWEEN fifty and sixty years ago there might be seen many groups of persons, early on a summer's Sabbath morning, quietly wending their way towards some neighbouring town or village, to attend a tent-preaching and communion—it might be at Carnock, Inverkeithing, or Cairneyhill, &c. At that time a journey of ten or even twenty miles on foot, to attend such an important occasion, was thought nothing of. Long before the period above referred to, it is recorded that at some of the communion occasions held at Dunfermline in the days of the Rev. Ralph Erskine, the tables began to be served at nine in the morning, and sometimes continued till twelve at night! Those communions had in his time been noted seasons, and were attended by vast numbers. They came from all quarters, some from a distance of forty and fifty miles on foot, and to the number, in some instances, of "*between four and five thousand communicants!*" Now-a-days one can scarcely realise such a fact as this; yet, nevertheless, it is so recorded in his journal. The period of the year for holding these great gatherings was generally when the daylight was at the longest, and at times when there might be moonlight, to accommodate those who had to travel long journeys.

In our remembrance, the people who were seen going to such out-door preachings were, as a rule, becomingly and comfortably dressed. Many of the men wore homespun clothing of hoddin grey, &c., while the women were attired in serge, camlot, Birsel-pea, bombazine, and bombazette dresses, which often did service for many years, and had graced many such assemblages. As a rule, they were quiet and douce in their demeanour, as became them on the Sabbath morning, and thus—

> " They took their steps from every side,
>   In casual bands, along the beaten way."

Men, women, and children, the rich and the poor, were to
be seen thronging towards the great tent meeting. The
aged and infirm were leaning on the arms of their sons or
daughters, and the little ones were being led by the hands
of their parents, or were trudging happily along by their
side. Some of the older women carried with them *creepie*
stools, to sit on when they reached the tent; and the
younger women, to save shoe leather, carried their shoes
and stockings over their arms, and performed the operation
of washing their feet and putting on their shoes at the
nearest burn or stream before entering the town. The
most of them carried refreshments to last all day—consisting, for the most part, of oaten cakes and barley
bannocks, butter, cheese, boiled eggs, &c. &c. While thus
wending their way to the great centre of attraction, the
young folks would sometimes naturally fall into each
other's company, and talk of matters congenial to those of
their own age. The old folks, as they leisurely paced
along, would get deeply involved in discussions on the
relative merits of the different preachers they were expect-
ing to listen to and to feast upon that day. One divine
would be spoken of as noted for his rousing denunciations
of the sins and frivolities of "a world lying in wickedness;"
another would be expected to be deep, dry, and doctrinal,
and to

> " *Wauken on some kittle point,*
>   *Some heretic put oot o' joint.*"

Some would be expected to give the people that day
"their kail through the reek," in the shape of fiery,
sulphurous declamation. Others, like the venerable Dr.
Brown of Whitburn, would be favourably spoken of, and
applauded for their quiet, loving, and convincing ways, and
so in this manner their peculiar merits would be enlarged
upon. While quietly jogging along, there was a deep
Sabbath stillness on all sides; there was the great, solemn,
blue dome of heaven above them, and an inexpressible
serenity in the morning air, refreshing to many a weary,
heavy-laden sinner. It resembled the scene so well described by Grahame add—

> " How still the morning of the hallowed day !
>   Sounds the most faint attract the ear—the hum
>   Of early bee, the trickling of the dew,
>   The distant bleating midway up the hill—
>   Calmness sits throned on yon unmoving cloud !"

When the vast gathering had assembled, and was seated, as it generally was, on the face of some rising ground or grassy slope, all leaned forward with sparkling eyes, and with evident signs of expectation. First one divine and then another would in turn mount the pulpit—which was usually a rude piece of carpentry, resembling a sentry-box on long legs—and address the people. All of them would do so in powerful, impassioned language, warning all present in solemn tones to "flee from the wrath to come." There was the "action sermon," the "fencing of the tables," and the solemn debarring of those who were unworthy to go there. At intervals, the overpowering strains of melody, proceeding from a thousand voices, would be re-echoed by the distant hills ; and then a deep, solemn feeling would prevail as some aged and well-known pastor with heart and soul engaged in prayer. By-and-by it might be Ebenezer Brown's turn, and on him every eye would be fixed, and every word listened to with breathless attention. His words would stir the hearts of many that day, and cause many a sob in that assembly. That beautiful oratory of his, with its natural and intense earnestness, devoid of art, which captivated and carried away Henry Brougham and Lord Jeffrey, would be heard to advantage on such an occasion as this.

While the tent-preaching was thus carried on outside, there was now and again a stream of people going in and coming out of the church adjoining. As the communicants were coming out of the church by the one door, and leaving the communion tables, crowds of others in succession were entering by the other door, taking their places, and sitting down. As they retired from the tables, they sang in solemn strains as they passed along the aisles to the read or intoned line,—

> " Some ancient melody, of style severe,
>   Their fathers sung in old reforming days."

Now and again there might be heard to arise some glorious psalm of David's such as—

> " God is our refuge and our strength,
>   In straits a present aid."

Or it might be—

> " I joy'd when to the House of God
>   Go up they said to me."

in which all the people joined, as they slowly and solemnly passed along to the door, in order to enable a fresh crowd of intending communicants to take their places, the last words of the minister falling on their ears, *" Go in peace, and may the God of peace be with you."*

Principal Robertson, the historian, when a youth, attended one of those gatherings, and years after, he spoke of the sermon he heard. He said, " It was delivered in a strain of natural and profound eloquence, and a strong impression was produced on all, and such was the effect, that I recollected more of that sermon than of any I have ever heard. Even yet, when I retire to my studies, the recollection thrills through my mind."

As time went on, flagrant abuses now and again came to light, and marred the usefulness and the influence of those wonderful gatherings. Tent-preachings were being gradually discontinued fifty-five years ago. Dunfermline, once so noted for them, gave them up. Inverkeithing and other places followed some time after. It was found that a great deal of drinking and other evils were indulged in, and that a large sprinkling of the " baser sort " frequented those gatherings, and indulged in unseemly levity. They, however, served their day and generation well, and public opinion, which for many long years pronounced emphatically in favour of those great religious festivals, in course of time pronounced against them. There was the bar of public opinion then, as there is now, which carries with it great influence. The highest and the lowest in the land are influenced by it. Much as I admire and revere the marvellous genius of our own immortal Burns, I cannot help thinking that his

"Holy Fair" is unfairly drawn, and is an exaggerated bur-
lesque. No one will convince us that there was (as he
attempted to show) nothing but unmixed evil attending
those gatherings. While there were many evils latterly
developed, arising from those large promiscuous gatherings,
which were to be deplored, we may assume there was
also an incalculable amount of good done to many a poor
sinner, at such seasons of religious communion, the
extent of which the world would never know. Those who
attended such meetings from proper motives, and in order
to derive benefit therefrom, would be likely to obtain it,
and to have a word in season

> "Dropped in the heart's deep well."

Those, on the other hand, who went from unworthy motives,
and to have sport and fun, would also be likely to get what
they wanted at the same time. While we read that beautiful masterpiece, "The Cottar's Saturday Night," written at
the very time those great preachings were in full swing, we
are tempted to ask if this model cottar and his household,
including their daughter Jenny and her sweetheart, did
not attend and receive benefit "from scenes like these!"
Public opinion being then, as it is now, so supreme a power,
the family in question would doubtless grace those
assemblies with their presence, and they would be the very
kind of people that would be open to receive edification
and benefit therefrom.

While attempting to say a word in vindication of
the tent-preachings of the olden times, we must also
concede with much regret that there was such an un-
pleasant side of the picture, which presented itself to
thoughtful men. No picture can be perfect without its
light and shade, and it must be recorded that large numbers
were tempted to enter the houses of refreshment during
the time the services were being conducted, and to
indulge immoderately in drink. Those houses had usually
placed before their doors a stool, on which stood a large
tankard, with a "bap" on the top of it, as an indication
that ale and bread were to be had within. As the day

wore on, some of those places of entertainment did a great
stroke of business. Soon the effects became visible, and
the neighbourhood presented something like the aspect of
a fair. We remember well of hearing of the great
disturbances that sometimes occurred at Inverkeithing
preachings. There is an incident related with regard to
one of those unseemly scenes which occurred there. Some
of our townsmen had gone into a public-house to obtain
refreshments, and while partaking freely thereof, a great
disturbance occurred outside, and all of them rushed out
of the house to see what was the matter. The last man
to leave the room, quietly and unobserved, slipped into the
pocket of his long-tailed blue coat the remaining portion
of a cold leg of mutton which was lying on the table, and
with quite an innocent face joined his companions outside.
He shortly afterwards proceeded to the tent-preaching,
and demurely sat down on the grass amongst the throng.
By-and-by, a big rough-looking dog (and there were
several there along with their masters) came snuff, snuffing, and smelling about him rather unceremoniously, to
his great disgust and annoyance. He could get no peace,
so at last he was reluctantly compelled to disgorge himself
of his ill-gotten plunder, and taking it out of his pocket,
threw it to the dog, saying—"*There it is! Tak it, ye
nasty, thievin' brute that ye are!*"

In connection with those great preachings, an incident
once happened which may be known to some of our
readers, but it is, we think, worthy of being recorded here.
It was usual for the minister's wife to provide beforehand
for the great demands that were expected to be made
upon the hospitable larder, through the influx of clergymen who were expected from a distance to assist at the
tent. On an occasion of this kind, the thrifty wife of a
minister belonging to this neighbourhood had provided
beforehand, amongst other things, a nice small beaf-steak pie,
and it was placed amongst some other viands on the larder
shelf. Two of her sons, young growing boys, were sorely
tempted to partake of that particular dish, their ordinary
fare being doubtless at that time what Burns called "*the*

chief o' Scotia's food!" The two at last fell foul of the savoury pie; they carefully and neatly cut round the crust, and took that off bodily, then regaled themselves with the contents. To add insult to injury, they filled up the vacant space with grass, and on the top thereof, they placed a small slip of paper, bearing the following text of Scripture, *"All flesh is grass!"* They then carefully replaced the pie-crust, and left the dish where they found it, and went their way. The utter astonishment of the guests at the dinner-table, "when the pie was opened," may be imagined—it cannot be described. The apt Scriptural quotation showed a degree of acumen and keen sarcasm not to be met with every-day! One of those boys afterwards became a most distinguished preacher, unsurpassed for natural oratory, as he was for a noble, generous heart.

Although it may perhaps be a little out of place here, another incident, connected with our Fifeshire divine, the Rev. Mr. Shirra, may be mentioned. At Kinghorn, as at other ferries about that period, it was the practice of the boatman whose turn it was to sail, to call all persons, loungers and passengers, from their potations and lurking-places about the town, and to shout from the one end of Kinghorn to the other:—"The boat, ahoy! to Leith, ahoy!" Mr. Shirra was preaching in the Burgher tent there one day, when he observed the well-known Tam Galloway, with some boatmen and passengers, going down to Pettycur. He stopped short in his discourse, and addressed them with an energy peculiar to himself:—"Boatmen, ahoy!" The boatmen, passengers, and others at once stopped:—"Boatmen, I hear you cry, 'The boat, ahoy! to Leith ahoy! but we cry, salvation ahoy! to Heaven, ahoy! You sail aneath Skipper Gallowa' there; we sail aneath Christ! We hae Christ for our skipper, the Holy Ghost for our pilot, and God himself at the helm! Your boat, let me tell ye, is but a bit fir deal frae Noraway, but the keel o' our boat was laid in Bethlehem, built in Judæa, rigged in Jerusalem, and launched on Mount Calvary! We hae the cross o' Christ for a helm, a cedar o' Lebanon for a mast, and the redemption o' mankind for a freight. Your voyage under your earthly skipper, short as it is, may end in shipwreck and disaster; but our voyage, long as it may be, with Christ for our skipper, will end in everlasting joy and in glory unspeakable! Slip awa noo my freends, for 'time an' tide will no man bide,' but mind what I've said to ye; dinna swear, or tak the Holy Name o' God in vain, as ye were wont to do, and I'll pray for ye!"

MINISTERIAL VISITATIONS AND EXAMINATIONS.

THE annual ministerial diets of visitation and examination were regularly and faithfully gone through by the parish and other ministers about sixty years ago. It was usual for them to announce from the pulpit on Sabbath that they would visit a certain locality during the ensuing week. It was also the custom for those who expected a visit from the minister to have their dwellings put into extra good order, and this arose from a laudable desire to show him all the respect they possibly could in their humble way. In many houses, too, it was the practice to have a kebbuck of cheese, and some whisky in the bottle, in order to treat the minister, and he was deemed very unsocial if he declined the proffered hospitality. It was the almost universal custom of the times, and it was often a severe ordeal for the minister to go through. I have heard it said that some ministers in those days were obliged to calculate the number of families they intended to visit in one day, by the number of glasses of whisky they considered themselves able to take! It gave offence if they did not drink a full glass in the houses where whisky was offered to them. This custom was carried out from a kindly motive, but we must now condemn it, and consider it ill-judged and mistaken kindness.

I remember well of seeing the Rev. Mr. Chalmers, the respected colleague of the Rev. Allan M'Lean, of the Abbey Church, going his rounds long ago. He called at mostly every house, for all were in his parish in those days, though they did not attend the Parish Church. He inquired kindly for the welfare of the inmates, and before leaving intimated that he would be happy to meet them at the house of some well-known neighbour, for the purpose of being examined as to their Scriptural knowledge, and also to receive religious instruction. The ministers were usually attended by a beadle. Some clergymen were very strict in their examinations, and it was deemed by many, both of the old and young, a trying ordeal to pass through. Clergymen were then regarded with a far greater amount of fear, respect, and reverence than is given to the same profession now. When it became known that the minister was to "*veesit*" a certain neighbourhood, there was a general flutter in the several dwellings. The furniture and firesides got an extra polish up. There was also much searching of hearts before-hand, and searching of the Single Book and Catechisms, Larger and Shorter. At these examinations some answered their questions very well, and passed through the trying ordeal creditably. Others sat like "condemned thieves," with a scared look and downcast expression—their agitation so great that when it came to their turn to answer the minister they got quite dazed, and both memory and tongue hopelessly failed them. Those of them who had the use of their tongues sometimes committed many ludicrous blunders. Occasionally the answers given to questions were as wide of the mark as that once given to the Rev. Mr. Chalmers of the Abbey, by an applicant who waited on him for infant baptism one day at the manse. The minister, to test the man's Scriptural knowledge, asked him—"What is baptism?" To which he replied—"Thirteenpence-halfpenny, for I paid it just the noo!" For many years after, this unfortunate slip caused the man to bear the nickname of "Thirteenpence-halfpenny."

As a rule, the church-going people were well informed in Biblical history, and in the theological questions of the day. It has been well remarked that those diets of examination were "schools of theology for the people, and the absence of which has not found any proper compensation in our times." No doubt the "hearing and asking questions" has a very venerable antiquity to recommend it. Many persons in the walks of humble life made theology a regular study, and were very often severe, intelligent, and outspoken critics at "preachings" and other gatherings, and remarked sometimes that the sermons of certain preachers contained far "mair din than doctrine;" or that they were "neither edifeen' nor divertin'." and one minister, who came from Jedburgh, and who was noted for his very long prayers and sermons, was irreverently called "Cool the kail!" It occasionally happened also that working-men were more than a match for the minister at those pastoral visitations, and some were inclined to argue certain points with the minister. Some pastors differed as much from others in their mode of catechising the members and adherents of their flocks, as they differed from each other in the style and weight of their oratory. Many were very abstruse in their preaching, and were sometimes so in their pastoral examinations too. Such questions as these were often put :—Whether is faith or repentance first ? What is the best way to resist the temptations of Satan ? Explain what is the Covenant of Grace ? &c. &c.

Chapter and verse were always expected to be given by those who answered questions. On one occasion, an old woman was asked by a clergyman at one of those diets of ministerial examination, "What are the decrees of God ?" Being unable to answer, she meekly and timidly replied, "Indeed, sir, He kens that best Himsel !" There is a story told about the Rev. John Law, late of St. Margaret's Church, Dunfermline, who at a gathering of this kind, held at the mining village of Berrylaw, was putting some of the members of his church and the young people "through their facings." Amongst those who had failed in giving satisfactory answers to their questions was a voluble and forward young woman, a coal-miner, who asked leave to put a question to the minister. He allowed her to put the question, which was to the following effect:—"Hoo mony links are there in oor gin-pit chain ?" He, of course, could not answer, so she pertly remarked, "Ilka ane kens aboot their ain trade best !" While it was usual to ask the old and the young to answer questions out of the Assembly's Shorter Catechism, they were also sometimes requested to repeat from memory psalms and verses of psalms, such as the 23d, 100th, or a portion of the 119th Psalm.

At that period no household was deemed respectable if it did not in some form or other have family worship, at least once a day. The man or the woman was shunned who openly disregarded the sanctity of the Lord's Day, and who did not attend, or was not connected with, some Christian church or other. All this may be deemed, in these so-called refined and enlightened days of ours, narrowness, bigotry, &c., but it was the state of matters nevertheless. This it was that constrained our national bard to say—

> "From scenes like these old Scotia's grandeur springs,
> That makes her loved at home, revered abroad."

William Chambers, in his memoir of his brother Robert, records the case of an old woman who was the exact type of many women who lived at that time in Dunfermline and the neighbourhood, and it affords a good illustration for our purpose. "She was a great stickler on points of controversial divinity, a rigorous critic of sermons, and a severe censor of what she considered degenerating manners. As the wife of a ruling elder she possibly imagined that she was entitled to exercise a certain authority in ecclesiastical matters. In presence of a number of her neighbours she thought fit to lecture her minister on the subject of his wife's dress : "It was a sin and a shame," she said, "to see sae muckle finery."

"The minister did not deny the charge, but dexterously encountered her with the Socratic method of argument. 'So, Margaret, you think that ornament is useless and sinful in a lady's dress ?'

"'Certainly I do.'

"'Then may I ask why you wear that ribbon around your cap ? a piece of cord would surely do quite as well.' Disconcerted with this unforeseen turn of affairs, Margaret determinedly rejoined in an undertone, 'Ye'll no hae lang to speer sic a question.' Next day her cap was bound with a piece of white tape ; and never afterwards till the day of her death did she wear a ribbon or any morsel of ornament. I am doubtful," he says, "if we could macth this out of Scotland."

He also refers to the general practice of sermon criticising long ago by working-men. When a few of them met together of an evening at his lodgings, "the conversation turned chiefly on sermons. Each visitor brought with him experiences as to how texts had been handled on the preceding Sunday ; on which there ensued discussions singularly characteristic of a well-known phase in the Scottish mind."

This kind of conversation was usually heard in our own Dunfermline, especially on a Sabbath evening, if one or two friends met together in a neighbour's house. A great deal of their talk in those days was on controversial divinity. As already stated, books were scarce and dear, and consequently, with the scarcity of money also at that time, the range of literature was to working-men very limited indeed, and it was chiefly confined to books of a religious class.

To show how well acquainted some of the old people were with their Bibles, a curious incident, which happened in Limekilns Church, shortly after the ordination of the Rev. Mr. Johnston, may be mentioned. On one occasion, after the preliminary services, he rose to give out the text ; but after turning over the leaves of the Bible for some time, he gave out the words, adding that he had forgotten at the moment where to find the text. Hearing this, one of his audience told him at once where it was, for which he was thanked from the pulpit. The same thing never occurred again during his very long, able, and successful ministry.

As an example of the facility and the habit that some possessed of quoting Scripture, the following case may be recorded. A man in Cairneyhill village, who was indebted to another, had often been craved for the amount he was owing, and one day he was again asked for payment, when he quietly and solemnly told his creditor, "Let patience have her perfect work !"

There was in Fifeshire some amount of jealousy and a spirit of rivalry between the United Secession and the Relief bodies. This was at a period when it was the usual custom for people, especially the weavers, who were fond of debating religious and political subjects, to criticise the

ministers' discourses of the previous Sunday. As a rule—
which was very commendable—every man preferred his
own minister, and there was often disappointment felt
when the minister was "awa frae hame," and some other
less popular man took his place. Two old worthies met
one morning, and each was heartily "roosin'" his own
minister for the many gifts and graces he possessed. The
Secession man said to the other—"Man, oor minister is a
wonderfu' preacher. When he's layin' aff his discoorse I just
sit glowerin' at him wi' perfect amazement, an' often, often
I say to mysel, 'It's really a blessed mercy that Providence
didna permit you to be an infidel, for if you had been an
infidel, wi' your most extraordinar ability, ye wad hae
pushioned (poisoned) Europe!' Na, na, I want nane o'
your *guid warks* men, or preachers o' cauld morality; gie
me a speerit-rousin' preacher, that'll hold the deil under
the noses o' his congregation an' mak' their flesh creep.'"

Whilst many of the clergymen of the olden days were
"deep, dry, and doctrinal," and were terribly opposed to
preaching in favour of "guid warks," there were some here
and there who descended to descant on topics of every-day
life, and to adopt the practical, not only in their mode
of preaching, but at social meetings. A reverend and
esteemed friend of the writer once heard a preacher
introduce at a congregational meeting the subject of
savings banks, and expatiate on the virtue of retrenchment
and economy, and he did it in this wise:—"You must
relinquish your smoking and your snuffing; instead of
silks and satins, you must put up with linsey-woolsey;
instead of tea and coffee, you must be satisfied with the
'halesome parritch, chief o' Scotia's food;' and instead of
treating yourselves to a grilled slice from the monarch of
the flood, you must be content to hold masticating converse
with a far higher dignitary—a Glasgow magistrate."

Speaking about ministerial visitations, the ministers of
Dunfermline were, as a rule, very attentive in the matter
of visiting the sick or the bereaved. One of the ministers
of the town once paid a visit of condolence to one of his
flock, whose wife had recently died. The bereaved man

was busily engaged with his supper, consisting of porridge and milk, when the minister went in. The worthy pastor gave expression to the deep sympathy he felt, spoke in feeling terms of the man's great loss, and tried to console him as much as possible. Meantime the disconsolate widower continued to ply his spoon vigorously, saying to the minister at the same time, with a wonderfully steady voice—"Aye, it's an awfu' loss I've met in wi'; she'll be a very sair missed woman. I was just greetin' afore I began to my parritch, an' I intend to begin again, as soon's they're a' suppit!"

THE TEMPERANCE CAUSE AND Mr. JOHN DAVIE.

PRIOR to the introduction of the Temperance movement, about the year 1828, drinking customs were universal over the land. At births, christenings, marriages, and funerals, at marketings, bargain-makings, indenturing of apprentices, and even at Presbytery dinners, strong drink was liberally provided and indulged in.

Dunfermline has the honour of taking the lead, first in the Temperance cause, and afterwards in the Total Abstinence movement. An eminent advocate for this movement, Mr. Robert Rae of London, says that "the first of these societies was formed at Dunfermline, Fifeshire, on the 21st September 1830, and was called the 'Dunfermline Association for the Promotion of Temperance by the relinquishment of all Intoxicating Liquors,' Mr. John Davie being the founder of it."

Another gentleman, belonging to Glasgow, who was one of the "early heroes" of the cause, says that "I believe the credit of drawing up the first 'total abstinence,' 'teetotal,' or 'Nephalist' pledge is to be traced to the ancient city of Dunfermline, in Fife;" and in *Chambers' Encyclopædia*, under the head "*Temperance*," it is recorded that on the 21st of September 1830 Mr. John Davie and several other members of the *Temperance Society of Dunfermline*, pledged themselves to total abstinence from all intoxicating liquors—*small beer excepted*, and wine on sacramental occasions; and in the course of the two following years Total Abstinence Societies were started in Glasgow, Paisley, and other places. It may be remarked here that the "small beer" above referred to was commonly known as *treacle drink*, which was much used by working-men at what formed the almost universal breakfast meal in those days.

It has been mentioned elsewhere in these reminiscences that the drapers of Dunfermline used to keep in

their back shops, bottles filled with different kinds of liquor, in order to stimulate and refresh their customers, especially those coming from a distance, as almost every one travelled on foot in those days, there being then no railway trains and omnibuses running to and from the neighbouring towns and villages. This back-shop drinking led to great abuses; some thirsty customers would make purchases in different shops, and get themselves sometimes into a muddled and helpless condition. Mr. John Davie, who we are happy to say is still to the fore, and still in the front, as consistent and as earnest an advocate as ever for the abolition of strong drink, ventured strongly to condemn this baneful practice. He and his much respected and energetic partner in business (the late Mr. David Reid) urged that this drinking should be discontinued, and it was soon abolished. At the time he advocated the abolition of this, a warm-hearted friend of his implored him not to speak of doing away with this good old-established social custom, for if it were done away with, they might just as well *put on their shop shutters at once!* Mr. Davie's course was clear to himself and to his own conscience, and no living man need have tried to dissuade him from his purpose. He was at last successful, and the change was soon found to be of incalculable benefit, morally and otherwise, to the drapers themselves, and to the general public. Through good and through bad report he has kept on the even tenor of his way. For many years it required no common amount of courage to face the bitter opposition and to bear the sneers and the ridicule that were often cast on the advocates of the total abstinence cause. They were then in a woful minority, but, as the Rev. George Gilfillan once said with much truth, "Minorities have done the real work of the world, and they are doing that real work up to this hour. John Hunter, the celebrated anatomist, announced a lecture on anatomy in London, and although he probably knew more about that science than any man in the city, yet when the hour of lecture arrived, he found nobody waiting to hear him.

That was being in a minority with a vengeance! Yes, there was one person present,—the door-keeper,—and the doctor addressing him said, " John, take down that skeleton, and place it beside you on that seat, that I may commence my lecture with—' Gentlemen!'"

Mr. Davie is allowed to be, if not *the first professed total abstainer* in Scotland, amongst the very first. On that eventful evening of the 21st September 1830 he dictated the first total abstinence pledge in the country, and signed it along with his small band of six or seven followers, all of whom had previously belonged to the Dunfermline Temperance Society. This latter Society allowed the use of wine and beer, but not spirits ; but this did not meet the views of Mr. Davie, who strongly advocated entire abstinence from every kind of drink which contained alcohol, and the result has shown the wisdom of his decision.

The cause is now progressing rapidly on all hands and in all countries. In Great Britain there are now numerous societies, leagues, and alliances, all of them working earnestly in behalf of total abstinence. "The United Kingdom Railway Temperance Union" alone, has now branches on nearly all the large railways of this country, and has a membership of 10,000 employees. This has not been brought about without the anxious and unceasing labours of such men as our townsman. Mr. Davie attended the very first meeting held in Glasgow, where a union was formed of the different societies in Scotland, and he joined that union. He also attended at the formation of the "Scottish Temperance League," joined it, and was made director of it for many years. He likewise attended the first meeting of the "Alliance," held in Manchester, was elected a member of the council, and is a subscriber to it at the present day. A misunderstanding having arisen between some of the members of the "Scottish Temperance League" and the "Alliance," which he and Dr. M'Culloch tried unsuccessfully to dispel, they left the latter, and formed the "Permissive Bill and Temperance Association for Scotland." Of this he was two years vice-president, and latterly president for five years, and is still a member of it. He was also an honorary secretary of the "International Temperance Convention," held in the Hall, Grosvenor Square. At one of their sittings a paper of his was read, which was received with much favour, and attracted considerable interest and attention, entitled "Some Incidents in the Early History of the Temperance and Total Abstinence Movements." This paper was published in the Official Report of that most interesting Convention.

It has been said with force and truth, that "if a man dies for his flag, the world calls him a hero, but if he is prepared to die for a principle, he is called a fanatic: yet the latter is the nobler of the two." To show that our townsman is not a man of one idea merely, it may be mentioned that he had a hand in helping on and supporting the London Temperance Hospital, and the International Arbitration and Peace Societies. He has also been a strong advocate for Woman's Suffrage, and is an opponent of Vivisection. It may also be mentioned that, while he has been so closely identified with the temperance cause for about sixty years, he has for the past forty years adopted and advocated a vegetarian diet. Now that he is far advanced in years, his eye does not yet appear to be dimmed, nor his steadfast faithfulness and unwavering constancy to the temperance cause he has loved so well to be in the least abated. It must gladden his heart in his declining years to see the great progress this cause has made, and, like an old and successful warrior, he can now look back upon the past with a degree of honest pride and satisfaction, and forward to the future with undiminished hope. Some of us may not be inclined to go his length, but every one, be he total abstainer or not, must admire and esteem him for his works' sake.

AUTHORS AND THEIR WORKS.

A VERY large number of persons connected with Dunfermline have, during the course of the present century, entered the various fields of literature, the most of them with an earnest endeavour to elevate, educate, and amuse their fellow-men. Space will only permit of little more than a mere catalogue of the names of the writers and the titles of their works. The names of those who have written pamphlets, stray verses, and fugitive pieces are innumerable, and few of them are recorded here. As will be seen, the most of the books herein mentioned are on subjects of a substantial character. Alas! like most of the works of man, many of them are soon forgotten, and as time progresses they will be like "a tale that is told." But others of them, which have shed some gleams o'er life's highway, may continue to edify and elevate the coming generations of men.

Rev. DAVID BLACK, Chalmers Street Church.
"The Covenanter's Directory ;" also, Sermons on Death.

JOHN MALCOLM, Baker.
A work "On Sacred Music and Psalmody."

Rev. HENRY FERGUS, Relief Church.
"History of Dunfermline," "The Testimony of Nature and Revelation to the Being, Perfections, and Government of God," &c. &c.

WALTER BELL, Tailor.
Poems on various subjects.

Rev. JOHN FERNIE.
"History of the Town and Parish of Dunfermline," "Sermons on Important Subjects," and other works.

DAVID PATON.
"History of Dunfermline," with illustrations ; and many other small works.

ARCHIBALD HAXTON, Teacher.
"Arithmetic for Schools."

JOHN MILLER, Senior, Printer, &c.
Author of many small volumes.

JOHN JOHNSTON, Teacher.

"Introduction to the French Language," "The Bard and the Belted Knight."

MRS. JOHNSTON.

"The Saxon and the Gael," in four volumes, published in 1814; writer to *Tait's Magazine*, &c.

ANDREW MERCER, Drawing-Master, &c.

"History of Dunfermline," "Summer Months among the Mountains."

MRS. BONTHRON, Cairneyhill.

Book of Poems.

REV. GEORGE BELL BRAND, St. Andrew's Church.

Lectures and Sermons.

JAMES RANKINE.

"The Dunfermline Songster, for the use of Schools," &c.

DR. JOHN MACKIE, Physician.

"Sketch of a new Theory of Man."

WILLIAM BLAIR.

"The Highland Maid," and other popular songs.

THE HIGHLAND MAID.

" Again the lav'rock seeks the sky,
    And warbles, dimly seen,
And summer views with sunny joy
    Her gowany robe of green.
But ah ! the summer's blythe return
    In flowery pride array'd,
Nae mair can cheer the heart forlorn,
    Or charm the Highland maid.

" My true love fell by Charlie's side,
    Wi' mony a clansman dear.
A gallant youth—ah ! wae betide
    The cruel Southron's spear.
His bonnet blue is fallen now,
    And bloody is the plaid
That aften on the mountain's brow
    Has wrapped his Highland maid.

" My father's shieling on the hill
    Is cheerless noo an' sad ;
The passing breezes whisper still,
    ' You've lost your Highland lad.'
Upon Culloden's fatal heath
    He spak' o' me they said,
An' falter'd wi' his dying breath,
    ' Adieu ! my Highland maid.'

> " The weary nicht for rest I seek,
>   The langsome day I mourn,
> The smile upon my withered cheek
>   Can never mair return.
> But soon beneath the sod I'll lie,
>   In yonder lowly glade ;
> Mayhap the stranger passing by
>   Shall mourn the Highland maid."

M. BARBIERI, Limekilns.

Gazetteer of the Counties of Fife, Kinross, and Clackmannan.

EBENEZER BIRRELL, Land Surveyor.

Tables of Land Measuring.

Rev. ALEX. FISHER, Queen Anne Street Church.

"Theological Gems," &c.

ROBERT FLOCKHART.

Several clever poetical and other pieces.

Rev. JAMES YOUNG, Queen Anne Street Church.

"Our Refuge," "The Remembrance and Imitation of departed Ministers."

Rev. Dr. M'MICHAEL, Relief Church.

"The Pilgrim Psalms," &c.

Rev. Dr. PETER CHALMERS.

"On Duelling," "History and Statistical Account of Dunfermline," &c.

ANDREW EWING SHOOLBRED.

Book of Poems, &c.

HENRY BEVERIDGE.

A translation of D'Aubigné's "History of the Reformation," and other works.

ANDREW THOMSON.

"Scotland ; its chief Towns, &c., in verse, for the use of Schools," &c.

HENRY SYME.

"Local Musings," and other poetical pieces.

ALEXANDER MACANSH.

"The Social Curse ;" also Essays, Poems, &c.

WILLIAM GLASS.

"Moses and Christ."

Rev. Dr. EBENEZER HENDERSON.

Eminent Linguist and Divine. He published works on Iceland, Biblical researches, Commentaries, &c.

EBENEZER HENDERSON, LL.D.

"Annals of Dunfermline," "Life of Ferguson the Astronomer,' &c. &c.

Rev. JAMES MACKENZIE.

"Our Banner and its Battles," "History of Scotland," &c. &c.

Sir JOSEPH N. PATON, LL.D.

"Poems by a Painter," "Spindrift."

Mrs. MORTON.

"Clarkson Gray, and other Poems," with illustrations.

ROBERT ANDERSON.

"Sketches of Russian Life," "The Fortune-Hunter," translated from the Russian, &c.

WILLIAM HORNE.

"The Nature and Contents of Scripture Revelation compared with other forms of Truth." A Prize Essay, for which he received £100. Also the Rector's (John Stuart Mill's) Prize Essay, for which he received £25, while a student at St. Andrews University.

ANDREW CARNEGIE.

"Round the World," "Our Coaching Trip," "Triumphant Democracy," &c.

ELIZABETH ALLISON.

Book of Poems—now being arranged, we believe, for the Press.

JOSEPH HUTTON.

Volume of Poetical and other pieces.

DAVID K. COUTTS.

Poems and Songs.

Rev. ALEX. MITCHELL, North Parish Church.

On "The Book of Jonah."

Rev. CHARLES MARSHALL, Free Church.

"Lights from the Smithy : Lays and Lectures."

ALEX. BRUNTON.

"Life of Sir William Wallace."

Rev. CHARLES ROGERS.

"Leaves from my Autobiography," &c.

Dr. WILLIAM SMITH.

"On the Books of Moses."

Rev. ROBERT FRENCH.

Volume of Sermons.

Rev. ANDREW BRYDIE.
   "On the Sabbath."

Rev. JAMES WHITE.
   Sermons.

Rev. JOHN MACFARLANE, D.D.
   "Mountains of the Bible," "Life of Rev. Dr. Lawson of Selkirk,"
   "The Night Lamp," "Altar Fire," "Life of Rev. Dr. Archer,
   London," "Pulpit Echoes," being Sermons preached in Kin-
   cardine, Glasgow, &c., and other works.

DAVID BEVERIDGE. [1]
   "Culross and Tulliallan, or Perthshire-on-Forth, its History and
   Antiquities."

In addition to the above list of authors who have published their works, we may mention the names of—

GEORGE THOMSON, known the world over as the able and
accomplished correspondent of our national bard, Robert
Burns, and who set several of his beautiful songs to music,
who was a native of Limekilns, parish of Dunfermline.
His father, from whom was descended the wife of the late
well-known Charles Dickens, was a teacher in that village
for some years. It may also be interesting to record here
that Robert Burns himself paid a visit to Dunfermline in
October 1787. When he was shown the stone slab underneath which, it was believed at that time, there rested the
remains of King Robert Bruce, he knelt down and kissed
it with fervour.

ROBERT GILFILLAN, poet, was born in Dunfermline in
1798. He published a collection chiefly of songs and
ballads, which was well received, and passed through
several editions. When but a boy he joined a band of
"guisers" about New Year's time, and he chanted a song
of his own composition on the death of Scotland's hero at
that period—Sir Ralph Abercrombie. He got many pence
and *hogmanays* that night, and was greatly admired and
praised by his companions. The family went afterwards
from Dunfermline to reside in Leith. A public dinner

---

[1] Mr. Beveridge is the son of the well-known translator of D'Aubigné's
"History of the Reformation," and is a nephew of the late Mr. Erskine
Beveridge, Manufacturer.

was given to him in Edinburgh by his admirers years after that, and a silver cup was presented, in testimony of their appreciation of his character and genius. It was his custom to submit his songs to his mother and sisters as he wrote them, for their judgment, by which he was often guided. While reading the manuscript of "Fare thee well, for I must leave thee," to his mother and the rest of the family, his sister and a young lady—a cousin of his own who was present—were so overcome that they burst into tears.

> "Fare thee well, for I must leave thee,
>   But O ! let not our parting grieve thee ;
> Happier days may yet be mine,
>   At least I wish them thine, believe me !

> "We part ; but, by those dew-drops clear,
>   My love for thee will last for ever ;
> I leave thee ; but, thy image dear—
>   Thy tender smiles will leave me never.

> "O ! dry those pearly tears that flow ;
>   One farewell smile before we sever.
> The only balm for parting woe
>   Is, fondly hope 'tis not for ever.

> "Though dark and dreary lowers the night,
>   Calm and serene may be the morrow ;
> The cup of pleasure ne'er shone bright
>   Without some mingling drops of sorrow !"

The following song by Gilfillan, which is famed the world over for its great beauty and pathos, is, we think, worthy of being referred to here. There is space for only the first and last stanzas.

> "Oh ! why left I my hame,
>   Why did I cross the deep,
> Oh ! why left I the land
>   Where my forefathers sleep ?
> I sigh for Scotia's shore,
>   And I gaze across the sea,
> But I canna get a blink
>   O' my ain countrie !

> "There's a hope for every woe,
>   And a balm for every pain,
> But the first joys of our heart
>   Come never back again.

> There's a track upon the deep,
> And a path across the sea,
> But the weary ne'er return
> To their ain countrie !"

Robert Gilfillan was apprenticed when a lad to Mr. Kirk (of Transy), a tobacconist in the Kirkgate and afterwards in the High Street, corner of Chapel Street. His master, I remember, was a curious looking man; he was stoutly built, and though well dressed had a good deal of the antique in his appearance. He usually walked in a bustling, half-trot manner. He wore a wig, and often carried his hat in the left hand and a stout staff in his right. When any one addressed him, or asked him a question, his answer invariably began with, " *What, what, what ?*" One of the poet Gilfillan's earliest efforts was to compose an epitaph for his master, which ran as follows—

> " Here lies Transy, wi' neither staff nor hat;
> When Satan comes to take him, he'll cry, 'What-what-what !'"

There might be added to the above array of literary names belonging to Dunfermline, many others who were considered a power in their day and generation. Such as William Sharp, correspondent for the *Scotsman*, and the writer of many very clever poems and *bon-mots*, a number of which appeared from time to time in *Punch*. There was also Colin Couper, baker, son of Mr. John Couper, manufacturer, Pittencrieff Street, and brother of the Rev. David Couper, minister, of Burntisland. He was a very able man, and a most vigorous and trenchant writer. He was correspondent for the *Fifeshire Journal*, and also wrote for other papers and magazines. The following specimen of his ready repartee is given, not because of its particular pungency, but because of its being the only specimen that occurs at the moment to the writer of these *reminiscences*. Some friends met together one night, and amongst them a large corpulent tallow-chandler, who was regarded as a " character" in the town. In the course of the evening this worthy said to Mr. Couper quite seriously, " They tell me, Colin, you're very clever; could you try your hand on

me and mak my epitaph?" Without a moment's delay
the following was there and then produced—

> " Here lies a tallow-chandler stout,
> Who ne'er did miss his mark,
> But Death hath put his candle out,
> And left him in the dark!"

No doubt it would have been very interesting to the
readers of these pages could there have been extracts and
quotations given from many of the works above referred
to, but want of space entirely precludes this from being
attempted.

While speaking of authors, and those of a literary turn
in the city, it may be mentioned that a considerable portion
of Pollok's *Course of Time* was written by that gifted author
while he was staying in Dunfermline for the benefit of his
health in 1826 and 1827; and mention must be made of
the conspicuous position taken up for many years by Mr.
John Miller and his son, dating from 1804, and afterwards
by Mr. William Clark and others who have followed. All
of them endeavoured to assist literary aspirants, and have
taken a keen interest in local literature. Special mention
must also be made of the late Dr. E. Henderson, whose
name, as well as that of his uncle, the Rev. Dr. E. Henderson, is in our list. Few men have ever shown a more loyal
regard for the honour and credit of their birth-place than
Dr. E. Henderson did for his native city Dunfermline.
From his earliest years he carefully hoarded up every scrap
of historical information he could lay his hands upon in
connection with it. An absence from it of more than thirty
years across the Border did not lessen, but rather intensified,
his regard for it. The *Annals of Dunfermline* testify in
some small measure to his industry and research throughout a long lifetime. In August 1859 the freedom of the
burgh was publicly conferred on him for his antiquarian
researches and in recognition of his services in connection
with the restoration of the burgh to its ancient status as a
city. He was at that time entertained to a public dinner,
presided over by Robert Robertson, Esq., then Provost of
Dunfermline.

THE NETHERTOWN "WEICHT."

FEW of the present generation will know what the Nethertown "Weicht" really was. It was an old sort of drum,
which was only brought out to the light of day, or at night,
on very rare and special occasions. It was kept concealed
latterly in "Threshie Charlie's" garret. Whenever the
"weicht" was brought out it was considered *a caution.*
There was something up, and, like the "fiery cross" of old,
the news spread like wildfire, and every one spoke with bated
breath. The "weicht" belonged, I believe, originally to the
"Friends of the People," a secret political society which was
founded in Dunfermline about 1794 or 1796. The "Friends,"
according to Dr. E. Henderson, were all *incog.*, and had
periodical meetings, presided over by one whose cognomen
was "Cato." It is said that they had the Pittencrieff
estate mapped off and allotted amongst their members.
There were many similar political societies established
throughout the country about this period. It is understood
that the publication of Tom Paine's *Rights of Man* and
Age of Reason, and the contagion spread by the French
revolutionists in those days, which afterwards brought to
many a French home untold misery, had much to do with
the origin of this secret society. The once well-known
Sir Francis Burdett was a leading member of it, and he
was at one time committed to the Tower of London for
his outspokenness. The "weicht" was brought out sometimes at the Nethertown Races, and at great political gatherings, figured at night mobs, and at times when there were
strikes in trade. This at least is certain, that on one of the
occasions where the dreaded "weicht" figured, a banner
was carried which bore the following "strange device"—

> "May Tories' hides become drum-heads
> To beat republicans to arms !'"

There has been much commotion in this country recently
regarding the Franchise extension, and many flags, banners,
and mottoes were exhibited, but nothing has appeared to
match the above.

THE CHARTIST MOVEMENT.

DUNFERMLINE sympathised deeply and was prominently identified with the Chartist movement. Many meetings were held, and the town was frequently visited by many itinerant lecturers and political orators. Collins of Birmingham, I remember, was a frequent visitor, and a very temperate and able public speaker he was. There was Fergus O'Connor, with his tall, portly figure, and his fiery, impassioned, Hibernian declamation. There was also Frost, who advised that the people should petition for their rights with *pens of steel and ink of red !* The Chartists of Dunfermline were greatly concerned with the question of "moral" or "physical" force. Some few were in favour of adopting physical, but an overwhelming number were in favour of using moral force.

During this great Chartist agitation, a general and *entire cessation from work took place in the town and neighbourhood of Dunfermline !* It was expected by those who were instrumental in inaugurating this novel device that the whole country would follow suit. The movement was, however, only confined to this neighbourhood, and lasted but for a week or ten days. There is no doubt that if an entire stoppage of work such as that at Dunfermline had spread and become general throughout the country, it would certainly have brought on a great crisis of some kind or another ! On the morning of this great "moral" strike, a man was heard to say to another, as he was in the act of putting the shutters on his shop-window, " *Thae shutters 'll no come aff till we gain the Charter, the hale Charter, an' naething but the Charter !*" A week or so sufficed to show that the country was not ripe for such a great and startling movement all at once. As the years have glided past since then, we have quietly, and by degrees, gained almost all the "six points" that the political veterans and pioneers of those old days fought and longed for with heart and soul.

DUNFERMLINE'S OLD REFORMERS.

Going back to the period when the great Reform movement was at its height, now upwards of fifty years ago, what an amount of excitement there was all over the country, and in Dunfermline in particular. What processions and speech-making, what great crowds! It is computed that at least 10,000 persons, including inhabitants and strangers from a distance, accompanied the great Reform procession of May 1832. About 4000 persons took part in the procession, five men abreast. Many curious emblems and devices were carried. One carried a beautiful model of a loom in full working order, with the man driving the shuttle. Another carried a model of a pirn wheel, with the figure of an old woman filling bobbins. A printing press was worked as it proceeded along on a cart, and slips were printed and thrown to the crowd on all sides. The great meeting was held in the Glebe, west end of Nethertown. Provost Kerr took the chair, and after he had said a few words the hustings fell. No lives were lost, but some were severely injured.

There were many who distinguished themselves for years on the platforms of the public meetings held in the town about that time and subsequently. On Parliamentary and other occasions, Messrs. James Inglis, Thomas Morrison, Erskine Beveridge, Alex. Halley, Joseph Paton, Henry Davidson, Robert Kilpatrick, Andrew Fleming, and others, figured very prominently. The most of them were well informed men, and several of them were excellent public speakers, and ready in debate. Those meetings were often full of life and excitement. When a Whig candidate offered his services to the electors, or when a Whig representative came to give an account of his stewardship, he had to pass through a most scathing ordeal, now known as the "heckling process." Mr. Inglis was quiet, pointed, sarcastic, and merciless in his remarks. Mr. Morrison, again, had more of the style and vigour of a popular orator; he could hold and fascinate an audience for any length of time, and sway it whithersoever he chose. Mr. Inglis had a great amount of natural genius, strong common sense, and mother-wit; and while Mr. Morrison was well endowed with these qualities, he was also a well-read man, had innumerable dates, facts, and figures at his finger ends, and was ready at a moment's notice to meet and confute an opponent!

> "His desperate grasp thy frame might feel
> Through bars of brass and triple steel."

He had a peculiar way of shouting "Hear, hear!" when an opponent was addressing a meeting, and it was a signal that a storm was brewing. It was then whispered from one to another, "*That's Morris*," and every one then looked forward to seeing some exciting work before the meeting was over. I remember as if it had been yesterday, a meeting held in the Guildhall to hear Lord Dalmeny (father of the present Earl of Rosebery) give an account of his stewardship as the Parliamentary representative for the burghs. He was then a very young man, inexperienced, and not over three or four and twenty years of age. He was about the middle height, perhaps under, straight, and very well made, with a finely formed head, and a most gentlemanly bearing. He wore, I remember, a dark blue frock-coat buttoned, and he looked every inch of him one of Nature's nobility. It must have been a sore trial to him, a young Whig, to appear in Dunfermline and give an account of his political doings before men who were much older, and far abler and more experienced in the field of politics than himself—before men who had made this subject a study from youth upwards, and who had been veterans in many political fights—before men who had ardently endeavoured to

> "Know the seasons, when to take
> Occasion by the hand, and make
> The bounds of freedom wider yet."

At that meeting James Inglis and Thomas Morrison, both of them advanced Radicals, gave his Lordship a warming, as they say in England. Mr. Morrison made a fierce onslaught upon his Parliamentary shortcomings. I stood close to the platform, and watched the fray.   On the whole, his Lordship bore his castigation pretty well, but now and again he could not conceal his emotion, and winced under the storm of scathing invective hurled upon him by Mr. Morrison. But when Mr. James Inglis took him to task, the colour left his Lordship's face.   Mr. Inglis' questions and remarks were so dreadfully sarcastic, so incisive, and withal so quietly and coolly put, that it was a most severe trial for any young man to pass through.   Many things have happened since then, and the silent grave has long covered the three principals who figured at that political "pass of arms."   It is so long since, that I have forgotten all the *pros* and the *cons* of that eventful meeting, but I shall ever remember two of the questions put to Lord Dalmeny by Mr. Inglis.   They were something to the following effect:—"Did not your Lordship support the vote for £70,000 to build and repair stables for the horses of Her Majesty?"   The answer was, "Yes, I did."   "Did not your Lordship vote against a certain application which was made to Parliament for £30,000 for educational purposes?" His Lordship admitted that he did.   Mr. Inglis required to say scarcely anything more on these points, but just to put the questions and answers in juxtaposition, and leave his audience to judge for themselves.

I remember being at another large political meeting, which was held in Queen Anne Street Church, when Lord Dalmeny was present to meet his constituents.   He and his friends occupied "the range" in front of the pulpit, and there were upwards of 2000 persons present.   His Lordship was most severely heckled that evening, so much so that the Rev. James Young came forward and said it was a most unbecoming and unkind thing to treat his Lordship in that savage manner.   A great howl was at once raised against Mr. Young for his interference, and I recollect well of hearing, amongst other things, a man shout from the far gallery—"*Abide by your callin', Maister Young; abide by your callin'!*"

SOME OLD WORTHIES OF THE TOWN.

LET us briefly refer to some of those worthies who long ago lived and moved about Dunfermline, but who have all gone to the silent land, and have joined the "great majority."

Mr. James Inglis held for many years a very prominent position in Dunfermline. He was looked up to with respect by his townsmen, and his public utterances always carried great weight with them. He and Mr. Thomas Morrison for many years fought hard to advance the cause of political, religious, and social liberty, when the advocacy of such views was very far from being so popular in this country as it is at the present day. We are now entering into the enjoyment of many political and other privileges and advantages which the early and persistent efforts of such men as he and Mr. Morrison had paved the way for. As Mr. Inglis was so well known in public life and in his native town, and as a slight reference has been made to him in Dean Ramsay's book, it will not therefore be deemed out of place if we make an observation or two upon his life and character in these reminiscences.

Mr. Inglis was a leading and an influential man in Dunfermline at the great Reform Bill period in 1832. His face was a familiar one on the hustings, and at many a public meeting in those days. He was also a powerful advocate for the abolition of slavery, for the repeal of the Corn Laws, and, above all, for the extension of the franchise. He sprang from a family which had been distinguished for its attachment to the principles of civil and religious liberty. His father, George Inglis, was one of the original members of Gillespie Church. He, too, was a seceder, and also a Liberal in politics, when such views were held by a mere handful of unpopular men.

At a comparatively early period Mr. Inglis connected himself with the Scottish Baptists, and was for some time, along with Mr. David Dewar, conjoint pastor of that body. The last decade of his life was spent peacefully, and in harmony with his long and faithful public career. At an advanced age, and after many years of labour, he was privileged in his declining health to spend his last years "Sabbatically, as if on the shores of the eternal world, or in the outer courts as it were, of the temple that is above the tabernacle of Heaven."

As a public speaker he was very effective; he always spoke to the point, and closely rivetted the attention of his audiences. He was never tedious, but, like the late Rev. Dr Johnstone of Limekilns, always stopped when he was done. He was clear in judgment, and yet cautious in his actions. He had a great fund of mother-wit and sagacity, and an occasional touch of sarcasm. His trenchant addresses were often sprinkled with old-fashioned phrases and good broad Scotch—so telling and so full of force and power. Many a time it has been our privilege to hear him address public meetings, and to admire his ready tact, good sense, and genuine humour. I remember well of seeing thousands of the men of Dunfermline assembled at the bottom of the High Street one evening, to hear the result of a keenly contested election. There were no telegraphs or railways in those days, and the final state of the poll was sent by messenger on horseback from Stirling. On that particular occasion the result was a great disappointment, and the defeat was as keenly felt as it was unexpected. I forget who the defeated candidate was; it might be Johnston or Colonel Thomson. Several of the local orators attempted the difficult task of addressing the disappointed assemblage from the town-house window facing High Street. Mr. Inglis' turn came; he spoke stirring words of hope and comfort to the vast gathering, and great cheering followed. I remember yet his concluding words, and they were to the following effect:—"Do not be downcast and disheartened, my friends; no great cause ever triumphed till after many reverses and many disappointments. You have fought a good fight and done your duty well, and be assured our principles will triumph in the end. Far better, my friends, to be unsuccessful in a good cause than successful in an ill ane!"

The following incidents relating to Mr. Inglis, although well known to many of the older residents of the city, may not be generally known to those of our readers at a distance, and they are worth recording here. Many years ago a chaplain was wanted for the prison of Dunfermline, and as Mr. Inglis was member of the Prison Board, he, along with other members, had to elect one out of the two candidates who presented themselves. The day of election came, but he was unsuccessful in carrying his favourite man. The majority of the members of the Board elected one who, although a most worthy and good man in all other respects, had proved unsuccessful as a preacher, and in consequence had almost emptied his church, so that it had to be closed. After the election of this gentleman, Mr. Inglis quietly and sarcastically remarked—"*Weel-a-weel, the man has preached his kirk empty; I only houp he'll preach the jail empty too!*"

There is another circumstance related in connection with the same well-known citizen, showing the readiness and pungency of his satire. A gentleman who held a very prominent official position in the town long ago, sometimes forgot himself by taking more stimulants than were good for him. He and some of his acquaintances were standing one forenoon at a street corner, when they espied Mr. Inglis approaching. One of the party made a bet of half a mutchkin that he would not have the courage to speak to Mr. Inglis as he passed. It was at once taken up, and when Mr. Inglis came forward (nicely dressed in his suit of black, as all the manufacturers usually were), and while he was passing, the other said to him, "Fine morning, Mr. Inglis; how are you to-day?" The reply was awfully cutting and sarcastic, "Thank ye, James; *I'm sober!*" He then passed on. Another instance may here be given of his quiet humour and sarcastic turn of mind. He had been much troubled with a clock which he had in his warehouse, and which took fits of standing still. One day he entered the place unnoticed by his apprentice John, who at the time was idling, and amusing himself by driving the pendulum. John at length observed that his master, who was at his desk, was looking at him, and feeling ashamed, he left the clock and slunk away to his work. His master made no remark at the time, but some time after quietly said to the young man, "John, ye micht stap awa' up to Bobby Macara's, the watchmaker, an' tell him to come doon an' tak awa' that clock, for I canna afford to keep a man to ca' the pendulum the hale day !"

There was a strike amongst the weavers of the town long ago, in consequence of some misunderstanding as to the rate of wages, and Mr. Inglis ventured to go in with his brother manufacturers, and take their side in the dispute. During that strike the people of Dunfermline suffered very severely, and so did the manufacturers. Whilst it was going on, one of the weavers of the town was heard to exclaim that " Jamie Inglis ought to be hanged for trying to tak doon the wages !" This remark came to Mr. Inglis' ears, but he took not the slightest notice of it at the time.

After this strike was over, some years of great prosperity followed, and then, unfortunately, came one of the severe periodical stagnations in trade. Great suffering and distress prevailed amongst many of the families in the town in consequence of that depression. Amongst those who came in for a great share of the hardship that existed, was the above-mentioned weaver, who with his wife and family were in sad distress, his looms being all idle, and his means of living gone. He went round the different warehouses from time to time soliciting a job, but without success. A friend of his asked him one day if he had called on Mr. Inglis. He said no, as he considered it of no use calling there, because that manufacturer was doing little or no business at the time. His friend urged him to " use the means," and to call at that warehouse as he had done at the others. He reluctantly promised to do

so, and he called the following day without having the
least hope of success. To his surprise Mr. Inglis told him
to call back the following week if he were passing, "at
ony rate," and he would see if anything could be done for
him, at the same time he distinctly informed him that he
could make no promise of anything whatever. The poor
fellow called back at the stated time, but with no hope in
him. To his great astonishment and satisfaction Mr.
Inglis took him into the warehouse, and pointed to where
a web was lying on the floor awaiting him, Mr. Inglis
even had the kindness to assist this poor weaver in
putting the web on his shoulders, and he said to him as
the man was going out of the warehouse door with it on
his back, and a grateful heart—"Noo, Tammas, if Jamie
Inglis had been hangit five years syne, ye wouldna hae
gotten that web the day!" This was an instance of
heaping coals of fire on the head of a poor fellow-mortal,
which I am sure has few equals in its way, and to this
poor weaver, if he was a right-thinking man, it was a
most crushing punishment.

Mr. David Dewar was one of the chief colleagues of Mr.
Inglis on political platforms, and also as lay preacher and
pastor in the Baptist Church. He died in 1852, after a
long, useful, and busy life. He had a strong desire to
promote the religious and the secular advancement of both
old and young. He was warm-hearted in his disposition,
and was sometimes imposed upon by the undeserving.
For many years he figured prominently amongst the
Baptists of the town. I believe he succeeded Mr. Thomas
Morrison, father of the late respected Bailie Morrison, as
pastor of the Baptist Church, Dunfermline. I never
heard Mr. Morrison preach, but he was considered a very
able man and a fluent speaker. I have, however, on
several occasions listened to Mr. Dewar, and heard him
discourse with much fervour and unction on the subject
of adult baptism, when he endeavoured to show its
warrant in Scripture, as opposed to infant baptism. On
those occasions there were usually three or four grown-up
persons to be immersed, and a full congregation assembled.

After his discourse was over, he retired to a side-room, and soon returned into the chapel, his limbs encased in long waterproof boots. He then proceeded to dip the adults one after the other, and after a prayer, breathing forth intense fervour, the service was concluded with many impressive and forcible remarks on the nature and importance of the solemn work in which they had just been engaged. Like some other pastors in the town, he had to complain sometimes of the irregular attendance of some of the Baptist flock. He used to say that some got unwell on Friday, they were worse on Saturday, and very bad on Sabbath, but all right again on Monday! He was open-handed and generous, and it was usual for him to have a large boilerful of broth, beef, &c., made ready on Auld Hansel Monday, that all the poor around the neighbourhood might have the comfort of a good, warm, and substantial dinner that day. It was also his custom to assist in the culinary operations himself on those occasions, and there he was to be seen with his bluff, honest face, and in his shirt sleeves, working away, the picture of happiness and contentment. After all, there is much wisdom in the remark, that " a true man is just as much a man when his coat is off as when it is on!" On the great morning of Hansel Monday, he, like many other employers of labour in those days, had all his old servants and workmen gathered around him at breakfast, and there he sat in their midst like a patriarch of old, bearing in his countenance the dignity of years, the genial grace of a well-spent life, and having within him a boundless love for all his fellow-men. Old David Dewar acted like some one of old, who once said, " I expect to pass through this world but once ; if, therefore, there be any kindness I can show or any good I can do to my fellow-beings, let me do it *now;* let me not defer or neglect it, for I shall not pass this way again !"

Old John King was one of Dunfermline's worthies, comparatively unknown, but a good man and a true. Many a time have we listened with a feeling of awe while passing his door at night, between nine and ten o'clock, to the loud strains of family worship proceeding from his humble dwelling. The wrestling earnestness of the man could not be exceeded. It came from the very depths of his heart, and was expressed with intense fervour and unction. The same might be heard every morning. His wife was rather hard of hearing, and his voice was usually pitched on a high key. If a number of rollicking, happy hearted, noisy boys happened to approach or pass by his door, while the old man—" the saint, the father, and the husband"—was so engaged, there was instant silence and a reverent demeanour. Those light-hearted lads knew instinctively that this man was, as "Jeemes the door-keeper" termed it, "in close grups" with the hearer and answerer of prayer, and in the near vicinity of Heaven's Eternal King. They passed by thoughtfully and quietly, although it might be only for a few moments' duration. There were many homes like this in Dunfermline long ago, where the morning and evening sacrifices were faithfully offered up by those who lived ever conscious that the present life is only "a small gleam of time between two eternities, and no second chance to them for evermore!" The fear of death was not so strong with many of them as the fear of doing a dishonest, untruthful, or mean action.

And old Mrs. Ross, I have a very pleasing remembrance of her. She was a widow, ninety years of age, and was the sister of the Rev. Dr. Black, minister of the Burgher kirk, Chalmers Street. She was hale and hearty at her great age. She lived a number of years after the decease of her brother. Often, when a youngster, have I sat at her feet on a "creepie" in the winter nights, listening attentively, but with an eerie feeling, to her stories about the witches, ghosts, kelpies, and fairies of her own young days, also about *wraiths, death-warnings, &c.* She seemed to be a firm believer in them, and although she was a very religious, good-living woman, she was fully persuaded of their existence. She belonged to Inchdairnie, Fife-shire, and that locality appeared to have been in the olden time a favourite haunt of such ghostly beings. I have heard her seriously tell of a house in that locality in which a murder or some great crime had been committed, and which had one night been pulled down by the fairies. The owner of the building tried to rebuild it, but it was in vain; as soon as the building was up a certain height, the fairies in the night-time pulled it down again. No doubt the loneliness and gloom of country life in the long, dark nights of winter had a tendency, as they yet have in some districts, of embuing the mind with feelings of a superstitious nature. The howling of the tempest, the roar of the waterfall, or the distant rumbling of thunder, were listened to, and believed to be monitions from the unseen. It is recorded that " Dr. Samuel Johnson longed all his life to see a ghost, but could not, though he went to Cock Lane, and thence to the church vaults, and tapped on coffins. Foolish Doctor! Did he never so much as look at himself? The good Doctor was a ghost as actual and authentic as heart could wish. Well nigh a million of such ghosts were travelling the streets of London by his side."

This kind-hearted old woman lived alone, and yet she never felt alone, for *One* was ever near her, with whom she held close communion. Every evening, except Sunday, she was at my father's fireside, which she left punctually as the eight o'clock bell rang. She then went to her lonely dwelling, lighted her cruisie which hung by the chimney, had what she called "family worship," put on the gathering coal, and retired to sleep the sleep of the just, with her door always unlocked and unbarred. More than half a century has passed away since she was called to her fathers, and her remains now calmly repose in the Abbey Churchyard of Dunfermline—

> " Forgotten as the world forgets :—
>   But He who rules the world has marked,
>   And sealed her silent unknown grave,
>   Till harvest time."

" The Bishop " was well known in Dunfermline fifty-five years ago, and he hailed from Masterton. I remember his appearance well. He was about the middle height, was

HOMEWARD BOUND.

stoutly built, and had a very large and finely formed head.
His head, I remember, was like that of the celebrated
player at draughts—"The Herd Laddie." It was large
and high, and resembled very much the form of the head
of Napoleon I., as seen in the portraits of that great
monarch. To most people abstruse and difficult calculations are irksome in the highest degree, but to the Bishop
deep arithmetical problems were quite a recreation and
pastime, as logarithms were to Napoleon. He was a
wonderful man, considering the scanty opportunities there
were for bringing out his peculiar talents. The poor
stone-nappers on the road-side used to get him to measure
the cubic contents of their work, which he willingly did
for them, without any recompense. The road surveyor,
whose duty it was to measure the bings of broken road
metal, and pay the men accordingly, was always afraid to
dispute the Bishop's measurements, as he was found to be
invariably accurate. His ordinary garb was a suit of
moleskin or fustian, the coat in surtout fashion, and he
was usually very far from being particular in his personal
appearance. Much of his time was occupied in mounting
looms, and he was, like Sandy Luive, expert at killing a
neighbour's pig now and again. He was always very
ready to assist others in any kind of work. He had a
great faculty for doing the arithmetical part of the loom
mountings, and this was a qualification which few men
possessed, especially with regard to the putting up of high
mountings. If a large round ball of worsted yarn were
put into his hand, he could come by outward measurement
wonderfully near the exact number of yards the ball
contained. Mr. Haxton, the Rector of the High School,
who was an excellent arithmetician, and the author of a
work on that science, which we school-boys used to call
"The Haxton," once got into controversy with the Bishop
on some questions of this kind. They tried to puzzle
each other, and one of the questions which the Bishop sent
to the Rector for solution was as to the cubic capacity of a
certain *whin-bus!* The Bishop in my young days was
looked upon as a Socrates; he was a quiet-living man,

very unassuming in his ways, and was regarded with a great deal of respect and admiration. His calculating powers were most astonishing, and had he been taken by the hand in his youth, and had his talents been properly directed, he would doubtless have become a most distinguished man. Many a one tried hard to puzzle him, and to beat him with arithmetical calculations, but in vain. He had a system peculiarly his own, which he never revealed, or was unable to reveal, and he always had an easy victory over those who attempted to cope with him.

THE INVENTIVE FACULTY.

FIFTY or sixty years ago there was quite a host of our townsmen who possessed in a high degree an original and inventive turn of mind, and whose thoughts were ever bent in the direction of mechanical pursuits. They were what we may call some of

The lichts o' ither days.

There was more originality, I think, amongst those old working-men than what can be found now. Folks now-a-days seem all to be cut out of the same pattern, and there is less individuality of character. Many of them tried their hands at the "perpetual motion" craze, but alas! to little purpose. Before that period, some of them had distinguished themselves by such feats as weaving in a loom a gentleman's shirt of fine linen, complete in all its parts, without one stitch of needlework in the whole, and showing great ingenuity. Henry Meldrum, of the Nethertown, was the first to perform this feat here; then David Anderson (who afterwards went to Glasgow) wove one more elaborately, which he presented to King George IV. through the Secretary of State, Lord Sidmouth. Going as far back as 1719, we find that James Blake, who had the credit of introducing damask weaving into Dunfermline, wove a napkin having on it a Latin inscription referring to 1649, when Charles I. suffered at Whitehall. No doubt some keen Jacobite got him to weave it. This napkin was long ago in the possession of Mr. Lawrence Wilson, who went to Canada. Then there was David Paton, who was endowed with great natural talent and originality, and who wrote and printed, with illustrations (of his own design), several small *brochures*. He had a taste for mechanics, and invented curious tide clocks, magic lanterns, &c. &c.; was fond of drawing and making woodcuts, and moreover had an intense love for his native town and all that belonged to it. An ingenious townsman also invented a machine for rocking his baby's cradle. The time of his wife being very much taken up with her pirn-wheel, and with bobbining yarn and other domestic duties, he found that the rocking of the cradle was sometimes a serious drawback to the carrying on of her other work. This called forth her husband's inventive powers, and he soon produced a cradle-rocking machine. But he told a friend afterwards that it turned out to be a failure, for, said he, "*it maks sic a blastit noise that it waukens the bairn!*" The "Sluggard's Alarm" was an ingenious machine, invented by a Dunfermline man for arousing himself in the morning. At a given hour the clockwork raised the blankets off him, made a great noise, and compelled him to get out of bed. The ingenuity displayed in very many instances by the weavers of Dunfermline showed their natural aptitude for the description of industry for which the city has so long been famed. Some years after David Anderson performed the feat of weaving the shirt for King George, with its most elaborate design—the British Arms woven in it of colours and gold, &c.—he also wove a chemise for our present Queen. It was composed of Chinese tram silk and net-warp yarn, and had no seams. The breast bore a portrait of Her Majesty, with the dates of her birth, ascension, and coronation, underneath which were the British arms and a garland of national flowers.

WILLIE CANT.

Amongst those whose tastes lay in the direction of mechanics and invention was the well-known Willie Cant, one of Dunfermline's sons. He had an eager faculty for this particular pursuit, and his walk was out of the beaten track of his fellow-townsmen. He was the inventor of various contrivances; but the one by which he was at that time best known was his apparatus for enabling him to "walk" upon the water. This peculiar machine, consisting of paddles attached to his feet, distinguished Willie very greatly in 1822, when King George visited

Scotland. Thousands of spectators assembled to see him walking across the water at Leith Roads, towards the warship which had conveyed the King from London, and also to witness the landing of His Majesty. An old doggerel ballad, written at that period by a townsman, has the following stanza :—

> " There goes Will Cant, the genius ;
>   He's a kind o' second Peter,
>   For he walks upon the deep blue sea
>   By paidlin' wi' his feet-er ! "

Willie Cant invented, amongst other things, the first machine that was ever tried for beaming webs. It proved exceedingly useful, was a great success, and saved much time and labour to the weaving community. In 1835 he invented a machine with rollers for yarn-bleaching purposes, which machine is used at the present day, and is found of much service. Had he secured some of his inventions, by patent or otherwise—such as the one for the more rapid manufacture of " cuddie-heels " for boots and shoes—it might have been of great pecuniary benefit to him and his family ; but his ideas were eagerly caught up and acted upon by others, and Willie, alas ! in spite of his varied talents, always remained " poor as a church mouse."

DAVID HATTON.

" For oh ! the lichts are a' brunt oot ! "—*Ancient Ballad.*

David Hatton, universally known in Dunfermline sixty years ago as " fluteorum," was a most conspicuous individual, and one of the most original and curious characters the town ever produced. The " fluteorum," by which he was so well known, was a musical instrument, blown by bellows attached to his elbow, and it was of his own invention. In its construction he was engaged for about twenty years. Crowds of people went to see and to hear the wonderful instrument, and also to inspect his extraordinary collection of nick-nacks of all kinds. He was a weaver-grocer in Pittencrieff Street, and afterwards he went to the Cross Wynd. It will scarcely be believed, but nevertheless it is a fact, that amongst the other things he exhibited for some years was his own coffin. He charged one penny from visitors who wanted merely to see it, but to those who wished to see how well it fitted him, the charge was twopence. What a strange sight, to see this curious mortal lying and grinning in what was to be his long, last home! When he afterwards went to Orr Bridge to reside, he was very nearly smothered in this same coffin. He was exhibiting himself in it to some country folks, who for a bit of fun put on the lid, and fastened it with a screw nail or two. He never again ventured to show himself off in this thoughtless manner after that. He worked some time upon a machine for enabling him to fly, but it came to nothing. It turned out as unsuccessful as the aërial machine constructed long ago by a man in Pattiesmuir. This man astonished the little village or hamlet by ascending to the top of his own chimney and leaping into the air with his pair of wings and his long tail strapped to him. His attempt at flying was a failure, for he soon fell most ignominiously on the top of a neighbour's midden. His own child ran into the house, saying to its mother "that the way his faither couldna flee was because he hadna a neb like ither birds!"

One of the whims which distinguished David Hatton very much, and caused some sensation at the time, was his widely known "mouse mills." In the newspapers of the day there was published the following graphic account of

Hatton's Mouse Mills.

"Mr. Hatton, of Dunfermline, has had two mice constantly employed in the manufacture of sewing thread for upwards of twelve months; and, that the curious may be entertained with a fair statement of facts, I hope you will give a place to the following description, which is by no means exaggerated, as I have often seen his mouse thread-mills, and thoroughly understand the amusing operation. The mouse thread-mill is so constructed that the common house mouse is enabled to make atonement to society for past offences by twisting, turning, and reeling from 100 to 120 threads per day (Sundays not excepted!) of the same length and equally with the enclosed hank, which I send as a specimen of their work for the inspection of the curious. To complete their task, the little pedestrians have to run 10½ miles. This journey is performed with ease every day. An ordinary mouse weighs only about half an ounce. A half-penny worth of oatmeal, at 15d. per peck, serves one of these treadmill culprits for the long period of five weeks. In that time it makes—110 threads per day being the average—3850 threads of 25 inches, which is very near nine lengths of the standard reel. A penny is paid here to women for every cut made in the ordinary way. At this rate, a mouse earns 9d. every five weeks, which is just one farthing per day, or 7s. 6d. per annum. Take 6d. off for board, and allow 1s. for machinery, there will arise 6s. of clear profit from every mouse yearly. The last time I was in company with the mouse employer, he told me he was going to make application to the heritors for a lease of an old, empty house—the Auld Kirk—in Dunfermline, the dimensions of which are 100 feet by 50, and 50 feet in height, which, at a moderate calculation, will hold 10,000 mouse-mills —sufficient room being left for the keepers and some hundreds of spectators. Allowing £200 for rent and taskmasters, and £500 for the interest of £10,000 to erect machinery, there will be a balance of £2500 per annum. This, sir, you will say, is projecting with a vengeance, but it would surely be preferable to the great South Sea speculation."

David Hatton left Dunfermline in 1829 for Orr Bridge, where he kept a small grocery store, along with his miscel-laneous collection of curious odds and ends. He had two large whale's jaw-bones placed over his door, which formed a sort of archway to the entrance of his strange dwelling. He had great crowds of visitors, coming from all quarters. For the benefit of the poor, he kept a charity box to receive donations from visitors. This box was opened once a week, then, stepping upon a platform at his door, he blew a trumpet blast, inviting all beggars and tramps to come forth and receive their share of the week's contributions.

AMATEUR SWEEPS AND BARBERS.

IN the olden times, when money was far scarcer than it is now amongst working people, when rigid economy in every direction was the imperative order of the day, and when one might walk the streets of Dunfermline without ever being pained by the sight of pieces of bread lying thoughtlessly about the gutters and footpaths, there were many persons who officiated as amateur chimney sweeps, and also as barbers. Many of them did it from a neighbourly feeling, and some for a glass of whisky, or some other small recompense.

It happened that the chimney of an old widow living in the south of the town required sweeping, and the ready services of an amateur were obtained. It was arranged beforehand that when he reached the chimney-top he would, before commencing work, drop down the chimney a bit of stone or brick, so as to give them notice to have all ready. An old sack having been carefully tucked in all round the fireplace to prevent the soot from flying about, the widow and her son Andrew waited patiently the expected signal. Thinking that it might be advisable to inform the man at the top that they were all ready and waiting, Andrew ventured to put his head into the chimney for that purpose. But, most unluckily for him, at that very moment down came a cloud of soot and a lump of brick, which struck him on the nose, causing it to bleed freely. He then turned to his aged mother, with his bleeding, sooty face and blinded eyes, and piteously said to her, "Mither, ye see what I've made by the soopin' o' your lum!"

Amongst the many amateur barbers who tried the shaving and hair-cutting business, there was a female in the neighbouring village of Charlestown who used to perform great feats in this way. Her shaving implements were often in very bad order, and this was the chief difficulty she had to contend with. One day a sailor came to her to get shaved, and Jean's razor appeared to have been uncommonly blunt that day, for, after rising from his trying ordeal, with his bleeding face and moistened eyes, he said to her, " *If this is skinnin', it's tolerable ; but if it's shavin', it's awfu' ! awfu' !*"

After the Disruption, as it was called, in 1843, when upwards of 400 ministers of the Church of Scotland nobly left their pastoral charges for conscience sake, and at an early period of the history of the Free Church, there were found many active and enthusiastic volunteers who did good service in the way of collecting money for the new and struggling cause. They laboured in season and out of season, and the Free Church has had its reward. Amongst others who collected subscriptions was a most energetic young lady, who one day waited on a poor cobbler to ask for help. He told her that he had on an average only about five shillings a week, and therefore could spare nothing from his family. She found that the man neither drank whisky nor smoked, and she was at her wit's end, but did not like to be beat ; so all at once a bright idea occurred to her. She found that he did not shave himself, and that this operation cost him twopence a week. She then, with a woman's ready wit, asked him if he could not buy a razor and shave himself, and give the weekly money to the sustentation fund. The old cobbler mournfully shook his head, and said he was afraid that he was "noo o'er auld i' the horn to shave," and he had never tried it ; " but," he added, " *if you'll come round twice a week and shave me, I'll gie* YOU *the tippence.*"

HUMBLE LABOURERS IN THE "SEEDFIELD OF TIME."

MEMORY calls up to remembrance the faces and forms of many of those who were well known in their own little sphere long ago. We remember well Old Halliper and J. Stirling, who worked with their antediluvian hand-shuttles, a mode of weaving utterly unknown to the young of the present day, and at which the present generation would stare with astonishment. Often in passing have we gazed into their small, dim shop windows, and seen them eidently driving those ancient shuttles, throwing them in from one side with one hand, and deftly catching them with the other. There they were laboriously engaged from "the screigh o' day" on some narrow "hunger'em" or "dice-aboot," working for a poor wage on a diet of "muslin kail" without "kitchen," but nevertheless eagerly bent on gaining an honourable and honest livelihood. Whilst working thus laboriously with their rude implements, little did they imagine that, in a short half-century or little more, hand-loom weaving would be a thing of the past, that there would arise in Dunfermline immense piles of buildings containing thousands of power-looms, the

"Offspring of the scheming brain;"

that science would so change the face of the earth—that railway trains would be actually tearing away through the bowels of the Ferry hills, and underneath our cities and rivers, like angry demons breathing forth thunder, fire, and smoke! Whilst thou, *Halliper*, art now sleeping the sleep that knows no waking, the world is driving headlong onwards in its orbit, day and night unceasingly. We are gaily and unconsciously traversing and plunging through boundless, untracked, unspeakable immensity. Whether asleep or awake, whether living here or like thee in the silent grave, our ponderous globe, with its load of oceans and continents, is sweeping through a firmament of rolling stars above us, beneath us, and around us—on, on, ever on!

So in the little social circles of men, there is constant rest-lessness, a ceaseless desire for something better, and something beyond. Could it be possible for thee, O Halliper! now to rise from thy narrow bed and look around, what changes would meet thy gaze! Couldst thou behold the roaring, smoking factories on all sides of thee, with the mighty engines and looms, and screaming steam whistles, and then see our railway trains driving along like the whirlwind, without any horses or visible means of propulsion, and above all get a glimpse of modern society, the strangeness and the novelty of thy surroundings as compared to the easy, slow-going, humdrum pace and quietude of the Dunfermline of long ago, would, we fear, almost make thee fain to creep back to thy silent bed, and seek shelter there from the din and turmoil on all sides! For a penny we can get every morning the news of the previous day from the ends of the earth; the poor dim flickering farthing dip, that required on thy part watchful care and constant snuffing, has given place to a clean and brilliant artificial light, and the wide Atlantic can now be crossed by our magnificent steamers in seven or eight days' time. Let us hope that all those things are preparing the way (it may be through much tribulation) for the time that's "*comin' yet for a' that!*"

Deacon H., the *wricht*, he, too, has long since quitted this mortal sphere; he and his hammers, chisels, and planes have for ever vanished. But we remember his workshop well, his wooden bench, and the row of sharp-edged tools in the rack behind him. He was sometimes a wee "crabbit," or short-tempered, to youngsters intruding into his *sanctum*, but I was somewhat of a favourite, on whom he seldom vented his temporary spurts of ill-humour. Often have we stood watching the curling shavings fly from his great jack-plane, and, awe-struck, beheld him busily putting together the *ultima domus* of some poor fellow-mortal who had gone the way of all living. While there, we would look with awe profound on the long black *dead deal*, and the black-painted spakes and tressels that stood in the dark corner of his shop. Often have we watched him tacking on the flimsy adornments that were soon, like the poor tenant of that narrow domicile, to be given over to corruption and decay. Alas! little do any of us know but that the timber which is to form our own little dwelling may now be silently growing for us; yea, even perhaps awaiting us in the stack of some joiner's woodyard!

Auld *Coat Wull* has long ago sung his *Nunc dimittis*, and has for ever passed away. Far removed is he now from the wild, tricky loons, who on a Halloween night would fill his house with clouds of smoke from their "Jenny reekies," making him start up and swear that his house was on fire! Gone, too, has *Marget*, his spouse (who kept a perfect model of a milk-house, although not much of a model herself to look at), whose chin was adorned with a few straggling hairs, which gave her the trouble of being her own barber in a primitive but most effectual way, as we have seen— her shaving utensils being a *lighted candle in the one hand, and a wet dishclout, ready for application, in the other!*

And *Lang Tam Cant*, maker of birds' cages, with his long bandy legs, will nevermore be troubled, as he was on Halloween occasions, with the *wild, royed laddies* thrashing at his door with cabbages and runts pulled from some neighbour's kailyard, without leave being asked or obtained, giving him, poor fellow, the trouble of a fruitless chase down the streets, backyards, and closes, which was the very thing the youngsters delighted in.

Hughie the Cobbler, too, we remember with his rosety ends, and his lapstone, hammering his bend leather into shape, and surrounded as he was by a veritable infirmary of old and dilapidated boots, shoes, and "bauchels." His surroundings, dreary enough and most trying to his artistic skill, many of the shoes being past redemption—soles, welting, and uppers ruined—they, like an old, useless musket, standing in need of a new stock, lock, and barrel! Yet, nevertheless, there was a silver lining to the dark clouds that environed him, in the shape of his shrill-toned fife, which had graced many a public occasion in Dunfermline, where he distinguished himself, and it was a solace to him in his lonely hours by the fireside.

And *Johnny Ross*, long since gathered to his fathers, we have now vividly in our remembrance. Light may the sod lie over the kind old man! Sometimes have we ridden in his rickety cart, drawn by some aged and infirm nag, which had now come into the hands of its last but kind-hearted master. No sumptuous car or first-class carriage in after years could compare with a ride long ago in the poor, jolting, bone-shaking chariot, over the rough, round boulders and deep ruts of Dunfermline streets. Unfortunate thou often wert though, Johnny, time after time, in the choice of thine ancient, spavined, broken-winded steeds, which caused thy faithful spouse to remind thee, when thou wer't going to the fair to purchase another one, *" to be sure an' get a guid ane this time, Johnny, though it should cost ye fifteen, or even auchteen shillins!"*

Andrew, or *" the Doctor"* as he was familiarly called, on account of his knowledge regarding bees, birds, &c., I have now before me, plainly visible to the mind's eye, and as he appeared in the flesh long ago. He was in some of his ways and habits the representative of a certain class of workmen who lived in the city. He was over the middle height, sparely built, and was somewhat careless about his personal appearance. His mouth had a twist to one side, and his aspect and dress were usually far from being tidy. Yet this poor hand-loom weaver was in reality a diamond in the rough. He possessed a very kindly heart 'neath his mean exterior and his somewhat uncouth manner. The *Doctor* was a well-read man, had quite a store of general information, and a fair knowledge of botany, natural history, ornithology, and other subjects. He never was a very successful operative, and consequently his wages were small, averaging perhaps not more than about eight shillings per week or so. Yet Andrew left behind him when he died a library worth about £50 or £60! Out of his meagre wage he sometimes spent as much as two or even three shillings per week on his books and aviary. A friend, for whom the doctor had a great respect, met him one day on his way to a bookshop to make a purchase, and he advised him rather to spend his small savings on a beefsteak, as he seemed to be more in want of that than of books. Andrew took his friend's advice, but remarked to him a day or two after, that he had made a great mistake, for he had nothing now to show for his money, the beefsteak was gone, but if he had purchased a book he would have had something to show, and to keep. The fresh eggs he generously gave to his canaries and breeding birds would have often been more appropriately bestowed on himself, but his own bodily comfort was the last consideration with Andrew. He was noted for his fine collection of feathered pets, and he spared no expense in getting first-rate breeds of canaries and other birds. He had also some fine pigeons, and he once took a fancy to importing a nightingale or two from England, and he tried by every effort in his power to rear them, but it was all in vain. This venture cost him money he could ill spare, it proved a complete failure—the northern climate was fatal to those matchless and most extraordinary songsters.

The Doctor was fond of old, out-of-the-way kind of books. One Sabbath morning he was lying on the grass reading and watching a bee-hive which was about to swarm. A friend came up to him and said, "What's this you're readin' the day, Andrew?" He replied that it was the "natural history o' the devil, a very rare and queer book!"

He was one of a reading clique in the south side of the town, and was greatly given, not only to reading but to the collecting of books. One of his companions named Wastit (Westwood), had been attending a sale of books and other effects, belonging to David Aitken of Blacklaw, and had bought a great load of old works. On his way home with them that night, he called at the *Doctor's* to show him his bargains, and the books were most carefully and lovingly examined and commented on. While this was going on, Wastit let out that, in addition to these, he had also "boucht a great big muckle lump o' a theological book, they called it *Ambrose*, and that it was said to be ane o' the *Auld Fauthers*, for which he did not care." It struck Andrew that this was the works of the celebrated Isaac Ambrose, so he asked "Whaur is the book?"

"Weel, it was sae awfu' heavy, I wasna able to carry 't, so I just flang 't awa." "*Ye monster!*" exclaimed Andrew, "*dae ye ken what you've done? Its ane o' the auld fauthers you've flung awa! Oh! man, whereaboots did ye leave it?*" Wastit told him as near as he could the spot where the book had been thrown away, so Andrew started at once, and cold, dreary, and dark though the night was, succeeded in returning about midnight, and in triumph, with the bulky volume, which he found lying at the root of a hedge.

His friend Wastit and he, and his other literary associates, often "*niffered*" (exchanged) books with each other, and the Doctor got the character of liking a big bargain. He possessed a book which was greatly coveted by Wastit, and this man proposed to "niffer" with the Doctor no less than a whole encyclopædia for it, a work for which he himself probably had not got room, or had got tired of. This was too good a bargain to be lost sight of, so it was agreed to. One night as old *Rachie*, the Doctor's mother, was sitting by the cheek o' the fire taking a quiet smoke, the door opened, and in came Wastit with a burden on his back, which he carried in a bed sheet. "What's a' this?" cried the old woman, "whaur are ye gaun?" "I've brocht some big books to Andrew." "Books, did ye say? ye're to bring nae mair books here! My certie, we've far mair o' them than we hae room for, or can mak' a guid use o'." In spite of this protest, Wastit was looking round the small kitchen to find some place whereon to deposit his burden, and meanwhile the Doctor, who had heard the altercation, came in from his loom, which stood behind the box-beds, and told Wastit to lay the books on the floor-head, till he "socht oot a place for them." "He'll do naething o' the kind," said Rachie, "there's nae mair books comin' here, I'se warrant!" The big quartos were at last thrown down on the earthen floor, amid the protests of the old woman. "Is thae them a'?" asked the Doctor, "No the half o' them," said his friend. "Losh preserve me," said Andrew's mother, "the books are no to come here, for oor wee house is crammed fou o' books, birds, and birds' cages; did ever onybody see the like o' 't?" "Whist, whist, mither! if ye only kent the value o' the licht o' knowledge." "The licht o' a snuff-pen! Gif ye had ony respect for the licht o' common sense, it wad be tellin' ye! Just look at the window, the drawershead, the kist, and the twa box-beds there, a' heapit up wi' books, its enough to anger a saint!"

The Doctor, honest, well-intentioned fellow that he was, in his poor, straitened environments, and with a soul eagerly thirsting for knowledge, had bit by bit, with his hard-earned savings, gradually accumulated a large collection of books, many of them old and second-hand. The difficulty of finding room for them was now becoming the question of the hour, and he anxiously pondered over the subject, but tried in vain to find a solution of it. Andrew had gone beyond the limits of human endurance, and his mother, kindly body that she was, had borne a great deal of inconvenience, in order to encourage and humour him, for he had been a good, warm-hearted son to her, but a most unexpected catastrophe was at hand.

It appears that the shelves which were around the inside of the two old-fashioned box-beds, and also the tops of the beds, were heavily laden with volumes, and Andrew had occasion one evening to resort thither for a book to show to some of his cronies, who were sitting round the fire discussing some literary matter or other. In reaching over for the volume in question, the old, top-heavy, wooden fabric came suddenly down upon him with a crash. There were deals, bedding, books, pigeons, and birds' cages, mingled in one mass of confusion! The wreck was unexpected, complete, and terrible to behold, and nought, alas! but the legs of the poor Doctor could now be seen. No pantomime could surpass it! His cronies rushed to his rescue, but amid the extraordinary wreck it was some moments before they could make up their minds as to what was best to be done. His father, too, greatly alarmed at the crash, came running " ben " from his loom; but at length Andrew, whose position was now critical, yelled out to his comrades—"*Ye monsters! if you've ony pity in you, draw me oot quick, for I'm near killed!*"

LOCAL CHARACTERS.

AULD BESSIE BITTEM THE SPAEWIFE, AND OTHERS.

" Forgotten generations live again,
Assume the bodily shape !" &c.

THE young people of the present generation will scarcely be able to credit the accuracy of the following incident, which occurred in Dunfermline long ago. It is a fact, nevertheless, and after all is not greatly to be wondered at, when we consider that it happened at a period when Dunfermline (and Scotland in general) was in a very primitive condition as compared to what now is.

Auld Bessie Bittem was looked upon by her neighbours with somewhat of an uneasy kind of feeling. She was regarded as one who was "no very canny," and whom it was unsafe to disagree or to meddle with, and whose curses or prayers were equally to be dreaded. Even her big black cat did not escape suspicion, and was looked upon as a sort of emissary in some way or other. One day Bessie appeared at the side of Johnnie K.'s loom, and said to him, "Johnnie, ye'll gang the morn and howk my wee pickle tatties—eh ?" " Deed an' he'll do naething o' the kind," shouted Kirsty, his wife, from the kitchen. " He has mair need to dad awa' at his loom, an' get his cut oot." Bessie replied, " He'll maybe no get his cut oot ony the sooner for no howkin' my wee pickle tatties." " Ye'll better let me gang," said Johnnie to his wife, in a sub-missive tone. " Ye'll no gang your tae length," said Kirsty. " Ye auld near-be-gaun jade, an' ye'll no let him howk a wee pickle tatties for a puir auld body like me ! Ye'll no be ony the richer for't, I weel a wat ! Noo, mind ye, I'm tellin' ye !" shouted Bessie, as she toddled out of the shop, followed by her black cat.

Johnnie had scarcely resumed his work, when out flew his shuttle, and fell on the floor. He got off his loom and lifted it up, and then tried again, but with a like result. Out it sprang once more, giving him the trouble and delay of going for it, and lifting it with a sad, sorrowful heart, and a deep sigh. He considered himself bewitched, and it appeared as if a "judgment" had come upon him sooner than he expected. He then, as his only resource, took the shuttle to the kitchen, and sitting down before the fire, with a very doleful face, having in the house

> "Neither vervain, nor yet dill,
> That hindered witches of their will;"

nor yet had he

> "Roan tree and red thread,
> That put the witches to their speed,"

So, therefore, in order to break, if possible, the spell that hung over him, he began by solemnly drawing the shuttle three times through the smoke, dolefully saying as he did so, "I kent hoo it wad be, I kent hoo it wad be!" He then turned to his wife and said, "O Kirsty! ye micht hae mair sense than contrar' that auld witch Bessie Bittem!"

PURSUED BY A SHARK.

Amongst "the lichts o' ither days" in Dunfermline, there was a very curious man, who was much given to exaggerating (to put it in the mildest way) while recounting any of the wonderful feats he had performed. One evening he was telling some friends at his own fireside of a most miraculous escape he had made from the very jaws of an immense shark in the Firth of Forth. He said that on a fine summer day he went down to the seaside to bathe, and it was not far from Rossyth where he took off his clothes and entered into the water. He was enjoying a fine swim, was about a mile from the shore, and near to the rock or little island called the Dhu Craig, when all at once there appeared the fiery eyes and open jaws of a monstrous shark approaching him! He plainly saw that it was now a matter of life or death with him, so he was put on his utmost mettle. As he was a good swimmer, he struck out with all his strength and with all his speed. In this way he swam twice round the Craig, but could not find a landing-place. Still the fierce, burning gaze of his deadly enemy was ever upon him, and the hungry monster was silently but surely drawing nearer. It was clear to him now that there was nothing left but either to kill, or be killed and eaten up bodily. So, being an expert swimmer, as he said, he skilfully and quick as lightning dived below its belly, and instantly ripped the monster up with his knife, and killed it there and then! His listeners were thrilled with the account of this extraordinary adventure, looked on him admiringly, praised his astonishing bravery, and, above all, his dexterity in the swimming line. The wondrous feats performed at the Carnegie Baths in these modern days were of course nothing to that! His wife, however, who was occasionally a thorn in his side, from a faculty she had of sometimes putting most inconvenient questions, spoiled the effect of this fine story by asking him before his friends—"*But, John, whaur did ye get the knife to kill the shark wi'?*" This untimeous question nettled John very much, and he exclaimed, "*Od, woman, what's the use o' bein' sae particular!*"

Another worthy in the Nethertown, who was also much given to boasting, was told by a customer who was in his shop one day that he could dance a hornpipe within ten inches of circumference. "Oh," said the other, "that's naething; I could dance a hornpipe within six inches of circumvention."

A REAL HERMIT.

Few places could boast of having in their midst such an extraordinary person as the following, whom I am now to introduce. He was a genuine specimen of the hermit species. Between thirty and forty years ago an individual named Thomas Bamburgh, a native of Charlestown village, was brought up to Dunfermline Poorhouse. His character and history are alike strange and astonishing. In early life he displayed a singular obstinacy of disposition. He appeared to have been endowed with the obstinacy of a hundred mules! When a boy of little more than ten years of age, he showed a very great partiality for a seafaring life, and was most anxious to get his mother's consent to his becoming a sailor. This she would by no means grant, and sternly opposed the very mention of such a proposition. The consequence was, that after the frustration of his wishes he secluded himself from the society of his fellow-men, and lived for more than twenty-five years of his life in a small garret, unseen and alone! His mother, a widow, lived in the apartment right below the garret; and although she had been so near her son as to hold some daily conversation with him, and to put his food up to him through a small aperture in the ceiling, yet for many years together she never got a glimpse of him! The last time she saw him was about fifteen years previous to her death. After her death there was no one to care for him, and the authorities ordered that he should be brought to the Dunfermline Workhouse. It was with considerable difficulty, and only by a stratagem, that he was compelled to leave his solitary abode; but after being fairly secured and on his way to Dunfermline, he became in some measure reconciled to the great change, and to those who had been the means of bringing him from darkness into light. His weird, unearthly, unkempt appearance, and his extraordinary habiliments, caused, as might have been expected, great surprise. He lived for some years in the Dunfermline Workhouse, and got somewhat reconciled to the faces of his fellow-men.

TEAPAT ROBBIE.

It has been well observed that history repeats itself; we see this every day, not only in the political world, but also in social life. Some persons are beset with a particular idiosyncrasy, which takes entire possession of them, and becomes the ruling passion. I knew a man who lived in the New Row, and who would cheerfully travel on foot a dozen or twenty miles to see a new kind of tulip or a new pansy, so keen was his taste for flowers. Others, of an antiquarian caste of character, would travel and procure an old pot, an old coal-scuttle, or an ancient door-handle, and would willingly exchange, like Aladdin, handsome new lamps for old ones. Teapat Robbie lived in Mastertown, near Dunfermline, many years ago, and he was distinguished for his strange and inordinate attachment towards old teapots: this was his one idea. I remember his appearance well. He was a tall, round-shouldered, powerful man. He had usually an untidy appearance, was generally bare-headed, and wore thick, heavy tackety shoes, but no stockings. Every time he was met on his way home to Mastertown (and few persons cared to meet him alone), he was sure to be found carrying the trophies he had collected in the shape of old earthenware teapots. New ones, or any other sort of crockery, he would not look at. He visited Dunfermline almost every day, and when he had a successful "take," he might be seen going homewards with his prizes slung by a cord round his neck. In this most peculiar "industry" he succeeded in nearly filling an outhouse with his teapots. Those ceramic treasures he guarded with miserly care, and woe betide the man, woman, or child who dared to put a hand upon his household gods! They were lovingly preserved and greatly admired by him, and, like children, they had their several names, such as the "Old Captain" and the "Young Captain," &c. &c. When in a rage, as I have seen him on his way home, caused, it might be, by some thoughtless boy venturing to touch the teapots which he carried, it was fearful to see the tall, wild-looking man stamping his foot and bellowing like a bull in a strange mysterious language of his own. His conduct, poor fellow, was the outcome of a poor, weak, bewildered brain.

FRANK WEIR.

Long ago there was a class of men belonging to the "Blue Gown" fraternity, who were professional and licensed beggars, and wore badges to indicate their calling. The last of the race in this neighbourhood was one known

as " Cardugan," but whose real name was Hutchison. He
died in 1819. After the days of the " Blue Gowns," there
were large numbers of wandering waifs and others who
preferred a nomadic life, and who might be seen on all
hands plying their vocation as mendicants, some of them
from choice, and many from necessity. They used to have
meal-pocks slung over their shoulders to carry the oatmeal
and other scraps that they received from those who were
hospitably inclined. Some of them were made welcome
to a meal, or to a bed in the barn or garret. Many were
very entertaining, and were in fact like a newspaper, doing
duty in the way of communicating the country and town
news, and the gossip of the day.

Frank Weir, about sixty years ago, took his rounds all
about Dunfermline and neighbourhood, ostensibly for the
purpose of selling broom or heather besoms, but in reality
he was to some extent a mendicant. He was quite an
original, and many curious stories are told regarding him.
He was a tall, weird-looking figure, wore his hair long, was
black-a-vised, and usually wore a long coat or cloak over
him, which apparently added to his great height. He did
not, like some mendicants, go from door to door, but had a
round of certain houses and families where he knew he
would be made welcome, and would enjoy their hospitality.
In those old days it might be a " cog o' porridge," " a
bowlful o' kail," a bit of bread and cheese and a cup of cap
ale, &c. Anything was acceptable to Frank. He was
very droll sometimes, and very expert with his answers
and remarks. He liked a dram, and with regard to some
of the better class of houses that he visited he would
remark that " they were guid meat houses, but bad drink
anes !" Amongst other places he visited was Pitfirrane,
where he was sure to be welcomed in the kitchen, and
asked to partake of the food that was going. One day he
met in the grounds Sir Charles Halket, who appeared to
be in bad humour, being annoyed about something or
other. Frank made obeisance to him in passing, and
Sir Charles told him to " go to h—ll." Frank slunk
away, " pocketed the affront," and wisely said nothing,

resolving to bide his time. For a good while afterwards Frank did not put in an appearance at Pitfirrane. When at length he did go there, he again happened to meet Sir Charles, who kindly asked him where he had been this long time. Frank told him that he had been away to the place to which Sir Charles had sent him the last time he was at Pitfirrane. "Where was that, Frank?" "Ye ken, Sir Charles; it was the ill place ye sent me to." "What were they doing there, Frank?" "They were just doin' there what they are doin' here; they were takin' in the rich folk an' keepin' oot the puir!"

Further on, under the title of "Sweethearting under difficulties," there is an authentic incident recorded of a young man who attempted to descend the inside of a chimney in a neighbouring village. A similar kind of story is told of Frank Weir. It happened long ago, when the minister of the first charge in the Dunfermline Abbey Church lived in the Kirkgate. One day his dinner was all prepared, and set down in the parlour ready for him. Frank from some neighbouring window observed the tempting dishes, and as it was more than he could resist, he without delay went down the minister's chimney, and, all covered over with soot and dirt from head to foot, and with his long, black, hairy head and beard, he sat down quietly and commenced on the eatables placed on the table. Immediately thereafter the servant happened to go into the room where he was, but she ran out in a moment screaming "Murder!" When she came to herself in some measure, and was able to speak, she told the alarmed household that "*The deevil was sittin' ben the hoose eatin' the minister's denner!*"

BOBBY GOW AND DAFT ARCHIE.

On the streets of Dunfermline there were to be seen specimens of real *naturals*, who used to wander about with their meal-pocks slung from their shoulders, trying to pick up the crumbs for a living. There were two who were specially well known—"Daft Archie" and "Bobby

Gow." They were kindly treated by many; but, poor things, they had to bear much rough usage from the wild school-boys and others who, for a bit of mischief and fun, delighted to set their "birse" up. Bobby was straight and well formed, but under the middle height; and though he wore a contented, perennial smile, was a poor, harmless, happy imbecile. Archie in his appearance was the reverse of Bobby. He was tall and muscular, had stooping shoulders, and a slouching gait, and generally walked right in the middle of the causeway for fear of a sudden attack. He had a big gaping mouth, and it gave great fun to the boys to get Archie to stand with his mouth opened wide, while they tried to pitch a copper or two into it. He had a cunning, suspicious look always about him, and was sometimes dangerous to meddle with. Like Bobby, he never was without his meal-pock, ready for the chief business of life. Archie never ventured beyond the precincts of the town, but Bobby wandered about all over the parish. Bobby was a far greater favourite with the public than Archie, and consequently was not nearly so much molested as the other. Poor Archie, who lived with his mother, was, I remember, very unkindly used by the boys in the streets now and again. He was withal somewhat clever and droll in his remarks, and he sometimes put curious out-of-the-way questions to those who addressed him. It was his habit to pay a brief visit to the different churches on Sunday forenoons; and when asked why he did so, he said that his "mither liket to hear the forenoon's sermons." As for Bobby Gow, he was ever wandering about, and it was great fun both to old and young to get him to stand in the street and repeat his well-known and strange rhapsody—"*Halley Petik, Halley Petoe,*" &c. &c., always finishing up this singular piece of rubbish with the words "*Bee, wee, wee, wee, woe!*" the last word given with a thundering shout, which might easily be heard in a quiet day half a mile off. The terrific finish up always gave uncommon delight to his youthful audiences.

The opening of the Dunfermline Poorhouse cleared the streets of those poor half-witted creatures, and provided for them a clean and well-ordered home.

HOGMANAY AND AULD HANDSEL MONDAY.

THE story of Hogmanay and Auld Handsel Monday is an
old one, and has no doubt been often told ; but, like the
strains of an old and stirring melody, the recital of it
anew—

> " Calls back from out the spectral past,
> Remembrance of the vanished faces,
> That peopled hours too bright to last
> In years that fled with lightning paces ! "

Long ago, *Hogmanay*, the last day of the year, which is
generally understood to be of Pagan origin, and Handsel
Monday, the first Monday of the year, Old Style, were
regarded in Fifeshire as the real holidays of the year.
In Aberdeenshire, Christmas or Yule-tide has always been
considered such ; while many other places kept New
Year's Day as the chief holiday season in the year. The
approach of Hogmanay and Auld Handsel Monday was
looked forward to with the keenest interest by old and
young (by the young especially) in Dunfermline. For
weeks previously, working-men were universally saving
and industrious—" on the push," as it was then familiarly
called—to meet the extra demands upon them at those
times of universal hospitality. It was a usual thing for
master tradesmen to give their men and boys a supper on
Hogmanay night, or a breakfast on Handsel Monday
morning, if family reunions did not prevent. In some
cases a small piece of money would be found beneath each
person's plate. Previous to Hogmanay, much consideration was given by the youngsters as to what disguises they
would adopt on that eventful night — what piece they
would " act " at the different houses they intended to visit
—whether it were to be the conflict between " Norval
and Glenalvon," or " Here comes I, Gallashan, Gallashan,
Gallashan is my name," or a bit out of the play of " Rob
Roy," or out of the " Gentle Shepherd," &c. Sometimes
they would arrange to be dressed up as gipsies and nonde-

scripts, so that their own mothers would scarcely be able to tell who they were. The warriors were to have blackened faces and long beards formed of yarn ravellings ; while their swords were to be made, not of Damascus steel, but of a piece of hoop-iron, got at Cooper Dick's or some other cooperage : and all this was to be accompanied with song-singing, fiddle-playing, and other wonderful exhibitions. Those important matters arranged and settled weeks beforehand, Hogmanay was ushered in by the younger portion of the community paying visits during the day to their friends, relations, and acquaintances, in order to get their "Hogmanay" from them. The usual salutations given when they unceremoniously opened the doors of the houses they visited were—"*Hogmanay, Mistress !*" Or—

> " Rise up, guidwife, an' shake your feathers,
>   Dinna think that we are beggars ;
>   We are bairns come oot to play,
>   So let us have our hogmanay !"

Others would say—

> " My feet 's cauld, my shoon 's thin
>   Gie 's my cake and let me rin."

Or—

> " Here come the guisers,
>   Never been before,
>   Not to beg nor borrow,
>   But to drive away your sorrow."

In other cases they would begin the proceedings by singing a song or a chorus, and thus they would go from one house to another. As the evening set in, numerous bands of grown-up persons, male and female, sallied forth with their "false faces," and their extraordinary guises on, to sing and "act" at the houses of friends and acquaintances. In many instances money was given to them, but the most of the guisers did it for the fun of the thing. There were usually refreshments offered and accepted, consisting of bread and cheese, currant loaf, hogmanays (or three-cornered biscuits), and in some houses whisky to those who were grown up. As a finish up, the guisers would all join in the following refrain :—

> "God bless the master of this house,
>   And mistress also,
> Likewise the little bairnies,
>   That round the table go.
> May your purse be full of money,
>   Your cellars full of beer,
> We wish you many a Hogmanay,
>   And many a good New Year."

Hogmanay day (being, as already mentioned, the last day of the year) was considered by many a very lucky day for being married on, and hence there were large numbers who preferred that day for this important event. In consequence of this, Mr. Rankine had an unusually long list of "cryings" to proclaim on the Sabbaths previously in the Parish Church of Dunfermline.

AULD HANDSEL MONDAY.

> "How is it, growing old, that what we've seen
>   In earliest days, should cling to memory yet,
> When all the interval of life between,
>   Compared to *that*, seems easy to forget?"

Auld Handsel Monday came in about a fortnight after Hogmanay, and was of all days the first and foremost of the year. It is now a thing of the past, and New Year's Day, though held with perhaps more outward decorum, but with far less enthusiasm, has taken its place. It is perhaps well that the change was made, for the advent of New Year's Day is now regarded everywhere as the most important epoch in all the year. To the young, this season of festivity had a most peculiar fascination. Every spare copper was hoarded up for weeks previously, in order to purchase a long, tin *touting-horn*, or for the materials to make a flambeau, to be lighted and carried about on the great morning. Those boys were considered fortunate who had secured the remnants of torches borne at the masons' procession on St. John's night, which took place in

December. The following lines are taken from a poem written by a townsman, Mr. R. Anderson, who for a good number of years resided in St. Petersburg, and who died recently in his own native city. The subject is here introduced with great fidelity and vigour.

" A laddie o' the brave langsyne,
  Ae Sabbath nicht lay doon at nine,
  He sleepit soun' an' wauken'd fine
    An' fresh for Handsel Monday.

" His flambeau's made o' hemp an' tar,
  His trumpet's there, to rout an' roar
  Wi's little drum, to deeve an' daur
    The ghaists o' Handsel Monday.

" Bob then got up withoot a licht,
  An' gae his face a hurried dicht,
  Pat on his claes—a happy wicht,
    Prepared for Handsel Monday.

" Then stealin' oot an' doon the stair,
  Tam, Jack, an' Sandy, an' lots mair,
  Were waitin' him—be 't foul or fair,
    Ready for Handsel Monday.

" They waited till the Auld Kirk bell
  Struck twal', then at the final knell
  The laddies a' set up a yell—
    Hurrah for Handsel Monday !

" From every close-mouth oot they ran,
  Wi' lichtit torches every one,
  Routin' their horns loud an' gran',
    To bring in Handsel Monday.

" The biel-fires blaze, the flambeaux flare,
  The yells an' shoutin' fill the air,
  Douce bodies frae their windows stare,
    An' say—it's Handsel Monday.''

. . . . .

The festivities connected with Handsel Monday commenced immediately after the clock proclaimed the solemn hour of twelve on Sunday night. Many persons, old and young, made a practice of "*clipping the wings of the Sabbath,*" by retiring to bed some hours earlier than ordinary. The "gatherin' coal" had been put on and happed more carefully than usual, so that a good fire could instantly be made. In many cases the excitement prevented sound sleep, and the stroke of the midnight hour found many hundreds of persons bustling about, ready to sally out into the cold, dark night, some with blazing flambeaux, many first-footing; some with long tin horns, blowing a blast sufficient to arouse the soundest sleeper. In a brief space of time the usually dark and sombre streets of Dunfermline at that early hour were now all alive with fun and noise, and the blazing torches seen flitting about in the dim, dark distance gave them a weird-like aspect. What with the noise of horn-blowing, the merry shouts of parties going along first-footing, singing, and fiddle-playing, the slumbers of many quietly disposed persons were sadly disturbed. But after all, who would not forgive them? Did not that eventful morning come only once a year to cheer and gladden them?

The parties who went to first-foot—and dark complexioned persons, or *black-a-vised* ones, were preferred, being considered the more lucky — never went empty handed, for this would have been a serious omission. They often carried with them some buns or shortbread or oatmeal cakes, and usually had a bottle of whisky, sometimes ginger wine, and sometimes a "het pint," composed of hot spiced ale, with eggs beat up in it, or broken buns or biscuits called "bakes." These drinks were brought to the bedsides of the old people, their privacy being in some manner invaded, but amongst friends and neighbours this was not deemed out of place in those times. Old as well as young were expected at that early hour to partake of the drink that was offered to them, and this was for good luck and a merry Handsel Monday. It was considered undesirable to be your own first-foot, and cases have been known in which paterfamilias returning home after twelve has been kept waiting outside till some one else arrived.

The breakfast on that morning was of an unusual and elaborate character. It might be that during a great portion of the year many had enjoyed what Burns calls "the chief o' Scotia's food," but this morning it was a complete change of breakfast fare, to please old and young. It was

to the young especially a red-letter morning to be remembered.   Fat or kail brose was often made.

As the day wore on, many kindly visits were paid by
friends and neighbours to each other, and the rites of hospitality were freely given and received.   Feuds and quarrels, if
any existed, were then made up and forgotten.   There was
always a hearty salutation offered to callers, and a blithe
" Come awa' ben an' rest ye," cordially given ; while at the
same time the best the house could afford in the shape of
refreshments were set before them.   There was abundance
of plain, substantial fare provided for all visitors who
crossed the threshold on that hallowed day.   During the
most part of the week very little work was done.   They
were usually termed the "*daft days*," to indicate that it
was a period of joviality to old and young.   On the Monday
and Tuesday, at least, not a stroke of work was done.
Every one was free to "lift the sneck" of his neighbour's
door without "tirlin'" thereat, and walk in *sans cérémonie*,
and wish his friends "a merry Handsel Monday, and mony
o' them."

> " There was an open door, that friends might dander in,
>   An' taste the kebbuck, an' tell a' the news."

All were usually dressed in their Sunday garb ; and as
every kind of work was at a complete stand-still, the day
had something of an extraordinary aspect about it.   Neither
a Sabbath nor a Saturday look it had.   The youngsters
would receive their "handsel" from friends, neighbours, and
visitors ; and in those days a penny or a sixpence would, in
many instances, be more prized by the young folks than
perhaps a ten pound note would be in after years.   During
that day and Tuesday, refreshments stood ready on the
table, the dresser, or sideboard, for callers—precisely as it
is the custom at the present time in New York to treat
friends and visitors on a New Year's Day.   The only difference was, that in Dunfermline there was the large
" curran' loaf," *specially baked for the occasion*, the homely
kebbuck of cheese, the beautiful shortbread (such as no
other country can produce), farrels and oatmeal cakes

(having carvey seeds), along with ginger wine and the unfailing "Jeroboam," the whisky bottle; while in New York, expensive wines, brandy, cakes, and confectionery are liberally supplied. An American visitor once remarked that at New Year time in Scotland it was nothing but cakes and cheese and whisky, and whisky and cheese and cakes, all day long! Two or three days after the festivities the tired youngsters were sometimes treated to a cupful or two of salts and senna to put their sorely tried stomachs into their usual state of efficiency.

Many of Dunfermline's sons and daughters will look back with pleasure, yet with a degree of sadness, to the vanished Handsel Mondays and Tuesdays of bygone years! A famous season it was for the reunion of friends and members of families, who were scattered far and wide, and when far fewer facilities existed for meeting than now. There were many happy family gatherings, reunions, and private social meetings as those evenings fell. It might be cold and dreary outside, but within, the fireside presented a happy and an animated appearance. Every face was lit up with smiles, and the hand was ever ready with the grasp of friendship and love. The old and the young met together; children's children were there, beneath the old rooftree, and "weary carking care" was for the time being cast to the winds—

> "It was the hour when happy faces
> Smiled around the taper light."

Songs were sung, stories told, and games and pastimes engaged in, with a heartiness and a homeliness that are now almost unknown. It seems to us as if our modern songs do not touch the heart, and they seem to have but a transitory existence, unlike the songs of bygone days. A song worthy of the name never gets threadbare, for, like the sunshine on the everlasting hills, it is ever new and ever beautiful.

All vanished now are the old worthies who fifty years years ago presided at those friendly reunions—the men who graced with their hoary heads and venerable presence the frugal and hospitable board of those happy homes on the nights of Auld Handsel Monday and Tuesday, where young and old could freely say—

> " Happy we 've been a' thegither,
> Happy we 've been ane and a',"

and who, when the hour of parting came, could join hands and hearts, some of them for the last time, in singing that soul-stirring and grandly pathetic national song—

> " Should auld acquaintance be forgot !"

A SATURDAY AT THE SEA-SIDE.

> "The golden long ago !
> I keep with care the old and trusty key,
> Which ope's the treasury of jewelled shells
> I gathered from the sea—
> The sea of other years !"
>
> *E. Allison.*

WHO of our townsmen can ever forget the expeditions made to the sea-side in their young days, and all the charming associations connected therewith ? It might be to Limekilns, or Rossyth, or to both. The summer days of long ago looked sunnier and longer than the summer days of later years. "The bird, the bee, the butterfly, were on their lightest wing." No one then took any "thought for the morrow," but all laid themselves out to enjoy to the full the passing hours. While journeying along the dry and *stoury* roads, a flood of beautiful sunshine overhead, and every gowan and every wild-flower singing their own songs of praise to the Maker of them (if one could only hear them), the hearts of all could not fail to be impressed with the beauty and peacefulness of the scene. In such circumstances as these, Schiller's question is appropriate :—

> "Will nothing tempt thee here to stay,
> O ! time of golden joys to me ?
> Ah, no ! thy waters haste away,
> To join the everlasting sea !"

As they jogged along, if it were harvest time, fields of golden grain ready for the sickle would be passed on all sides. Now and again the lads would halt for a little, looking up to the clear blue dome, eagerly listening to the thrilling notes of the almost invisible lark, singing its morning hymn with all its might "at Heaven's gate." On their way they would now and again diverge from the beaten path to cool their thirst at some running spring, or to search some distant hedges or bushes for wasps or bees' bykes, brambles, or wild-flowers. Some of them, too, would gather green rushes, and make to themselves and companions *threshy caps.* As a change to the prospect, a field of turnips or beans would come into view, and this was a temptation which was hard to resist, for the turnips or beans in one's own garden-patch were not half so fair, nor half so enticing, as those that now came into sight. Discussions on themes congenial to happy-hearted school-boys would now and again spring up. That of birds and birds' nests would occupy a great share of the talk as they sauntered along. Critical discussions on birds' nests in general would ensue, and also minute descriptions of the special habits of grey and green linties, lav'rocks, pease-weeps, yellow-hammers (yites), and other birds. The particular size, colour, and peculiar markings of birds' eggs would be knowingly commented on, and it was wonderful what an amount of knowledge of natural history some boys displayed. Many of them could describe accurately the particular situations where certain birds preferred to build, how many eggs they usually laid, the colours and marking thereof, how long they took to hatch their young, and how soon the young ones were able to leave the parent nest, &c. &c. All these things were discussed with as much seriousness and earnestness as our School Boards sometimes bring to bear on the questions they have under review at their board meetings! Some of them would boast of the nests they had found out that season, of the beautiful eggs they had captured, and afterwards taken home and strung together like rows of beads to ornament the walls and ceiling, and they would tell of the nests of young birds (raw garbs, as they were called) which they had tried often in vain to rear. Unkind and cruel actions were frequently committed in those days, but done very often without thought and with no cruel intention. It has been said with great truth and force that "there is not one sin that we commit but has its effects upon our souls in after years." Those who are beginning life's journey should remember this.

After passing Primrose Farm, a halt would be called at Brankum Braes, as the place was named, and after a rest on the greensward, or amongst the broomy knowes, a search would be made for brambles, which used to grow there abundantly long ago. Proceeding onwards a little way, the sea would break upon the view, calling forth deep, strange, and fascinating thoughts. Arriving at the sea-side, there were the pitchers to be filled with whelks, lempics, and cavies (limpets and crabs), and after a long search amongst the wet rocks and sea-weed, the industrious were usually rewarded for their toil. Crabs were the great objects of attention, and some of them were very fine in quality, and although much smaller than the kind commonly known as partans, caught further down the Firth, they were richer in flavour, and not so rank. Some ludicrous mishaps occurred in the catching of those curious crustaceans, and the boys had to handle them very carefully for fear of being caught and severely crushed by their savage nippers and claws. Those creatures are famed for their pugnacity, and woe betide the thoughtless youth who sometimes ventures to put his hand behind some dark rock to capture them. Some of the mishaps I have seen in this way bring to my mind the story of the man who once went to a fish-market to buy a fish. He was noted for his stingy disposition. His dog, which was walking by his side, was suddenly caught by a live lobster, and it at once started away for home at full speed, the lobster holding on by the dog's tail like grim death. "Whistle for your dog to come back!" exclaimed the indignant fishmonger. "Na, na, ye can whustle for your partan to come back, if ye like," was the reply.

In wandering up and down amongst the rocks and sea-weed, trying to fill their pitchers with sea-fare, the incoming tide was a reminder that time and tide wait for no man—that the "happy hunting-ground" was being rapidly submerged by the rising flood, and an end put to all further search for that day. The scene was soon completely changed, for the long stretch of cold black-looking rocks, with their dark dripping sea-weed and tangle, were being rapidly hidden from view, and now the beautiful, calm, and mysterious blue sea came rolling slowly on in all its quiet and solemn majesty. A temptation was now offered, and advantage taken of the opportunity, to plunge into the clear blue flood and have a bathe.

After the bathe, races on the sea-beach were sometimes engaged in, and then a visit was paid to the ruins of the ancient fortress or castle at Rossyth—*Ross-hythe*, being "*the landing-place at the promontory*"—where Margaret (afterwards the beloved Queen of Scotland) and the royal exiles disembarked about the memorable year 1069. This place was in 1363 constituted by David II. a port for the use of the abbots and monks of Dunfermline, and also for the burgesses and merchants, for the export and import of all sorts of goods, such as wool, hides, skins, &c. The castle seems to have been erected long afterwards, about the year 1561; and it is a fact that it was occupied or visited for a brief period by Mary Queen of Scots. There the massive ruins stand—

> "Stern e'en in ruin, noble in decay,
> They seem as breathing forth defiance still."

In its palmy days it must have been an extensive and imposing stronghold. On a recent visit we measured the walls at the basement, and they were about ten feet thick in some places. The massive foundations of the "Chaple of the Castle," which stood on the west side, may yet be clearly traced. Often have we gazed with interest on the carved stone above the door in the south wall, which has lately been removed, and read its quaint inscription, to this effect—

> "In due time draw this cord, ye bell to clink,
> Whose merry voice warns to meat and drink."

Could those massive grey ruins but speak, what wonderful stories and scenes they might recall! Scenes of happiness and festivity, and also occurrences of perhaps a dark and tragic kind. But "here desolation holds her dreary court," and the old walls are dumb, so—

> "Waken not those whispers,
> They may pain your ears;
> Waken not the dust that deepens,
> Through the solemn years."

Rosyth Castle.

The following beautiful lines, by Goethe, on a similar old castle ruin, are very appropriate here, and may be quoted :—

> " Now gone are door and portal,
>   And all is hush'd and still ;
> O'er ruined wall and rafter
>   I clamber as I will.
>
> " A cellar with many a vintage
>   Once lay in yonder nook ;
> Where now are the cellarer's flagons,
>   And where is his jovial look ?
>
> " No more he sets the beakers
>   For the guests at the wassail feast ;
> Nor fills a flask from the oldest cask
>   For the duties of the priest.
>
> " No more he gives on the staircase
>   The stoup to the thirsty squires,
> And a hurried thanks for the hurried gift
>   Receives, nor more requires.
>
> " For ruined are roof and rafter,
>   And they hang begrimed and black ;
> And stair, and hall, and chapel
>   Are turned to dust and wrack."

A visit to this old, romantic, lonely keep was always intensely gratifying to youngsters. They had perfect freedom to wander about its ruined wall and chambers, and to perform feats of daring as they pleased. To scramble up to the sandy room, as it was called (because the floor of it was covered with sand and powdered lime), did not require much trouble. It was, however, deemed a somewhat dangerous feat to go up to the floor above, called the grassy room. There were only two ways of reaching this elevated part of the ruin—either by scrambling up by the broken circular staircase, where there was little or no foothold to be had, and where a slip or false step meant a deep fall to the bottom of the tower or staircase, or, worse even, broken bones; or by stepping up by the mullions of the large eastern window, which was also a perilous undertaking, for a fall to the outside meant a broken neck. It was wonderful how many boys escaped as they did, but serious accidents now and again occurred.

On the expeditions to Rossyth, some persons would, if the tides fell unusually low, manage to go out as far as the Dhu Craig, and there they would be able to obtain what the boys called "hairy hutchins," or sea eggs, technically named *Echinidæ*, or sea urchins. These shells or eggs are very pretty and peculiar looking, and many a parlour mantelpiece in Dunfermline used to be adorned with them.

The waning of the sun in the western sky, and also indications coming on of a sharpened appetite, led the boys to think of betaking themselves homewards. Wearily they sometimes wended their way back, some of them tired, footsore, hungry, and sunburnt, and in some cases lame from cut feet, or smarting under the stings of bees or wasps. And so it is that, amidst the most pleasing of our earthly joys, there are often painful drawbacks mixed up with them. Roses and thorns grow together on the same stem. Reaching home at last, bearing with them in their well-filled pitchers the spoils of the day, on which they set great store, they were ready for the luxury of a substantial homely meal. From kind and loving hands this was soon obtained, and such justice done to it as only hungry boys can do. They were then by-and-by well prepared, after their long ramble, for a night of sound, healthy, unbroken slumber, far away in the realms of dreamland.

THE CHOLERA TIME.

WHEN the terrible scourge of *Cholera morbus* first made
its appearance here on the eventful 2d day of September
1832, it caused great consternation on all hands and
amongst all classes. The first person who was attacked
and died in the town was a man named Messer, a weaver
in Baldridge Burn. The disease spread very rapidly, and
was very deadly. It continued from that date till the 17th
November, when the town was declared to be free from
the fearful pestilence. In that period there were 349 cases
and 158 deaths. While the epidemic was at its worst, there
were from *fifteen to twenty-four funerals daily.* Thursday,
October 11th, 1832, was observed as a solemn fast-day, on
account of the awful spread of the disease. A temporary
hospital was opened in the Lancasterian School, Rolland
Street, and all around the building was boarded up with a
high fence of boards, and in the building itself there were
long rows of beds for the patients. A woman named
Brunton, sister-in-law to Willie Cant, was the head nurse.
A covered-in cart was got to accommodate the numerous
patients who were brought from all parts of the town.
Those who listened to the peculiar hollow rumble of that
cholera cart going along the streets night and day, conveying the dying to the hospital and the dead to their narrow
homes, would never forget its ominous sound; it was of itself sufficient to breed cholera. If two or three neighbours
were sitting around the fire of an evening conversing, an
instant silence and a nameless fear would take possession
of them all, if the doleful, hollow sound of that cart were
heard approaching. So deadly and so terribly rapid was
the disease in its course, that few people ventured to follow
the cart with the remains of their relatives to the graveyard, for fear of infection. The bodies were buried in
trenches in the new burying-ground opposite the Frater's
Hall, and in some cases there were five or six, and even
more, put into one grave. For years after, this portion of

the burying-ground was regarded with feelings of awe and dread by those who passed it by. It was solemnly pointed to as "the cholera graveyard." When the disease was at its height, and the sound of that dreadful cart was heard every now and again, it put one in mind of the state of London during the plague, when men went their rounds with carts, and shouted as they went along the streets, "Throw out your dead! throw out your dead!" I remember well how deep the gloom was that overspread Dunfermline at that time. Every morning there was the cry of lamentation heard in several houses over the town, and no one knew whose turn was to come next. This dreaded and deadly pestilence was supposed to hold in its hand "a roll of death warrants, and no man knew, as in the old Roman proscriptions, whether his name was or was not in that frightful roll!" If ever there was a searching of hearts, it was at that memorable period.

Poor thoughtless mortals that we are, divided from the unseen world by a very thin film, yet living jauntily here as if this were to be the place of our everlasting rest, it is only when we are brought face to face with such a deadly calamity as this, that we feel how entirely helpless and dependent creatures we are. Many were the solemn communings between friends and relations—between those who were near and dear to each other, such as husband and wife—during those dreary days and nights. No one knowing how soon the summons might come to them, the question was often asked—

> " One of us, dear—
>   Which one ?
>   May sit by a bed with marvellous fear,
>   And clasp a hand
>   Growing cold as it feels for the spirit-land :
>   Darling, which one ?
>
> " One of us, darling, it may be,
>   It may be you will slip from me ;
>   Or perhaps my life may first be done :
>   I'm glad we do not know
>   Which one !"

American Paper.

The authorities did all in their power to lessen and abolish every nuisance. The streets were well cleansed, tar barrels were burnt, and they sent up their smoky, lurid glare by day, and also in the darkness of night. Men went about with hand-carts or barrows, containing chloride of lime and vitriol, to fumigate the town, and everybody, I remember, wore a small bag suspended from the neck and under the clothing, containing a bit of camphor, to keep away the infection. Some of the folks in the town alleged that this scourge was a visitation sent by the Almighty to chastise the people for their great sins; others boldly declared that the whole thing was done by the doctors, who put poison into the public wells! This calamity, happening so soon after the Burke and Hare scandal, would no doubt lead a very small section of ignorant and stupid people to blame the doctors for causing the pestilence.

Both at that time and also in 1849, when this great scourge again visited the city, the doctors worked day and night, and with no mercenary object in view, for they willingly risked their own lives to save those of others. Amongst those who took some credit for their exertions was one well known in the town, Dr. Cameron, who kept a druggist's shop in the High Street. He sounded the praises of his cholera mixture, and sold a large quantity of it. He declared it was an unfailing remedy. He was one of the "characters" of Dunfermline—Dr. "Hollipotts," as he was familarly called. He was an old Highlandman, was kindly and genial in his way, and had seen active service as a surgeon in a Highland regiment. His skull had been fractured by a sabre cut or gunshot wound, and I have seen him show where it had been clasped by a silver clasp. He used often to walk up and down in front of his shop door, always prim and starched, wearing an old-fashioned high ruffled collar, and was always dressed in black suit and white neckcloth, and had his gold-mounted cane in his hand. Great numbers went to Dr. Cameron at that time to get his cholera bottle. When this fell disease afterwards appeared in 1849, it was again

very deadly, but it did not create the great consternation that it excited on its first memorable visit.   On its
first visit, Mr. Angus of the post-office fell a victim; there
was also the well-known Watty Bell, a jobbing tailor and
a poet.   Willie Nicol, too, commonly called "*the Blue
Beadle,*" was stricken with this disease while he was in the
act of digging a grave, and there were many other well-
known persons in Dunfermline carried off suddenly.   At
that time the town was neither properly drained nor was
it sewered, and there was an absence of a good supply
of fine, pure, wholesome water, such as is now to be seen
abounding in all quarters.

HAWKERS, PACKMEN, AND GAUN-ABOOT FOLK.

FEW in Dunfermline will be aware of the extent to which the manufacturers long ago were indebted to the large number of hawkers and packmen, who travelled everywhere throughout the country selling Dunfermline goods, &c. &c. Those men regularly attended the fairs in England, and bought linen and other goods from the manufacturers who went there with their merchandise. Some Dunfermline manufacturers in those old days went to the fairs held in Leeds, Preston, Chester, Shrewsbury, Wolverhampton, York, Wrexham, &c. &c., and sold their goods to the hawkers, who distributed them all over England. In course of time, this led to a warehouse being taken at Liverpool by Mr. Anderson, as a depôt for England, to which the "Scotchmen," as the hawkers were called, sent their orders. Many of those hawkers laid the foundation in this way of large fortunes, and became great warehousemen in Manchester, Bradford, Leeds, &c., and thus brought Dunfermline to the front as a manufacturing town. About fifty-five or sixty years ago there were very many persons, male and female, ever on the road in Scotland, acting as small itinerant vendors of all kinds of merchandise. Some of them did very well, and were able to retire, as they advanced in years, on a comfortable competence, or were enabled to set up small shops in their native places or elsewhere. There were at that period nothing like the fine shops we now have in town and country. Railways, steamers, 'buses, shopkeepers' vans, and cheap postage were then quite unknown. Those itinerant merchants, who abounded in the smaller towns, and who went from village to village, and from one farm-house to another, carried with them a wonderful assortment of wares of all kinds. In their oilskin covered baskets and in their capacious packs they carried needles and pins, tapes and laces, ribbons, woollens,

dress pieces, and shawls, worsted yarns and stockings—
in short, a miscellaneous assortment of goods, up to
watches and cheap sparkling jewellery, sufficient to please
all tastes. The arrival of a packman with his wondrous
collection of wares was always welcomed, and the opening
up of his pack or wallet, with its glittering treasures,
always gave uncommon pleasure to old and young.
Nothing could surpass the array of tempting articles
displayed, as one tray after another was brought forth, and
their contents shown to the admiring onlookers. Some
philosopher of old, it is said, while walking the streets of
a large city, said to himself, as he gazed into the beautiful
windows, "How many things do I not want?" so the
packman's audiences did not know the extent of their
wants till his tempting wares were laid out before them.
Like the itinerant tailors, they were usually a well-
informed class of men, and were very useful in the way of
spreading the news of the day, and telling of matters
political, ecclesiastical, and domestic. They were generally
treated with hospitality in rural districts, and as a rule
received as much food as served them till they reached
the next village or farm-house. If they were peremptorily
told—"We're no needin' onything the day, honest man,"
they would, if it were warm summer weather, likely ask
for "a drink o' water." This they usually got with a
large handful of oatmeal in it, which quenched the thirst,
and sustained the strength while travelling long distances,
infinitely better than beer or any other malt liquors could
possibly do. Hence the well-known phrase, "You're
surely ill wi' the packman's drouth." Sometimes they
would get a large basin of broth, or fine fresh milk and
bread and cheese, in exchange for the latest news which
they retailed. Before the duty was taken off salt, large
numbers of "salt cadgers" were to be seen everywhere
vending this first and foremost necessary of life. On his
arrival at a farm-town, the "sauter" is reported to have
addressed the sonsy, good-humoured mistress in something like the following fashion—"Weel, guidwife, here I
am again, the nearer to e'en the mair beggars ye ken.

Hoo's the guidman? You're a' meat-hale an workin'
some, I houp?" To which she would reply, "Come awa'
in bye, sauter, we're glad to see ye; we hav'na haen a lick
o' saut for twa three days, an' I was wonderin' what had
come o'er ye." "That's a bad job, mistress, but ye ken
it's better to be sautless than sillerless; but here I am, an'
I'll be glad to pitch my camp here for the nicht."

The packmen and travelling merchants knew instinctively the best places to arrive at towards the
gloamin' hour. They knew where they would be made
welcome, and receive a hearty supper of sweet milk and
sowens, potatoes and herring, bread and cheese, or whatever
was going in the family that evening. In many homesteads it was looked upon as a matter of honour, and an
urgent Christian duty, to relieve and to entertain the
"wayfaring man" as the shadows of evening fell. In the
memoir of Robert Chambers the publisher, written by his
brother William, it is mentioned that in some dwelling-
houses and farms long ago, shelter was given every night,
not only to hawkers, but also to groups of vagrant people.

> "Wha totters sae wearily up to the stile,
>   Wi' back sairly bent, and forfoughten wi' toil,
>   Wi' age-wrinkled face, an' the tear in his ee,
>   I wonder wha' this weary body can be?"

> "'Come in to the ingle and rest you awhile,'
>   Quoth Johnnie Graham's father; and then, with a smile,
>   An' a heart fou o' kindness, he held oot his han',
>   An' heartily welcomed the auld beggar man."

On a Saturday night, at some of the hospitable small
farms, there would sometimes be as many as twenty of
those "tramps," as they are now called, received by the
farmer, who gave them food and lodging till Monday
morning. Some of them, who had established for themselves a good character, were entertained in the Ha',
where the farmer, his wife, and the servants usually sat;
others were accommodated in the barn or outhouses, as
was the fashion in those times. "Such was the custom of
Branksome Hall." The family rather relished this society,
for from hardly any other source did they obtain the news
of the country. Many of those "gaun-aboot bodies" had

a wonderful amount of mother-wit and genuine humour, and a facility for making themselves agreeable wherever they went. Many of them, too, alas! were broken-down and wounded soldiers, who had been wounded at Waterloo in 1815, and who fought their battles over again at many a hospitable fireside and farmer's ingle in the long winter nights. In those quiet, easy-going times there was a great deal of the element of brotherly kindness prevailing in society. The same thing abounds now-a-days on all hands, but it is often shown in a very different manner. While there are numerous beneficent societies and schemes of all kinds now afloat, for the purpose of relieving human suffering and aiding the poor and the destitute—and all honour to them for this—we have, alas! in our midst huge workhouses, containing thousands of poor creatures, who are "cabin'd, cribbed, and confined," shut out from much of genial human sympathy, and from communion and companionship with Nature and Nature's works. To them we throw our crusts over a high wall, as if to a kennel of dogs. It is indeed sad to think that, in the midst of our high civilisation and boundless wealth, nine-tenths of mankind have to struggle so hard as they do against famine and destitution. What sight can be sadder than that of a band of modern "tramps," as they are called, waiting their turn to gain admission to the casual ward of a city workhouse? The officials, in quite a callous, business-like way, examine the cases before them, and generally assume that each one of the woe-begone applicants is somewhat of an impostor, addicted to begging, swindling, and stealing, as opportunity offers. But it sometimes happens that decent mechanics, and well-conducted labouring men, out of employment, wearily travelling from place to place on foot, are obliged to betake themselves at nightfall to the workhouse for shelter. Those men are treated like the rest; the deserving and undeserving, the honest and the dishonest, the drunken and the sober, all are looked on as alike by the cold, stern official eye, and all are treated alike, and usually worse than convicts are.

REV. MR. SHIRRA AND THE PACKMAN.

We shall close this by quoting the following quaint story, which is told regarding one of those packmen of the olden times, and the celebrated Mr. Shirra, the able but eccentric minister of Kirkcaldy. It is worthy of being repeated here.

One Saturday afternoon the Rev. Mr. Shirra was on his way to Doune to assist a brother clergyman, whose communion was on the following day. On his way thither he met a fellow-pedestrian, and they got into conversation. "May I ask," said Mr. Shirra, "what manner of occupation you are of?" "Please sir, I am a pedlar, or travelling merchant." "I am glad to hear that," said Mr. Shirra, "for I am a travelling merchant myself." "Indeed," said the stranger, "I should scarcely have thought that from your appearance. May I ask what you deal in?" "I deal," said Mr. Shirra, "in fine linen, and am on my way to Doune, where I hope to dispose of my goods to-morrow." "To-morrow!" replied the stranger, "I am thinkin' that ye hae forgotten that the morn's the Sabbath." "No, no," said Mr. Shirra, "I have not forgotten that, it is the sacramental occasion. There will be preaching at the tent, and a great gathering from Kincardine, Kippen, and many from Stirling, with some of whom I expect to do business to-morrow." "Weel," said the pedlar, "I have been a long time in the line, but I am happy to say I never did business on the Lord's Day yet, and I never saw any guid follow those who did. Ye're an auld man, sir; an' I would advise you, as a friend, to gie up the practice of sellin' on the Sabbath." "If you will not sell," continued Mr. Shirra, "perhaps you will buy?" "Na, na," said the pedlar; "if it's sinfu' to sell, it's as sinfu' tae buy. I'll wash my hands clear o' the business entirely; I'll neither sell nor buy on the Lord's Day." "Then you'll maybe come to the tent?" said Mr. Shirra. "That I intend to do," said the pedlar.

Our two travellers had now come to the Bridge of

Teith, where they parted, each taking his own road—Mr. Shirra repairing to the manse, and the pedlar to his humble lodgings in the town. In arranging that night what share he was to have in the services of the coming day, Mr. Shirra signified to his brethren that, if agreeable to them, he would like to preach the first sermon in the tent next morning. Punctual to the time, Mr. Shirra was at the tent. Casting his eye slowly and searchingly over the vast meeting, he discovered in the midst of it his friend and fellow-traveller of the previous day. The psalm and opening prayer being ended, Mr. Shirra rose and gave out his text, which was in Revelation xix. and 8th—"And to her was granted that she should be arrayed in fine linen, clean and white; for the fine linen is the righteousness of saints." Whether the pedlar had by this time recognised his friend and fellow-traveller in the minister was uncertain. It was not long, however, till there was no ground left on this point for uncertainty. After some introductory remarks, Mr. Shirra said he had come there that day to open the market of free grace; that he was a merchant, a commission merchant, commissioned by a great and rich king—the King of Heaven; that the article he was there, in His name and by His appointment, to dispose of, was "fine linen," which was the righteousness of Christ. After explaining its nature, and illustrating its properties, and commending its worth and value at considerable length, and showing in his own expressive language that there was nothing to equal it, or to be "evened" to it, he proceeded to counsel his hearers "to buy it." He showed that they had all of them instant, urgent, absolute need of it. There was no coming to the Lord's Table, there was no getting into heaven without it. It was to be had without price; it was to be had for the taking. Such, he said, was the Gospel sense of "buying." He then concluded—"And will no man buy this fine linen? Must I go back and say, 'Lord, Lord, there were many at the tent, many in the market, but none would believe—none would buy?' And will ye go back as ye came—poor and wretched, miserable and blind and naked? I put it to you again, 'Will no man buy?'" He then paused. There was an old grey-haired man at the foot of the tent, who, with his hands clasped and tears in his eyes, was heard saying to himself, "I'll buy, I'll buy; I'll take Christ and His righteousness." Mr. Shirra, hearing him, said—"The Lord bless the bargain! There is one man at least who has gotten a great bargain to-day; and as for you, my fellow-traveller, my brother merchant, come, oh! come, ere the market close, and buy likewise. If you do, you will make the best bargain you ever made in your life."

What effect this touching appeal had on the pedlar is not known. Although Mr. Shirra was considered very quaint and eccentric in his ways, he was admitted to be a man of much learning, and a bold, effective, and fervent preacher. If anything like the extraordinary sayings which he uttered were expressed now-a-days, some of the highly respectable, proper kind of folks would stare with astonishment and think the preacher mad. Mr. Shirra was a tall, portly, handsome man; his voice was rich and sonorous; and, like our own Mr. Spurgeon, he was followed by crowds wherever he went. His name has long been a household word in Fifeshire.

ITINERANT TAILORS.

" Ah, me ! how lovely is the golden braid
   That binds the skirt of night's descending robe !
 Day hath put on his jacket, and around
   His burning bosom buttoned it with stars !
 It is a joy to straighten out one's limbs,
   And leap elastic from the level counter,
 Leaving the breaking thread, the din of shears,
   And all the needles that do wound the spirit !"

O. W. HOLMES.

THERE were many persons about sixty years ago who
acted in the capacity of itinerant tailors, who went from
house to house amongst their customers, "all the year
round," doing work in the way of making, altering, and
mending garments—making "auld claes look amaist as
weel 's the new." Those tailors were often put to their
wits' end, and their skill was sometimes severely tested in
the earnest endeavour to create new out of old raiment !
" Clout the auld, the new 's dear," was the universal maxim
of the times, and it was wonderful what feats those men
could sometimes accomplish in the way of their business,
and to please customers. Their lot was somewhat of a
cheerful one, and in going from house to house they saw
much of life, and had abundant opportunities of studying
human nature in all its wonderful phases and aspects.
Many of them were gifted with an inexhaustible fund of
anecdote and humour. They could lilt a cheery song at
their work and at the fireside, and they were usually welcomed at the different houses where they were employed.
Newspapers were then scarcely ever to be seen, except in
the houses of the wealthy, or in towns where there were
newspaper clubs ; and so those tailors, packmen, &c., did
duty for our modern newspapers, filling up a gap in the
way of satisfying that craving for news which we all have.
As a rule, they had a scrupulous regard for honour, and
would not divulge the more private affairs of their
customers ; but, notwithstanding this, many droll stories

have been published regarding the treatment some of those itinerant tailors received at the hands of their more sordid customers. Some of the people they worked for were very poor; others were worse, for they were mean and stingy in their disposition, and very near-be-gaun, as it was termed, in all their dealings. Others, again, were very furthy in their ways, and with them the poor man's bite and sup were never grudged and never missed. Some of those tailors were very intelligent and well-informed men, considering their opportunities, and were able to take the measure of their customers very correctly in more ways than one. Those who tried to take a mean advantage of them were sometimes paid back in their own coin. It is not the first time that a tailor has dropped—by accident, of course!—his heavy goose into the porridge pot of a mean-hearted customer, and knocked the bottom out of it!

One of the most acute and far-reaching dodges I ever heard of for keeping those tailors honest, who did work at their own homes, was that practised in Inverness. In the case of those who gave out their clothes to be made at the shops or houses of the tailors there, Captain Burt relates in his letters that the following scheme was adopted. They bought "everything that goes to the making of a suit of clothes, even to the stay-tape and thread, and when they were delivered out, they were altogether weighed before the tailor's face. When he brought home the suit it was again put into the scale, with the shreds of every sort, and it was expected that the whole would equal the original weight!"

Some of the itinerant tailors kept an apprentice, who assisted them, and went round to their customers' houses, learning all the mysteries and experiences of that useful and venerable profession. On the occasion of those youths being bound as apprentices, there was sometimes a little treat or supper given, at which it is said the young lad's master would make something like the following remarks: —"When we are thegither i' the country, you an' me, at my customers' hooses, we maun aye mak the best o 't. At breakfast time I've seen parritch that could hae run a mile on a fir deal; but never mind, mak your breakfast o' them. At denner time tak' aye plenty o' kail—they're sure to be there; gin they be guid they're worth the suppin'; an' tak my experience, if they shouldna be guid, depend on't there's no muckle comin' after them. And thirdly, an' lastly, in regard to supper time I hae little to say: there's no muckle to come an' gang on—just potatoes an' milk. Still an' on, ye canna dae better than just tak plenty o' milk to your tatties, and plenty o' tatties to your milk."[1] Some of those tailors were somewhat more fastidious than others as to their diet. One had a great abhorrence of the relish of onions in his broth, and from his perch on the kitchen dresser he could notice all the cooking operations going on. One day he observed the mistress about to put into the pot a handful of the vegetable he detested, so he told her, "If you put any of that into the pat, I will not put a spoon in the kail this day! *Noo, mind I'm telling ye!*"

> "O! wha's the loon can clout the claes,
>   Canty Davie, dainty Davie;
> Wha the lassies' spirits raise,
>   Like little tailor Davie?
>
> "O! blithe is ilka body's hoose,
>   Whaur Davie sits an' cracks fu' crouse;
> Nae post-bag's half sae cramm'd wi' news
>   As tonguey tailor Davie?
>
> "The weanies round him in a raw,
>   He raises sic a loud guffaw,
> Ye'll hear the din a mile awa,
>   O' them an' tailor Davie.
>
> "The auld man's roomy weddin' coat—
>   Wi' age an' moths scarce worth a groat—
> Maks breeks to Tam an' coat to Jock,
>   An' spats to tailor Davie."
>
>   *Ballantine.*

---

[1] "Laird of Logan."

THE MAYGATE LODGE—MASONIC AND OTHER PROCESSIONS.

The old Mason Lodge in the Maygate was the scene of many an interesting gathering long ago. In that hall were held of yore the mystic meetings of the brethren connected with St. John's Lodge (No. 24), one of the most venerable lodges in the kingdom. There, too, a school was kept by Mr. Rankine, where he taught English, arithmetic, writing, and music. There Rennie, the teacher of dancing, kept for years his classes. There, too, the drawing academy was presided over by Mr. Campbell, teacher of drawing, and afterwards by Mr. Joseph Paton; and young men were there taught drawing and design, with a view to the improvement of patterns and designs for damask cloth. In that room were held many pleasant concerts, soirees, dancing assemblies, and singing classes in the olden time, when Mossman kept his shoe shop underneath. Above all, the "Penny Crush," or Saturday evening's entertainment. Little did the promoters of the Dunfermline "Penny Crush" conceive that their humble efforts in behalf of a cheap, fascinating, and wholesome kind of amusement for their fellow-townsmen would result as it has done, and prove such a great boon throughout the land to many thousands of their fellow-countrymen. Dr. George Macdonald has forcibly and truthfully remarked, "If I can put one touch of rosy sunset into the life of any man or woman, I shall feel that I have worked with God."

Some of the older citizens of Dunfermline will yet remember the grand Masonic processions that took place on the evening of St. John, in December. The St. John's and the Union Masonic Lodges used to fraternise together as that evening fell, and they paid a friendly visit to each other. When the brethren emerged from their lodge, every one held in his hand a lighted flambeau. The torches were then consigned to the care of some of

the numerous young lads who were waiting at the door
to receive them. The Masons then formed themselves in
procession, two abreast, walking in the centre, while the
torch-bearers walked on either side of them. The remains
of the torches (which were manufactured in Edinburgh)
afterwards belonged to those lads who carried them, and
they often again did duty on the morning of Han'sel
Monday. The procession was a very imposing spectacle.
What with the grand array of blazing flambeaux, sending
up their bright glare into the dark December night (at a
time when the street lamps of Dunfermline, fed with
train oil, gave but a dim and sickly light), what with the
merry music of the bands, the streaming of flags and
banners, and the gilded insignia of the brotherhood, borne
along by the more prominent members of that ancient
guild, it was a sight to be remembered! The spectacle
was especially imposing as the procession marched along
the High Street. The streets were densely crowded,
thousands came from far and near to see it. Hundreds of
smiling faces and fair and graceful forms were seen
looking down upon it, bending over the open windows,
and waving their handkerchiefs in all the streets through
which the Masons passed.

> "Soft eyes looked love to eyes which spake again,
>   And all went merry as a marriage bell."

In addition to the various emblems, devices, and insignia
of office carried along, there came along with them the
reverend chaplain in his gown and bands, the Rev. George
Bell Brand, the respected minister of St. Andrew's Church,
bearing with solemn mein a large Bible, which lay open
on a velvet cushion. A pair of compasses and a square
lay upon that portion of the sacred page referring to the
building of Solomon's Temple, that building where
originated the mysteries and methods adopted by the
Mason craft in the centuries following. After peram-
bulating several streets in this way, the bands playing
various national and stirring tunes, amongst the latter the
well-known air of—

> " Hey ! the merry masons,
> And ho ! the merry masons,
> And hey ! the merry masons
> Go prancing along !"

They adjourned to their lodges, where, amidst much solemnity, and afterwards much joviality, they spent the night.

Before this great annual festival, the brethren would sometimes vie with each other as to who would have the handsomest silk sashes and aprons for St. John's night. Many of them purchased their sashes and aprons in Edinburgh, but others were content to have home manufactured ones, probably the production of fair and loving hands, and many of them were regarded as excellent specimens of taste and fine needlework.

In those old days they had also St. Crispin processions, got up by the cordwainers of the town and neighbourhood. The colliers, too, had what were called *parades* now and again. They were attended by large numbers of colliers of both sexes, accompanied by bands of music, flags, &c., and thousands of onlookers. The first St. Crispin procession was held, I believe, about 1823, and was a most gorgeous affair. There were about 8000 spectators. Several towns in Scotland used to have their cordwainers' processions long ago. I remember seeing the last one that took place in Dunfermline, and which was carried out in a most imposing style. It was somewhere about 1839 or 1840. The showy dresses, uniforms, and brilliant equipages, also the insignia of office, &c., which were to be solemnly borne along, were obtained from the Edinburgh St. Crispin Lodge. Those who witnessed the demonstration will not be likely to forget it. The principal officials who took part in it were gaily attired. Some of them acted as aides-de-camp. They were mounted on horseback (perhaps for the first time in their lives), and while they rode their richly caparisoned steeds, they bore in their hands the flaming swords of State and Justice. The foremost to head the procession were heralds, who led the van on horseback, then spearmen, then gentlemen ushers, the sword of State, the chaplain in his gown and bands, the archbishop, two macers, and then came the most important and distinguished personage of all, the king! He had on his head a jewelled crown, and carried in his hand the sceptre of office, while he wore a gorgeous dress of crimson velvet and ermine, and bore on his breast badges and showy stars of diamonds. He had white silk stockings on his ample kingly calves, and silver buckles on his shoes. His long rich train of crimson velvet, lined with white satin, was borne behind him by six small and nicely dressed pages. He was supported by stalwart dukes and body-guards, and by the knight-marshal Crispins. The king was a tall, erect, stately man, of over six feet in stature, and as he walked along in the midst of this pageantry he had quite a majestic appearance. They could not have fixed upon a more suitable man to represent majesty than he. In the evening there was held a court or levee (in the Guildhall, if I remember rightly), where the public had an opportunity of obtaining an audience of the king and his consort, and seeing them seated on their elevated and richly adorned thrones, surrounded by their knights, equerries, and lords in waiting, clad in all the habiliments of office.

This grand and harmless St. Crispin display, like many others of a more truly regal description, has passed away, and is now "like a tale that is told." It will yet be remembered by a number of persons in Dunfermline who were privileged to witness it, and no doubt the recollection of the affair will call forth a quiet smile. The *soubriquet* of "the King" clung ever afterwards to the one who represented majesty on that great occasion. If one were asked years after, "Wha made thae boots o' yours, Jamie?" the answer was, "the King," or "King Crispin." Or another would remark that he "saw 'the King' wi' his leather apron on, standin' at his ain door, crackin' wi' Deacon Tamson," &c. &c.

THE GIPSY AND THE BLACK POCKET-BOOK.

"There's wee Tammie Twenty, the auld tinkler body,
Comes here twice a year wi' his creels an' his cuddy,
Wi' Nanny, his wifie, sae gudgy an' duddy,
It's hard to say whilk is the queerest auld body."

Ballantine.

WHILE everybody in this neighbourhood has heard of the Pattiesmuir College, and of the funny doings of the collegians there in the olden time, few are aware of the fact that long ago this now humble village of Pattiesmuir was historically and intimately connected with gipsy life; that in bygone ages it was "one of the headquarters of the Scottish gipsy!" In Gifford's *Memorials of the late Rev. Dr. Johnston*, of Limekilns, it is recorded that "the gipsies had a *palace* here, in which their kings were installed and crowned for life, deputations coming from every part of Scotland to pay court!" Just think of that!

Egyptians originally, they appear to have been always a wandering race, and were scattered over the whole of Europe, and parts of Asia and Africa. The increase of the population in this country, and the progress of civilisation, were the means of keeping them down, and now appears to be gradually extirpating them. To many persons, this wandering, "camping-out" kind of life would be most fascinating, and is so at the present day to some who have taken to it, and who have tried the novel mode of travelling in a large van, and living in thorough gipsy fashion, sleeping at night under canvas, and cooking their own food.

Those who can remember the Dunfermline of fifty-five or sixty years ago will yet have a recollection of the bands of dark-eyed, swarthy gipsies and tinkers that used to squat in the neighbourhood of the town at that time. Some of them lived about Calais Muir and other places, in kennels and under tents, and had usually a horse and cart, sometimes a donkey or two, with panniers slung across their backs, to carry their children and their other effects in. At a tinkers' hamlet they had always a number of young children and some aged persons amongst them, and also big towsy dogs, that prowled about the farm-towns at night in quest of food. There was always to be seen the fire, and the boiling-pot suspended outside on a triangle. They were considered to be not very observant of the Eighth Commandment, and had *tarry fingers*, so that farmers had frequent occasion to complain of their depre-dations. Many of them were very industrious, and not at all like some of the sturdy beggars that would neither work nor want. Some of the men made tin-ware of various kinds, repaired old pans and kettles, old chairs, broken-winded bellows, and also dilapidated umbrellas, &c.; others made horn spoons, heather besoms and *rainges*, and so forth; and the women hawked the manufactured articles far and near, from door to door—getting a bit of food here and there, telling people's fortunes, curing diseases by means of herbs and the state of the moon and planets—trying, in short, all schemes to "raise the wind." In telling fortunes, the palm of the hand was examined minutely, and the palm of the gipsy's hand had to be crossed with silver. We all remember the lines of Burns :—

> " The gossip keekit in *his loof*,
>   Quo' she, wha lives will see the proof,
>   This waly boy will be nae coof ;
>   I think we'll ca' him Robin.
>
> " But, sure as three times three mak nine,
>   I see, by *ilka score and line*,
>   This chap will dearly like our kin',
>   So leeze me on thee, Robin."

It is rather strange, but nevertheless true, that Adam Smith, the celebrated author of the *Wealth of Nations*, who belonged to Kirkcaldy, was stolen by the gipsies when he was a child of three years old, and was kept by them for some time.

The following authentic incident connected with the gipsy tribe happened in Dunfermline at the close of last century. Doubtless some of our older readers may have heard the story in their young days. It was published more than half a century since, but is worthy of being rehearsed here :—

Thomas Adamson, a substantial Fife yeoman, having been very successful one market day at Dunfermline, was enabled to stuff his little black pocket-book with bank notes. Thomas was in great good humour, as may naturally be imagined, and after having a hearty crack and a dram with some of his farmer friends and acquaintances, he was preparing to retire from the market, when he was thus accosted by a tall, swarthy complexioned man, in the dress of a drover of the better sort.

"Hoo's a' wi' ye the day, Maister Adamson ? Od, man I'm glad tae see ye; I've been seeking for ye owre the hail market."

"Weel, friend," said Thomas, "what do ye want wi' me, noo that ye've fund me ?"

"Is your cattle a' sold ?" asked the stranger.

"Every hoof o' them—a' gane, stump an' rump. I hae made a gude market the day."

"I think sae," was the reply, "an' sae I maun look to be ser'ed some ither gait."

So saying, the tall, swarthy looking man in the dress of a drover walked quickly away.

"I dinna like the looks o' that chield," said Thomas to himself, as he slowly left the market. "I never saw him atween the een before, and he doesna' seem to be a drover either. Gude forgie me! I houp a 's richt!" he ejaculated, as his thoughts and his hand simultaneously reverted to the black pocket-book. But, alas! the nest was empty, the bird had flown, the black pocket-book had disappeared, and Thomas Adamson stood like one suddenly transmuted into stone. At length he gave utterance to these broken exclamations—"I'm lost—I'm ruined—clean done—pocket-book an a'! I maun flee the country. Hoo can I ever look my wife an' weans in the face withoot my black pocket-book? The deil catch the lang, ugly villain by the neck! Gif I had him here, but od, I'd make him steal honest folks' pocket-books. As gude's a hunder an' fifty pounds sterlin', forbye seventeen an' saxpence in silver ! He's welcome to that, howsomever, if he gi'es me back the pocket-book an' the notes. But, oh ! what am I tae dae noo ? What am I tae dae ? "

This was a question much easier asked than answered ! and Thomas Adamson was not the man, in his present circumstances, to answer it either speedily or satisfactorily. He could do nothing but moan and say to himself—"What am I tae dae ? My pocket-book gane, an' my wife no here ! Was there ever sic a misfortunate deevil as Tam Adamson is this day ! Od, I'll gang back to the market ; I'll send through the bellman ! Fule ! that I didna think o' that sooner ! I'll hae oot the constables, and the militia, and the fire-drum. A' the toon shall hear o 't." And with this settled determination Thomas Adamson returned to the market.

In the meantime, his wife, having some little purchases to make, and not having been ready to accompany her husband when he left home in the morning, was on her road to Dunfermline. She had arrived within half a mile of the town, when she heard a sweet plaintive voice, singing as it were to a child, and on approaching nearer she could distinguish the words—

> " Sleep, baby, sleep !
> Though thy fond mother's breast,
> Where thy young head reclines,
> Is a stranger to rest.

Almost at the same moment she observed a young woman, in a red cloak, sitting alone in a lonely part of the road, nursing a child. As Mrs. Adamson came nearer, she perceived that the young woman's eyes were red with weeping. In country places there is little ceremony —every person speaks to one another—but even had it been otherwise, the disconsolate state in which the young woman appeared to be, awakened all the sympathies of Mrs. Adamson's nature. She therefore stopped and addressed to her the homely and kindly inquiry of " What's the maitter wi' ye, lass ? "

" Oh ! my husband ! my husband ! " exclaimed the young woman, in a tone of bitter but repressed anguish. " He has gone into the market, and I trust and pray that he'll not have occasion to repent his bargain."

" Is that a' ? said Mrs. Adamson. " Why, lassie, my man has gane to the market tae, and let him alane for makin' siccar bargains. I'se warrant his wife 'll no hae tae greet her een oot for the bargains he maks."

" Oh, but," replied the young woman, " you do not know whom you speak to, or what you speak about. Would that I were like you, good woman, or that *he* was like *your* husband ! But, oh, how widely different are our situations and destinies ! "

She burst into tears, and the kind-hearted and sympathetic Mrs. Adamson blubbered too, to keep her company. Suddenly the young woman started up, wiped her eyes, and looked in the direction of Dunfermline. " Did you not hear it ? " she said, rising and grasping Mrs. Adamson by the gown. " There, there again ! shouts of uproar and exultation. Oh, my God ! they will murder him ! No, no, it is over—it is nothing. If you only knew what I have endured to-day, you would pity me ; you would, indeed. From morn till now I have sat on this cold stone, with no one to smile on me, no one to comfort me but my baby ; and oh ! the agony of my thoughts, the torture of my feelings ! I have sat and watched the little birds as they flew about, chirping merrily when my heart was bursting, breaking ; and I have wished that I had wings like one of them, that I might fly away and be for ever at rest. But where could I fly to but to him, who, however cold he is to others, still continues warm to me and to his baby ? And could his wife forsake him when all—even his ain tribe— have gone against him ? No ! Even in the hands of his enemies, with the chains around his limbs and the rope about his neck—even then would I cling to him, and in that bitter moment of horror and despair I would testify to him and to the world the depth and intensity of my affection, and the strength and constancy of its endurance."

She paused, and Mrs. Adamson, who began to think the

woman was deranged, took the baby into her arms and
began to fondle it as people do with children. The young
woman continued—

" I can endure this suspense, this torture, no longer.
Every noise I hear fills me with alarm. If he does not
come to me I shall go to him ! "

She paused again, and then somewhat suddenly addressed
Mrs. Adamson—

" My good woman, might I request you to do me a
favour ? "

" Oh, ay ! " was the answer.   " Onything in my power ;
onything in reason."

" Just to take charge of my baby," said the young
woman, " till my return. I am going down to the market
to seek my husband ; I'll be back very soon."

" Oh, willingly," said Mrs. Adamson, " if you promise no
to bide long. I've business to dae in the toun mysel' ;
besides, I've to seek my ain man, and it'll no be very easy
to find him. He'll likely be in some public-hoose, an'
some o' his cronies round aboot him."

The young woman hastily, but fondly, kissed her infant.
Mrs. Adamson inquired if it was like its father.

" Heaven forbid it ever should ! " said the mother, with
a shudder.

" Eh, but it's a bonnie bairn, a sweet wee lamb ! I'll
just sit down here on the same stane ye were sittin' on till
ye come back, sae ye canna miss me."

" Thank ye ! thank ye ! " said the young woman ; " and
here, tak my cloak aboot ye till I return ; you will feel
cold, perhaps, and I will not require it."

She threw the red cloak around Mrs. Adamson's
shoulders, and then departed.

The child finding itself in stranger hands, soon began to
be noisy and troublesome, and Mrs. Adamson therefore set
herself most assiduously to sing it asleep. Just as she
had succeeded, and was making a comfortable bed for it
on her knee, a tall, swarthy complexioned man walked
quickly past her, threw a black pocket-book into her lap,
and as quickly disappeared.

"Eh, what's this?" said Mrs. Adamson to herself, too much astonished to observe in what direction the stranger had gone. "Whaur can this hae come frae. It's oor Tam's pocket-book, I do declare! an' what is better, it's fu' o' notes! Either it or me's bewitched, I think. But od, there's something no right in the wind. I wish that limmer were back for her brat. I houp she doesna mean to leave the bairn wi' me a' thegither! Gude forgie me! I wonder hoo oor Tam wad look if I brought hame a wean to him that's no my ain! Ay, I thought there was something wrang aboot the wench, an' I think yet she's dementit. I believe she's ane o' the show folk—greetin' in yon gait, and makin' me greet tae. But I wonder what Tam'll say to this strange kind o' wark—it's clean past my comprehension. There's ae thing clear, however, that he's lost his pocket-book an' I have found it."

Whatever might have been Mrs. Adamson's suspicions of the young woman, they were dissipated by her return, and as soon as she saw her, Mrs. Adamson asked if she had seen her husband.

"Alas, no!" replied the young woman. "I sought for him everywhere, but I could hear nothing of him."

"Weel-a-weel," said Mrs. Adamson, "there's your bairn, an' there's your cloak, an' noo I've but ae advice to gie ye, an' that is, to mak yoursel' scarce as soon's you can, for we're a' honest folk here, an' harbour neither robbers nor gipsy folk."

Mrs. Adamson then hastened to the market, where she found her husband in a state bordering on distraction. He had made inquiry of everybody if they had seen aught of his pocket-book, but no one could give him any information on the subject. As soon as he perceived his wife, he poured into her sympathetic ear the full extent of his misfortune.

"I canna haud up my head after this!" he exclaimed. "I may as weel dee at ance at the back o' some auld dyke; I'm clean ruined—pocket-book an' a'!"

"It's no sae bad as that, Tam," replied his wife; "come awa' frae the market, an' I'll tell ye something that'll maybe astonish ye. Hoots, come awa', man," she continued, dragging him by the coat.

"Get awa' wi' ye, woman!" said Thomas; "is this a time for your jokes and your astonishing stories? What hae ye got to say? Can ye no say it at ance? Od, woman, ye'll drive me mad!"

"Ou ay, Tam, but it'll be wi' joy, lad. Come awa' and hear my secret."

"Confound your secret," said Tam, in a fury; "I tell ye I've lost my pocket-book!"

"An' I tell ye I've found it!" said his wife, producing it, "an' here it is."

"Lod sake! so it is—the identical pocket-book!" cried Thomas, overcome with joy. "Whaur did ye get it?— but ye'll tell me a' that again. Let's see, though, if it's a' safe. Ten—twenty—thretty—forty, and three twenties, is a hunder, and five tens is fifty,—ou ay! a's here safe; an' I think, wife, ye weel deserve a new gown for your luck. Come awa' doon to Black an' Arnot's, the haberdashers on the Brig, an' I'll treat ye till a real braw ane!"

So saying, he clasped his black pocket-pook with an air of triumph, and with no less satisfaction gave his wife a smack which was heard over the market. Ever afterwards the story of the black pocket-book formed one of Thomas' most amusing stories, when he had around him a circle of friends at his cosy fireside in a winter's night in the olden time.

PENNY WEDDINGS.

About the beginning of the present century, penny weddings were being gradually discontinued, but before that period they were very common all over Scotland. After the marriage ceremony had been gone through at the manse of some clergyman or other, the invited guests who were assembled to receive the newly married pair and their attendants made contributions in money, seldom exceeding two shillings or so each, to pay the general expenses. The balance that was left over, in some cases amounting to a considerable sum, went to help the young couple to furnish their humble dwelling. There were often great gatherings on these occasions. An empty house or a barn having been previously secured, the party went heart and soul into the festivities, which were kept up sometimes for a day or two together. At those weddings they had the services of one or two fiddlers or a piper, the barn was cleaned and decorated for the purpose, and at night a few tallow candles or oil lamps were stuck round the walls, and gave what we would now-a-days call a poor, glimmering light. What with singing and dancing they had a lively time of it. Now it would be that a number of couples were seen to occupy the floor, gliding nimbly through reels, country dances, &c., laughing and shouting with all their might, so that

> "They made the barn shake with laughter,
>   They beat its flooring like a drum,
>   Battered it with Tullochgorum,
>   Till the storm without was dumb."

At stated intervals some official, usually the "best man," went round the company with a bottle of whisky in one hand, and a dram glass, probably minus a shank, in the other, while his attendant accompanied him with a plate containing oatmeal cakes, cheese, biscuits, &c., to refresh the perspiring company, and literally to keep up the steam. It must be borne in mind that those "penny weddings" of the olden time were hailed by old and young as a pleasing relief to the otherwise dreamy and comparatively monotonous life they led. The public amusements, entertainments, and cheap literature of that period were very limited indeed.

Some clergymen were often very much annoyed in those days with noisy bands of persons connected with "penny weddings" coming to their houses at all hours and from many distant places, to get the marriage knot tied. In many cases the conduct of those gatherings in the manse was very boisterous and unbecoming. The late Dr. Johnston, of Limekilns, as appears from his *Memorials,* having been very much troubled with such bands coming to his house from distant towns, determined to put a stop to it. Not very long after this resolution had been come to, a smiling couple, from a neighbouring town four miles distant, presented themselves along with the usual bands of attendants. In somewhat a severe tone he informed them that he *would not* perform the ceremony, and told them to go to their own minister and get it done. He was a kindly, warm-hearted man, but at times he could speak his mind in quite a determined manner, and he did so on this occasion. The poor disconsolate bride began to cry, and both bride and bridegroom solemnly declared that, "If he would only do it this time, they would never trouble him again!" "What could I do?" said Dr. Johnston, "I felt so much for the lassie that I married them, to the great joy of both." About the most comical case of this kind I ever heard of, was related by a reverend and esteemed friend of the writer, who has for many years been located on the south side of the border. A brother clergyman of his, who was long ago minister of the first charge of an Abbey Parish Church in the west of Scotland, was preparing to go to bed about eleven o'clock one night, when he heard a loud knocking at the door. He opened his bedroom window, looked down, and shouted, "What do you want?" One of the party replied, "Oh, Mr. Wilson, we're awfu' sorry to come sae late, but we want to be married!" "Go away," said he;

"this is not a proper time to come to any minister's house to be married; I am just going to bed. Go away, and come to-morrow morning, and I will marry you." "Oh, Maister Wilson! we were detained, an' couldna come ony sooner," replied the anxious bridegroom. "Well, that's your own fault," said the minister, "and I cannot be troubled at this hour." "Weel, Maister Wilson," exclaimed the alarmed bride, if ye canna come doon, ye micht gie's a word owre the window!" The idea of marrying a couple in the dark, with his night-capped head stretched over the window, and his sleeping "surplice" on, tickled Mr. Wilson greatly. He still persisted in telling the party to go away, and come back at a more seasonable hour, but they continued to return to the charge; and the bridegroom, in a whining tone, cried out, "Oh, Maister Wilson! if you'll only do 't, we'll never gang an' hear Mr. B—— again!" The ingenuity and earnestness of this rejoinder, at a time when it happened that there was much party feeling, of an ecclesiastical kind, running high in this particular parish church as to the colleagues, completely amused and overcame Mr. Wilson, who in due time descended to his study, admitted the party, and soon dismissed the happy couple united in the bonds of matrimony.

ABOUT PRECENTORS.

MANY in this neighbourhood will yet retain a vivid remembrance of Mr. James Rankine, who was the master of song and parish clerk of Dunfermline for about thirty years. He was indeed a master of song, and perhaps in no other place in Scotland could there have been found a man so thoroughly accomplished as a leader of psalmody. His genial disposition, his knowledge of music, his gentlemanly appearance, his fine voice, and his exquisite taste, made him a great favourite wherever he went. He was often a guest at Broomhall, and was much admired by the Earl of Elgin and his family. He died in 1849. His fine talents as a vocalist ultimately led him too much into company, and this proved very injurious to him and to his family. There is a story told in connection with him and the well-known Willie M'Nicol, the "Blue Betherel," as he was called. The latter had one day given Mr. Rankine some serious offence, which so exasperated him that he told Willie to "go to the d——l?" The "Betherel" thought proper to inform the Rev. Allan M'Lean, the minister of the Abbey Church, of the circumstance that Mr. Rankine had ordered him to go to the infernal regions. "But," added the "Betherel," "I fear, sir, that the devil will no be for lettin' me in there!" Mr. M'Lean merely replied, "Be thankful for that, William; oh! be thankful for that!"

A curious incident is related by the Rev. Charles Rogers, LL.D., of a Dunfermline precentor in the olden time, a good while before Rankine's time. There was a vacancy for a precentor in the Abbey Church. A young man in the town became a candidate. He was to be allowed to go into the *latteran,* and to make his appearance on the following Sabbath. On rising to the first psalm, he became quite nervous, and, suddenly overcome by seeing so many of the familiar faces of his townsmen intently surveying him, it was more than he could endure, so he darted from the desk, and in a few seconds disappeared. He did not go home, and whither he went nobody could learn. There were some very unhappy surmises, but no certain tidings could be learned of the runaway precentor. After the lapse of half a century, when almost all those who witnessed the scene had been gathered to their fathers, an elderly gentleman visited Dunfermline, and owned himself the hero of the story. He had gone abroad, and had become prosperous beyond all his expectations. He purchased the small estate of Navity, in the neighbourhood, and there erected an elegant mansion.

In the days of James Rankine, the leader of psalmody in the Abbey Church, there were few church organs to be heard in places of worship in Scotland. In Presbyterian churches, at least, they were quite unknown. With such an accomplished leader, and with the well-trained choir he had, those aids were not at all required. Artificial helps of this kind, which were called by our forefathers "kists o' whistles," are now almost universally used throughout the land. But there was a time when even musical pitchforks were not in general use in country places. Every artificial aid was then accounted an abomination and a devil's device. It has been recorded that the precentor of Carnock, near Dunfermline, thought he would be the better of a musical pitchfork to help him to pitch the tunes with. He sent word to the Dunfermline carrier to bring him one from Edinburgh. The worthy carrier, who had never heard of any other kind of pitchfork but such as were used in barns and hay-fields, purchased one ten feet in length! It was late on Saturday night before it arrived, and a message was sent to the carrier asking him to bring it to the church next day, and give it to the precentor. Next morning, the leader of psalmody was standing conversing amongst some of the villagers near the church-door, when the man appeared with the article in question, to the utter astonishment of the precentor. Like the god Neptune, with his trident in his hand, he came forward to the astonished group and said to the vocalist, "Aweel, John, here's the pitchfork ye wantit; but, let me tell ye, I never thought muckle o' your singin' before, an' I'm sair mista'en if ye'll sing ony better noo!"

THE WONDERFUL STARLING.

MANY years ago, two or three working-men belonging to Dunfermline, were taking a quiet saunter to the westward of the town, and at last they adjourned to a public-house in Crossford. It was on a Handsel Tuesday of the olden times, and they agreed to have a friendly dram together. Over their half-mutchkin many subjects were discussed, and amongst others the aptitude of some particular birds to learn to talk like human beings. One gave an instance of the gifts that a certain parrot in his neighbourhood was possessed of; another of a jackdaw that he himself had heard perform wonderful feats in this way, and something like the following colloquy took place. Except one, the names of those in the party are fictitious, but the incident itself is perfectly true.

Willie Berridge of Whirlbut.—"Od, that's an awfu' clever bird, that parrot up i' the fit-paith, belongin' to Geordie Tamson's son, wha has just lately come hame frae the Wast Indies. It can speak like onything, and whussle 'O'er the water to Charlie.' It seems that Geordie has gotten a grand cage for 't, at Locke and Hutton's hardware shop on the Brig."

Sandy Simpson.—"Ah! but I ken o' a far better ane than that. It belangs to Doctor Bowes, o' the Distellery Brae, and it beats a' for speaking. Not only can it speak plain, but it can also curse and swear like a trooper. The sailors learnt it tae dae that, an' also tae chow tobacco, on the road comin' hame in the ship! By the Yetts o' Muckhart, ye canna match that!"

Hughie Steenson, who had been a silent listener to the discussion, now said—"That may a' be very true, my friends, an', for onything I ken to the contrar, Dr. Bowes' parrot may be perfectly able not only to chow tobacco, but also to swallow his ain 'celebrated hive poothers,' an that's nae joke! But I can tell ye o' a far mair wonderful bird than ony you've mentioned. It's that o' a stirlin', an

it is keepit by a man in Guttersyde, an' that same stirlin'
is not only able to speak far better than ony o' the birds
you've spoken aboot, but while it can fluently say, 'Here's
to ye,' it can likewise swallow a hale gless o' whuskey!"

This fairly put the copestone on the debate, but it
turned out that the starling in question was one named
Stirling, a journeyman weaver to a certain deacon in the
south side of the town.

––––––––

LONGEVITY IN DUNFERMLINE.

"He liveth long who liveth well."

THIS city has long been regarded as a very healthy place. It has always maintained a low death-rate, except at the times when cholera made its ravages in 1832, and again in 1849. For example, it was only 16¼ per thousand in 1884. This healthy condition may arise from its fine dry, elevated situation, and from the circumstance of the houses not being so densely built together, as in many other towns and cities. The abundant supply of fine wholesome water, lately introduced, will no doubt tend to make it even more healthy than it has hitherto been. Except at the time when that deadly and mysterious visitant the cholera committed such ravages in 1832, the low death-rate has always compared favourably with that of most places in Scotland. As regards sanitary excellence, it must, however, give way to one or two villages in Haddingtonshire, which fairly eclipse Dunfermline, and of which a story may be told. A tourist passing through one of those villages, and observing the gate of the churchyard open, went in, and was greatly surprised to see recorded on the tombstones the large number of persons of very great age who had been buried there. He expressed his astonishment to the sexton, or gravedigger, and said that in all his travels he had never before seen in any cemetery such an array of long ages. The sexton, who was doubtless, like our own celebrated Blue Betherel, a bit of a wag, quietly said to the stranger, "Man, that's naething extraordinar. Awa' doon there, at the village o' Spat, they never dee; they're obleeged tae fell them!"

A PATRIARCHAL DINNER-PARTY.

"Those fading faculties are sent to say,
'Heaven is more near to-day than yesterday !'"

MANY persons in the city will yet remember that, about thirty years ago, a rather unusual festival took place here, called a "Patriarchal Dinner." It was held in the Royal Hotel, and was attended by most of the old men of the burgh. Why it was that none of the aged persons of the other sex were invited to join in the festival is not very clear, unless it was wished that none but "patriarchs" should be present. The rule adopted for admission to this remarkable gathering was that a man should be at least seventy years of age. This was the only qualification ; all men in the town of this age were eligible, whatever their social position in life might be. There were forty persons present, the youngest of whom was threescore and ten, and the eldest eighty-eight years. Mr. John Stenhouse occupied the chair, and Mr. Alexander Lowson was croupier. Messrs. Alexander Blair, David Barrowman, Alexander Inglis, and John Fotheringham were the stewards. It was a very pleasant and happy dinner party. What a fine array of "frosty pows" there were ! Old men full of geniality and fun.

"Where now the frosty pow was seen,
There ance was gowden hair !"

What laughing and joking took place amongst them, as they felt themselves grow young once more. Some of them had in their early days been officers and privates in the army, militia, or fencibles, and a great amount of mirth was evoked as they descanted on their military, volunteer, and other experiences by flood and field. The annual drillings on Kirkcaldy Sands in their young days were also commented on. That happy company of old men "fought their battles o'er again ;" the tales they told and the songs they sung were received with enthusiasm. The chairman, who had himself been a volunteer captain, ably presided over the meeting. He began the proceedings by very appropriately repeating the pathetic and well-known lines :—

> "I'm wearin' awa', Jean,
> Like snaw, when it's thaw, Jean,
> I'm wearin awa'
> To the land o' the leal !"

Some of those veterans afterwards reached upwards of ninety years of age, but, alas! death every year thinned the ranks of those who that evening attended the happy festival; and all of them have long since joined the great *majority*, and have met "*beyond the unseen shore.*" Few towns having a population similar to Dunfermline at that time, could muster so many at such a gathering as that of the 23d September 1859—men over the threescore and ten, all so hale and hearty, and so juvenile in spirits, no doubt the outcome, in most cases, of a well-spent life. The sum total of their ages was 3013 years. Their names and ages were as follows :—

John Stenhouse, seventy-four; James Dickie, seventy; Thomas Walls, seventy; Alex. Lowson, seventy-two; Andrew Ferguson, seventy; Robert Erskine, seventy-two; Alex. Blair, seventy-two; John Key, seventy-four; James Baxter, seventy-five; John Fotheringham, seventy-two; Andrew Wilson, seventy-two; John Anderson, seventy-two; David Barrowman, seventy-five; Robert Fergus, seventy-six; Charles Main, eighty-eight; David Stenhouse, seventy-six; James Mill, eighty-four; James Donaldson, eighty-three; John M'Kinlay, seventy-two; William Robertson, seventy-two; Thomas Coulter, seventy-six; David Marshall, seventy-two; David Mowbrie, seventy-three; James Hutton, seventy-four; James Page, seventy-four; Andrew Aitken, seventy-four; Duncan Robertson, seventy-two; Robert Walls, seventy-four; David Moir, seventy-five; Robert Philp, seventy-four; David Moir, seventy-four; Thomas Hoggan, eighty-three; David Black, seventy-three; John Brown, eighty-six; Peter Burt, seventy-four; Peter Garroway, eighty-two; John Hunter, seventy-four; Wm. Philp, seventy-three; A. Inglis, Golfdrum, seventy; A. Inglis, Pittencrieff, seventy-three.

THE HISTORY OF THE TRADESMEN'S LIBRARY.

The Dunfermline Tradesmen's Library, which long obtained a prominent position in the town, originated, according to Dr. E. Henderson's account, in 1808. At that period books were very scarce and dear. There were no shilling volumes and cheap editions such as there are now. There were no cheap weekly and monthly journals, no penny newspapers, nor the endless literary attractions that now exist on all sides amongst us. Like many important undertakings, it had its origin in a very humble way. Richard Gossman, William Carnegie, and Charles Anderson, weavers in Moodie Street, agreed to make a common good of the books each possessed; but finding their stock too small, they applied to some others, and a committee was afterwards constituted, composed of the following members, viz.: — Richard Gossman, William Carnegie, Charles Anderson, Ralph Walker, Deacon Letham, Thomas Main, John Syme, Andrew Aiken, and William Meldrum. Shortly after its institution the little library had to be removed to another place. On this occasion a *coal bucket* was washed out to hold most of the books, and in it they were taken away by William Anderson, while William Meldrum carried the rest in an apron. There were only about fifty volumes or so, large and small, in the library at the time of its removal to William Meldrum's house in the Nethertown. There it remained for a good while, the volumes gradually increasing in number, till it was removed to a room in Donald M'Kenzie's house, to which there was a separate entry by an outside stair. It was until then chiefly patronised by the men in Moodie Street and the Nethertown, and was called the Nethertown Library; but after the appointment of William Wilson as librarian it soon became famous, and numbers joined it from all parts of the town. The members now were numerous, and the nights on which it was open being few, great crowds were often seen standing on the outside stair, waiting their turn.

The Library was thereafter taken to a room in Abbey Park Place, behind Dr. Gibb's house ; then to one down Mrs. Vallance's Close ; then to a place behind Mr. Clark's book-shop ; and afterwards for years it was kept in a large room down an entry in the Kirkgate, at the back of the Townhouse. On Saturday nights, I remember, this place was often greatly crowded. The librarian, Mr. William Wilson, who was a most intelligent, well-read man, was a man of few words. He was most careful of his charge, very pains-taking, and a faithful, much-respected public servant for many years.

In the year 1819 there were three hundred volumes in the library, belonging to about thirty members. Down to that period there was no room rent to pay, no librarian or treasurer's fees, and everything was conducted with rigid economy. A short time after the formation of the Mechanics' Institute in 1825, the Tradesmen's Library and that of the Institute were united. As years passed on, and through judicious management, its extent and value greatly increased, and it enjoyed a long period of con-tinued prosperity. Doubtless, too, it was a source of untold pleasure and benefit to thousands of the readers who belonged to it, and it shed many a ray of light and hope into the homesteads of the working men and women of Dunfermline. Little did the small self-elected com-mittee at the outset of the library's career, ever imagine that it was going in course of time to be so great a power for good to many thousands, as it afterwards became. Truly those few humble men did something in their day and generation to advance the moral and intellectual eleva-tion of their fellow-men around them.

Notwithstanding the limited number and narrow range of the literary works they had in those days, they made a good use of such books as came in their way. They thoroughly mastered them, and were able to discuss the merits of many difficult points, and to speak intelligently on the literary, theological, and political questions of the day. It is recorded that the schoolmaster of our great national bard—Robert Burns—afterwards went to London, where he lived for a while and learned what good society was, and he declared "that in no meeting of men did he ever enjoy better discourse than at the hearth of the peasant father of Burns." The same thing may be said of many of the hearths of the working-men of old Dunfermline.

It is very greatly to be regretted that the bulk of the books now being issued from the great seething press, and being eagerly read, are works of fiction. Like a diet of sponge-cake, it tickles the palate at the time, but often leaves unsatisfactory results afterwards.

Amongst many of the readers in the Tradesmen's Library—and they were chiefly working men—there were some great book-worms, as they are called. Amongst the number, there was a very intelligent, but a rather curious, man who belonged to the Spittal. He was a most diligent reader, so much so that he performed the great feat of reading the greater portion of the twenty-eight volumes of the *Encyclopædia Britannica!* When he used to come to the library to exchange one of those big volumes, he always said to the librarian—"Let me hae volume neist, Maister Wilson!" This library is now merged into that of the Carnegie Free Library, a noble institution, the generous gift of one of Dunfermline's sons, who, strange to say, was born and bred in the same Moodie Street where, from small beginnings, the Tradesmen's Library first originated, seventy-seven years ago. Over the door-way of this beautiful new building are the impressive words, "Let there be light." Long may it continue to shed the true light of knowledge and of wisdom on all sides, and prove a priceless boon to the citizens of Dunfermline.

THE "ROARING GAME."

THE following incident was related to the writer of these *Reminiscences* many years ago, by one of the clergymen who figured in the story. This gentleman had occasion to spend several hours in the old grey city of Dunfermline, having been detained there unexpectedly. It happened to be on a Saturday in the dead of winter, and the frost was very severe. He did not think of paying a visit to any clerical brother on that day, as he considered that it might be inconvenient to call on a Saturday. To while away the time before the starting of his train, he went to the Curling Pond, and there he was heartily welcomed by the players, and invited to join them. He was an entire stranger to them all, but on the ice no introduction was required. He was dressed in travelling costume, and as he had all the appearance of a fine, tall, portly farmer, no one present imagined that he was a clergyman.

Along with this gentleman, and on the same rink with him, there was the Rev. Mr. Young, the genial and much-respected minister of Queen Anne Street Church. Mr. Young was present on that day, for he made it a rule to have his ministerial work finished before the end of the week. By-and-by about a dozen stones had been thrown up, and a very careful and critical shot was required, which it fell to the lot of Mr. Young to play. There had been much excitement, every one had been "soopin' his ain stane," and cheering like schoolboys when any good shots were played. All eyes were now fixed on Mr. Young—his skip, Mr. J. D. giving his directions to the following effect:—"Noo, Maister Young, draw up here, and pit a bonnie stane doon there, to mak a fine guard to thae ither stanes o' ours." This order should have been complied with at once, as the skip is considered like the master of a ship, whose orders are to be obeyed; but Mr. Young suggested what he thought, a better move, and began, in fact, to argue the question with his skip, which was contrary to

all rules and regulations. The latter gentleman then lost
all patience, and abruptly told Mr. Young to do as he was
bid. He then turned to the tall stranger at his side, and
whispered to him in a confidential kind of way, "Thae
deevils o' minister bodies, they think they've a' the wit in
the world!"

Many of our leading Scottish clergymen have always
shown a great love for this peculiarly healthful and ex-
hilarating winter's game. On the ice all classes, rich and
poor, stand on equal terms, and many working men leave
their wealthy competitors far behind as regards skilful
playing, and are intensely keen players. On one occasion
a minister was on his way to the curling pond, and some
persons observed him passing. One said, "I do not think
it's becomin' tae see the minister gaun awa' to the ice sae
often; it wad set him far better if he were makin' sermons
or veesitin' the sick." Another one, who was a keen
player, remarked, "Weel, lads, I think the minister is
quite richt tae gang an' get sic fine, healthy exerceese at
the curlin' pond: it's gude for baith sowl an' body. If I
were a minister, an' there was ony man i' my parish that
wadna tak at least ae day's curling every year, I can tell
you what it is, I wad keep him back at the Sacrament!"

As an example of how unceremoniously persons of rank
are sometimes treated on the ice if they happen to play
badly, a circumstance may here be related which occurred
in the west. A man named Hugh Conn, who was an
excellent player, was skip on the side of the Earl of ——,
and was directing his Lordship how to play the last stone,
on which the success of the game depended. "Dae ye see
this stane, my Lord?" "I can see part of it, Conn." "Weel,
ye maun tak it awa'." O! my Lord, dinna miss!" "Well,
Conn, I'll do my best." Up came the stone, on which all
eyes were intently fixed, but it was about an inch off the
mark. Poor Conn threw up his arms frantically, and exclaimed, "Oh, my Lord, I declare you would miss a hay-
stack!"

Another case is that of a man who happened once to be
playing on the same rink with a Scottish Sheriff. This

man was noted far and near as a splendid curler; but he had some years before been convicted of poaching, and had been sentenced to sixty days' imprisonment by this same Sheriff. As the game went on, it came to the turn of the Sheriff to throw up his stone, and the old poacher thus addressed him:—"Dae ye see that stane there?" "Yes, I see it." "Weel, Shirra, hit him hard; gie him sixty days!"

DUNFERMLINE RIOTS.

DUNFERMLINE, which has been noted for its usually quiet and law-abiding disposition, would now and again become the scene of lawlessness, and display a riotous aspect. About a hundred years ago, there were in the town occasional outbursts in the shape of meal mobs, when the dreaded "dearths" occurred, and when meal, which was the main staple of life, rose to famine prices; but the riots that took place fifty or sixty years ago were usually caused by misunderstandings regarding the question of wages, and trade disputes. Doubtless, the leaders of such tumults considered that there was good cause for the action which they took; but at the same time the great bulk of the inhabitants were always on the side of law and order, and were much shocked at the tumultuous proceedings of the unruly depredators. In dull times, when severe depressions of trade took place, or when yarn rose to a high price, and when profits diminished, there was a strong inducement on the part of the manufacturers to reduce the scale or "table" of wages, not only of the hand-loom weavers, but also of the large number of women who were employed as bobbiners. On such occasions there was a natural outcry raised against those reductions, and much angry feeling was shown towards the employers, which on several occasions culminated in open riot. There was one that I remember, at which the dreaded *Nethertown weicht* or drum was brought out, to warn all those concerned that *something was up.* A noisy mob soon collected, and as an onlooker at a distance, I saw the proceedings. The crowd gradually increased, and soon had a very threatening aspect; but I observed a well-known and much-respected Magistrate, followed by one or two other persons, go boldly into the very heart of the furious mob, and implore the ringleaders to quietly disperse. After a deal of trouble and opposition, he was at last successful, the *weicht* quietly disappeared to its dark hiding-place in an obscure garret, and the gathering thereafter melted away. It was a most daring thing to do; but, thanks to his extraordinary tact and force of persuasion, he accomplished his object—the mob slunk away, and peace was secured.

I remember seeing one or two other mobs on their way to wreak their vengeance on those who had incurred displeasure in connection with trades' disputes and strikes. They swept along at night, and the peculiarly ominous and angry sough of voices was heard in the distance. The ringleaders nimbly climbed up the public street lamps and put them out, leaving some streets in darkness. On they came pell-mell, the crowds consisting not only of men and lads, but also of women. Some of the foremost of them had blackened faces, and carried sticks in their hands. On arriving at the doomed houses the work of destruction went furiously on, and the women sometimes vied with the men in their efforts to destroy dwellings and looms. Both in the north and also in the south side of the town did those riots occur long ago, and the utter folly and wickedness of such proceedings afterwards became apparent, when the damage done to property had to be paid for at the expense of the public.

The question may be asked—Where were the police? The answer is, that those affairs were usually so secretly planned, and so expeditiously carried out, that the police were not aware of them till after all was nearly over. At that time there would be only one policeman (or town-keeper, as he was called) and an assistant, and what could they have been able to do in the face of a body of violent rioters, the most of them strong, active young men? The town-keeper had no costly staff of assistants, as such a thing was rarely required, and he was deemed quite a sufficient "terror to evil-doers" in those times. I think it is Novalis who has said, "Two things strike me dumb — the starry heavens, and the sense of right and wrong implanted into the heart of man." If there were no such sense implanted within us, where would we be in the midst of the large number of the evil-disposed, if there could be anything approaching to unanimity amongst them? After the rioters had nearly finished their work, a cry was raised, "There's the constables," and in a short space of time the mob took to their heels, and dispersed as hurriedly as if a troop of armed dragoons had made their appearance.

"Conscience does make cowards of us all!"

In the case of one mob, which was on its way to commit mischief, they passed a man named Barrowman, who asked some of the rioters what was the meaning of such a noisy crowd, and he was informed that it was a *collier's waddin'*! He quietly remarked that it was the biggest and queerest "waddin'" he had ever seen. In several cases much hardship was inflicted upon those who were entirely innocent of anything which could cause offence or be injurious to any human being.

In some instances, when the magistrates were apprehensive of riots, large numbers of special constables were sworn in and presented with official batons, and they were ordered to hold themselves in readiness to act when required. On two or three occasions I remember seeing troops of dragoons brought to the town to restore order, and give the well-disposed security against lawlessness. The Riot Act was also read in several instances when it was considered necessary, and when matters had assumed a dangerous aspect, and there was a fear of destruction of property, or of personal violence being offered.

One of the most extraordinary cases of rioting that ever occurred in Dunfermline took place in connection with what may be termed

THE IRISH EVICTION.

Coming down to 1850, we remember the great riot that then occurred in Dunfermline. It originated with what is called a "Navvy's farewell," which is usually given on the completion of some railway undertaking, when the navvies are about to leave a certain locality. Those orgies commence with a drinking spree, and often end in bloodshed or loss of life. This disturbance commenced on a Saturday, about eleven o'clock at night, when the public-houses were emptied, and soon large crowds collected around the navvies to see the fun. For a while the north side of the town quite resembled a Donnybrook Fair. A sham fight first commenced amongst themselves, then after that, the belligerents began to strike every person they could lay their hands on, and much personal damage was done.

On Sunday morning no disposition was shown by any party to renew hostilities,—everything looked peaceful and calm, and the tempest seemed to have passed away; but on Monday morning outrages were committed on two Irishmen who were employed hoeing a field of potatoes on Urquhart Farm. The poor men had agreed to hoe at a rate greatly below what women in the locality had been previously getting. A crowd rushed upon one of them, and threw him over a dyke. A rush was made upon the other; he tried to escape by getting into a drain, but was pulled out by the legs and handled roughly. In the course of the day a plan was concocted to compel all Irishmen to leave the town forthwith. Had the parties chiefly connected with the getting up of the plot been content to wreak their vengeance only against the navvies who had first caused the disturbance, there would have been some sort of excuse for their subsequent proceedings. The scheme of expulsion embraced the whole of the Irishmen in the town, some of whom had been residents there for many years, and had conducted themselves in an exemplary manner. They had at once to quit their workshops, their dwellings, their wives and children. Amongst those expelled was one named Frederick Lennis, who had resided in the town for twelve years, and was generally well liked. The mob succeeded in compelling about forty persons to leave their work, and they drove them on like a flock of sheep. When some of the band entered the shop where Fred was quietly working, unconscious of what was about to befall him, they immediately ordered him to quit work and come off his loom.

"What for?" said Fred. "For being an Irishman; all Irishmen are to quit their work and leave the town at once," said they. "Och, thin ye need not be in so great a hurry; allow me to work my cut out and get my pay, and thin, sure, I'll go paceably." As he appeared to be in no hurry to go, they proceeded to assist him in an uncermonious way. He then asked to be allowed to go home and see his wife, and get a clean shirt and decent clothes, but no time was given for that, and Fred had to go along with the flock of countrymen waiting at the door. As the band of Irishmen were marched down by Bothwell Haugh, he was hailed by an old acquaintence, who asked, "What are you seeking here, Frederick?" "Faith, I don't know!" "And what were you doing?" "In troth, I was doing nothing else but working at my loom." "And where are they taking you to?" "By jabbers! an' that I cannot tell. Had they been driving me the other way, I might have thought they were sending me home to the ould country, but this is the wrong road for that." Some of Fred's friends interceded for him, and he was allowed to go back. The mob having learned that an Irishman was at work in Mr. Whitelaw's foundry, a portion of them entered the foundry, and the man was ordered to leave. Mr. Whitelaw strongly remonstrated with the crowd as to the unreasonableness and cruelty of their conduct; but it was in vain, and so the man, to save any further disturbance, voluntarily left his work and joined his countrymen. The mob next proceeded to the factory of Mr. Erskine Beveridge, as several Irishmen were employed there; but a powerful body of the workers protected their Irish shopmates, and prevented the rioters from getting within the premises. One poor Irishman was found by two persons secreted in a field at the north side of the town. He appeared to be lying on his face dead. They went up to him and shook him, when, finding that they were his friends, he cautiously looked up, and asked them if the wild mob was away yet! The Irishmen, as they were unhoused, were put in position in the centre of the crowd, and driven along. The number captured was now about forty-five;

most of them were navvies, but some were weavers, shoe-makers, masons' labourers, &c. &c. When uncertain as to the nationality of the captured persons, they were told to pronounce the word *peas;* if they pronounced it *pays*, they were considered Irish! The intention of the rioters was to get their victims down to Queensferry, and to see them across to the other side of the Forth.

Provost Kinnis and Bailies Johnston and Ireland were now engaged swearing in special constables. The more well-to-do class came forward readily and in large numbers to enrol themselves, so that a sufficient force was soon collected, but not in time to overtake the rioters within the bounds of the burgh. The Sheriff-Substitute and Mr. M'Donald, Procurator-Fiscal, hired a gig, and proceeded without delay to North Queensferry. They arrived before the mob, having gone by another road. By the time the rioters had reached Queensferry, they had dwindled down from two or three thousand persons to about four hundred. The Irishmen were ordered by the Sheriff-Substitute to march into the quarry, which they immediately did. The mob was then cautioned, at its peril, not to pro-ceed further; and with this caution they ultimately deemed it advisable to comply, and in a short time they resolved to return to Dunfermline. Fearing that further outrages might occur, a messenger was despatched to Sheriff Mon-teith to request a detachment of the military, which was at once granted, and soon forty-five of the 13th Light Dragoons arrived. As they came by the way of Queensferry, the Sheriff asked the unfortunate Irish people if they wished to return to Dunfermline; and as they all, with the exception of six or seven, expressed a desire to go back, the Sheriff, with the military, accompanied them back to the town. They were all kindly sheltered in the Town-house for the night, and at an early hour next morning they proceeded to their various places of abode.

A lawless disturbance similar to the above occurred at the same time at Townhill Colliery, where about sixty Irishmen were employed. Incited by what had taken place at Dunfermline, the colliers resolved to expel all the

Irish people from the works. There had been a strike amongst the miners in Lanarkshire, and those at the Townhill were afraid that the Irishmen would work for any wage, however small, and they would have no chance of success if they struck like the colliers of Lanarkshire. In the course of the Monday they expelled about thirty of the more obnoxious of the Irish people, and, with the assistance of about three hundred Dunfermline weavers, they would have expelled still more; but in this they were frustrated by the boldness and determination of the manager, Mr. Mungall, who armed himself with a pair of pistols, and went straight up to the leader of the lawless mob and threatened to blow his brains out. At this juncture Bailie Johnston and Mr. Kilgour, the Town-Clerk, appeared, and after some little time the disturbance was ultimately quelled.

Some of the ringleaders in this serious disturbance afterwards got terms of imprisonment, and it is an extraordinary and a ludicrous circumstance that one of the young men convicted for his participation in the riot was the son of Irish parents! He was born in Dunfermline, however, but the inherent love of excitement, fun, and mischief was so strong within him that he could not resist joining in the fray.

CURIOSITIES IN NOMENCLATURE.

" What's in a name ?   That which we call a rose
By any other name would smell as sweet."

IT is highly questionable if Shakespeare is accurate in his answer to the question, "What's in a name?" Be that as it may, commend us to Fifeshire if we want to become acquainted with the extraordinary nomenclature of certain localities there. We have in Dunfermline our Whirlbut, Guttersyde, Hallybluid Acres, &c. &c.; but they are more than matched by the names of certain other localities in Fifeshire, as, for example, Coup-my-Horn, Purl Ha', Devil's Neuk, Bald Breekie, all near to Kennoway; Hunger-em-oot, near Tam's Ford, Largo; Cauld-Hame, near Kettle; Skirl-Bare, Cloven-Stanes, Foggy-Butts, Drake-Lands, Pluck-the-Pint, in the parish of Kettle; Hell's Kitchen, near Halbeath; Puddle-Dock, near Crossford; Isle o' Canty, near Gowkhall; Dog-Tour, Cutty-Gates, Gomorrah, Flaggis-Pat, Flynd-Loup, Penty-Ha', Stand-Still, Tilly-Lum, in the parish of Auchterderran; Punnel-Neuk, Coup-Owre, Blink-Bonnie, Hare-Stanes, Satan's Castle, Goat Milk, in the parish of Kinglassie; Shank-o'-Navity, near Blairadam; Conscience-Brig, Foul-Thoombs, near Cairneyhill: Dirt-Hill, near the Crossgates; and Galloway Tam's, near Pattiesmuir.

After all, there must surely have been a great amount of quiet humour amongst the Fife people of the olden times. Sydney Smith once ventured to say that it almost required a surgical operation to get a Scotsman to understand a joke. He evidently " calculated without the host," and was " swearin' at lairge " against Scotsmen when he made this foolish remark. Had he mixed a little amongst the folk o' Fife, he would have found out his mistake.

NEIGHBOURING VILLAGES ON THE DECLINE, AND HAMLETS NOW EXTINCT.

In the space of half a century, or little more, what changes sometimes occur in certain localities! How entirely different, for example, is the aspect of Dunfermline now, compared to what it was fifty or sixty years ago. The houses of that period, the badly paved and undrained streets, the dark pall that hung over the town in the long winter nights, relieved only by a few stray oil lamps, which served to make the darkness visible, were in striking contrast to what may now-a-days be seen everywhere. The furniture, too, of the dwellings, and even the dress of the working people of those old days, were very different from what may be seen now. While many of the little homely one-storey houses in the town have given place to smarter and more comfortable dwellings in all directions, and while, in short, Dunfermline has been progressing greatly in her material circumstances, several places in the neighbourhood have been gradually going to decay. Villages and hamlets, which fifty years ago or so were in a very thriving condition—such as Cairneyhill, Limekilns, &c.— appear now to be completely changed. Limekilns, which at one period owned about forty vessels, and gave employment to a hundred and sixty ship carpenters, was a bustling, thriving village; and Cairneyhill also, which could boast of having forty electors fifty years ago, now appears to be settling down into a dull, torpid state, with its many roofless houses, was at one time full of healthy village life and vigour. On every side there might have been heard the song of the hand-loom weaver, as he busily plied his shuttle; or he and his family might be seen working in his little croft, sowing the seed or reaping the crops.

At that period many females in this as well as the neighbouring villages of Torryburn, &c., made a living by tambouring, and afterwards by hand-sewing, which was carried on extensively in the locality. The tambouring-frame or the spinning-wheel used to go cheerily on in these villages long ago; but now, like many other places, they have had to succumb to the great "*economic conditions*," as they are scientifically called, that are regulating trade and commerce.

If we take the burgh of Culross, which has long been in a state of commercial decay, we find, according to Mr. Beveridge's account, that it was a very flourishing place when neighbouring burghs were in their infancy. Then as to little hamlets that were in this neighbourhood —such as Garvock, Drymill, &c.—we look for them in vain. Of those hamlets, where were reared peaceful and happy families, there is scarcely a vestige to be seen. They are now extinct—blotted out of the map as completely as if they had never been. The writer remembers the latter little hamlet well, with its four or five dwellings all tenanted, and where once issued the blue curling smoke from the chimney-tops on a summer's evening. Many of the younger portion of our readers will not know where it stood. Drymill was situated a few hundred yards to the westward of the Grange Road, and north-west of the large gasometer lately erected by the Gas Company. The small row of houses forming the hamlet had a clump of trees which grew at the back; beyond that, and not far from the burn, was a quoiting ground, where matches were often played in the summer evenings, and where numbers of persons from Dunfermline who felt interested in the game used to assemble, and watch with eager interest the exciting contests that sometimes took place. The Drymill men were considered good quoit players, and they also distinguished themselves at leaping and other athletic sports. Many an exciting match was played here in the days of yore.

The names of some of those who lived there were the Huttons, the Hoeys, and the Pitcaithlies. The Hutton family were tall, powerful men, athletes in their way, and they excelled in quoiting, putting the stone, and leaping, &c. Pitcaithly, who was a tall muscular man, kept a splendid horse called "King David." He himself died of cholera during the great epidemic which raged in Dunfermline in 1832. Many happy days were doubtless spent in the homesteads of Drymill, and doubtless some sad ones, too—

> " For muckle o' joy and sorrow
> Comes youth and age between ! "

The ploughshare silently turns over the sod where once stood the hearths and homes of the families who lived here. The hamlet of Drymill has completely vanished, and the fate which has overtaken it has fallen upon many thousands of humble dwellings and hamlets in the Scottish Highlands, and all over Scotland, during the past fifty years.

THE MINISTER'S PIG.

THE following incident actually occurred in this neighbourhood, and may be familiar to some of our readers. It is very cleverly told in rhyme by one who was much respected, and who was a credit to his native place, Dunfermline—the late Mr. Henry Syme. The story is worthy of being re-told in these *Reminiscences*, as other localities have been named as being the scene where the laughable occurrence took place. This incident happened at a period when the stipends of clergymen were very small compared to what they are now, and when in many cases it was found necessary to make a respectable appearance on very slender means. In several instances the wives of the ministers did much towards increasing the material comforts and the income of the hospitable manse, by keeping cows, pigs, and poultry, and supplying their neighbours with fruit and vegetables from their gardens or orchards, and with milk and butter from their dairies. It happened, too, in the old-fashioned days, when there was a greater amount of genuine fun abounding, and a *penchant* for playing practical jokes upon one another that does not abound to the same extent now-a-days. It illustrates the spirit of waggery and harmless mischief that then prevailed, which if attempted now might lead to serious consequences.

A young minister in Dunfermline, who had been presented with a small pig, found that the cost of its feeding was getting expensive for him as it grew bigger, and he resolved to send it out to Cairneyhill to a friend who had ample accommodation for it, and where board and lodging would be got free of expense for a while. The minister's man was directed to put it into a sack, and to carry it to Cairneyhill; and, as he was a sort of simpleton, he was enjoined to tell no one he met where he was going, nor what was his errand. So away he trudged with his precious burden on his back. Arriving at Crossford, he

met three acquaintances standing at a door, who hailed
him, and asked what he carried on his back. He informed
them that he dared not tell his errand, but this he would
say—it was neither a cat nor a dog he had in the sack. His
cronies said they would not inquire further, and did not
want to know; but they kindly asked him into the public-
house to share a dram with them, as he would be tired
with his journey and his burden. He tried to excuse himself by saying he could not well go in, for the minister
would never entrust him "with a pig again!" However,
the lads were so decent-looking and so kind, that he was
persuaded to leave his sack at the door just for a single
minute, and to go in for the "mouthful" which they
kindly offered. In a twinkling, one of the three lads
snatched the pig out of the sack, and put in its place a
young dog. Free from all guile or suspicion, the honest
beadle, after taking his dram, proceeded cheerily onwards with his burden, which he soon delivered up to
the minister's friend, along with many compliments from
his master. Great, however, was his astonishment to find,
on opening the sack, that instead of the pig with its long
white snout and cloven feet, a small black dog jumped
out, and shook itself briskly. The poor dumfounded beadle,
the picture of alarm, called loudly for help. He said the
devil had been busy since he left the manse, and had
transformed the creature from a pig to a pup dog! The
minister's friend was also bewildered at the man's tale,
and told him to carry back the cur to his master again.
"It's not a dowg, sir; it's a pig, sir, as sure's death; but
Satan has changed him from white to black!" He then
very ruefully put the dog back into the bag, carefully
tying it, and set out on his return journey. He soon drew
up to the alehouse door, and there he espied the same
three decent, quiet-looking lads very demurely standing
where he had seen them before. He at once told them
where he had been, and what a dreadful transforma-
tion had befallen the pig. They thoroughly entered into
his feelings, seemed as much astonished as himself, and
sympathised deeply with him in the strange disaster that

had happened; begged him, as he had yet a long journey with his burden, to go in and take a rest for a minute or two. This he was tempted to do, and instantly the dog was taken out and the pig restored to its old quarters in the sack. The unsuspecting beadle trudged along towards the manse, while many strange and gruesome thoughts passed through his muddled brain. He told the minister of the day's disaster, and that his Cairneyhill friend had at once ordered him to take back the dog immediately to his master. The young minister was much perplexed and greatly annoyed at what had happened, so in disgust he directed the man to untie the sack, and put the pig back into the sty again, "It's no a pig, sir; it's a black pup dog, as sure's death; I'll let you see for yourself!" On opening the sack the beadle screamed aloud with terror, and the minister was utterly confounded by the man's most extraordinary story!

THE REV. MR. HADDEN AND THE
SWEARING SKIPPER.

THE habit of profane swearing was unfortunately prevalent to a considerable extent amongst all classes of society fifty or sixty years ago. It was indulged in very much, not only by the poor, but amongst the affluent and well-educated, and the habit did not then detract in any serious degree from their social status in society. There is an authentic story, which we have heard related long ago, regarding the worthy Mr. Hadden of Limekilns (who was the predecessor of the late Rev. Dr. Johnston) and a skipper, who was a member of his church. At the period when the occurrence took place, Limekilns village was very different from what it is now; the forty vessels belonging to it were usually "laid up" during the winter months, and both masters and men had a pleasant time of it at home with their wives and families. This quiet, easy-going style of seafaring life would never do now-a-days, when the universal maxim seems to be, "The devil take the hindmost." But it was a fine "breathing time" for the seamen of those days, and they after all got to the end of life's journey with far more genuine comfort than the seafaring men of the present time can possibly do, who work without intermission from January till December. In those old times it was usually "wind and weather permitting," but in these go-ahead days of ours, such a cautious reservation is never heard of, and would be laughed at. During the time when the vessels were laid up and the sailors were at home, the village had a cheery aspect, and it was at this period that Mr. Hadden was taking a walk one day down Limekilns pier. He was a most worthy man and a faithful minister, having little guile about him, his weak point being a liability to be imposed upon sometimes, as the following incident will show.

As the minister approached one of the vessels lying in

the harbour, he heard loud and profane swearing proceeding therefrom. Although this vice was far more common at that period than now, still, to the sensitive mind of Mr. Hadden, it was painful in a high degree. On approaching nearer to the vessel he found that it proceeded from the captain, who was either a member or an office-bearer in his own church. The skipper now observed his minister standing on the pier, and he immediately came ashore, when the minister exclaimed—"Oh! David, I have been greatly shocked to hear you indulge, as you have just now been doing, in the sin of profane swearing; you, who are a member of my church, and who ought to be a burning and a shinning light unto the flock, and to the world around you." To this David meekly replied to the effect that he could never get the men to do their work unless he swore at them, and that he was in this respect just like the most of his neighbours, and it was the usual custom. The minister seemed to be incredulous as to this, and emphatically said so. The skipper then said he would soon convince him that his statement was true, so he quietly descended the ladder and went aboard of his ship. By this time it is surmised that some of the men had an inkling of the state of matters, for shortly after their master had gone on board, he ordered them in a loud voice to remove some ropes. To this order they paid no attention, he then spoke in a more peremptory tone, but with no better result. At last he stamped his foot on the deck and swore a good round oath, and instantly every man flew to his work, and did with alacrity what was ordered. Shortly afterwards the skipper came ashore somewhat triumphantly, and honest Mr. Hadden was obliged to confess that there was some truth in what the captain had said. He, however, took the opportunity of telling him what a dreadful thing it was that men should be so left to themselves, that they would not do their lawful work unless under a loud volley of oaths and curses.

BURIED WHILE IN A TRANCE.

ONE of the strangest and most startling incidents that the writer of these *Reminiscences* ever remembers to have heard related in his young days, was connected with the supposed death, and afterwards the burial, of the mother of the celebrated Rev. Ralph Erskine, who was minister in the Dunfermline Abbey, and afterwards of Queen Anne Street Church. Some of the older residenters of the city must also have heard it told.

It seems that Ralph Erskine's mother, while the family were living in Berwickshire, had a serious illness, which terminated, to all appearance, in death. There was great grief manifested by her loving and bereaved husband, and also by the other relations, as she was much beloved by them and by all who knew her. She was buried in due course, and on the evening of the funeral day the grave-digger, or some other person who was aware that when consigned to the grave she had on her finger a rather valuable ring, determined to obtain possession of it. After opening the coffin, and whilst he was engaged in the act of forcing the ring off, and actually cutting the finger and causing it to bleed, she returned to consciousness, having been in a trance. Her first words were, " Alas! alas!" The astonished grave-digger at once fled in terror, and she was afterwards able to proceed home. Whilst the bereaved husband and some relations were sitting sorrowfully around the dreary fireside that night, a knock was heard at the outer door. He at once started to his feet and exclaimed—" If my wife had been alive, I would have said that was her knock!" The servant was too much frightened to go and see who the visitor might be, so he ran to the door himself, and fell senseless at her feet when he saw her in her grave clothes, the sudden revulsion from great grief to great joy being too much for him. She lived for some years after this most extraordinary event, and gave birth to two children, one of whom was Ralph. I have told the story exactly as I heard it nearly sixty years ago, and as many others in Scotland have also heard it related long ago. There is nothing unnatural about the incident, for cases of as strange a kind have no doubt occurred, and can be well authenticated.

A RARE SPECIMEN OF THRIFT AND FORETHOUGHT.

IN olden times it was a common thing to hear people converse freely upon the subject of death, and even to wish for that event, *if they thought that their souls were well prepared for it.* Their minds dwelling thus familiarly on this subject, it lost much of its ghostly terrors. These remarks are made by way of introducing to the reader's attention an incident which happened long ago in a village not very far distant from Dunfermline.

A young woman, who was noted for her extraordinary thrift and keen forethought, one day addressed her old father, who was the village joiner, or *wricht*, thus :—" Father, you're gettin' gey auld an' frail noo, an' as ye hae plenty o' timmer i' the shop, what's to hinder ye frae makin' you're ain coffin ? It wad divert ye, as ye are no very thrang i' the noo, an' it wadna bring death ony sooner, an' the thing might be handy at ony time, ye ken."

SWEETHEARTING UNDER DIFFICULTIES.

An incident of a serio-comic character occurred in Pattiesmuir, near Dunfermline, which deserves to be recorded. This little place, like many other country villages in Scotland, could boast of having several comely damsels within its borders. Their fame was known far and wide to country lads who had an eye for the beautiful. It happened that a young man, who resided some miles distant, had taken a fancy to one of those blooming, buxom lasses. His suit was progressing smoothly and favourably so far; but the courtship was carried on under some disadvantages to the young folks, as they themselves thought, for the father and mother of the young lassie were very strict in all their ways. One evening the young man was somewhat later than usual in getting away from his farm work, and when he arrived at the humble dwelling of his lady-love, who expected him that night, he found, to his disappointment, that the inmates had all retired to rest. In those quiet-going, candle-saving times, when daylight was so precious, the maxim in all well-ordered families used to be—

"Early to bed and early to rise."

In this cottage the evening's family worship (which was then common in the most of families) had been past, and silence reigned in the dwelling. While the young man dolefully surveyed the back and then the front of the cottage which contained the dearest to him on earth, the spirit and sentiments of the cavalier in the old song came strongly over him—

"Her father he has locked the door,
Her mother keeps the key;
But neither door nor bolt shall part
My own true love from me!"

He had travelled some miles that cold, dark night to get an interview with his sweetheart, and great was his dis-

P

appointment. What was to be done? Was he to wend his weary steps homewards without seeing his beloved, and was he to come back some other evening? Would she be quietly sitting alone by the kitchen fire thinking of him? These were questions which occupied his thoughts. After some consideration, a bright idea flashed upon him, which he resolved to carry out, for it is well known that with those in his frame of mind "love laughs at lock-smiths!" It occurred to him that, rather than go home without seeing her, and rather than disturb the family by knocking at the door, he would mount the roof of the house, which would not be in the least difficult. He could then go quietly down the inside of the chimney to the kitchen. Any little inconvenience arising from soot could easily be got rid of, for a good shake would relieve him of that. Up to the roof he accordingly went, and at once cautiously commenced his descent. The top of the chimney was deceivingly capacious, but he found as he descended that it got alarmingly narrow. Coming to a bend, he got completely jammed, and in spite of his utmost exertions found he could neither get up nor down. Here was an unexpected dilemma—a thoughtless, disreputable-looking piece of business for him, a decent country lad. He was completely "cabined, cribbed, and confined" on all sides. After being covered over with sweat and soot, he became desperate, and was at last compelled to shout for assistance. This brought some of the drowsy villagers out to their doors, but there was some trouble at first in finding the quarter from whence the strange shouts proceeded. They looked east and they looked west, and the sounds seemed "near, and yet so far." They fell on the ears of the villagers like the strange notes of the cuckoo, which can be distinctly heard while the bird itself is usually invisible, or at least rarely ever seen. The extraordinary situation and circumstances soon dawned upon them, and became in course of time apparent. There was nothing for it but to take down a portion of the chimney and the gable of the house to relieve suffering humanity. A handy labourer was got, and after a while the prisoner was set free. His sooty, woe-begone appearance did not enhance his claims in the eyes of his lady-love and the family, nor impress the bystanders with a favourable estimate of his wisdom and good sense.

"FECHTIN' WHISKY."

"NECESSITY," it has often been observed, "is the mother of invention," and the truth of the statement was once exemplified in some measure in the case of a publican who lived in the neighbourhood of Dunfermline. This man was noted for his quaint humour and his old whisky, and used quietly to boast that he kept in his house all the different kinds of whiskies. He had the *braggin' whusky*, the *singin' whusky*, and also the *fechtin' whusky*! There was a deal of genuine humour here, as well as sound philosophy; for if we are observant, we may see how very differently affected some persons are from others, while under the influence of strong drink. "*In vino veritas*" is a well-known and universally established maxim.

One Saturday evening, this publican had a number of labourers and also sailors in his house drinking. A great quarrel arose amongst them. There were loud swearing, tumult, and fighting going on—so much so, that mine host thought there was going to be bloodshed, and that his house might be pulled down down about his ears. He well knew, from long experience, that there was no use for him to attempt to reason with such a band of half-drunken, excited men, so he thought he would in his extremity try strategy. He therefore, without a moment's warning, flung the door wide open and went boldly into their midst. Being lame, he brandished his crutch over his head, and shouted at the top of his voice—"Stop, men! stop. For goodness sake stop! Sit doon; it's a' my faut, it's me that's dune a' this mischief. I've gien ye the wrang kind o' whusky! I've gien

ye by mistak the *fechtin' whusky*; but if you'll a' sit doon
quietly, I'll bring ye in a mutchkin o' the very best *singin'
whusky!*" The effect was magical; peace was ultimately
restored, the company afterwards quietly dispersed, and
the wild scene of confusion "passed away like a tavern
brawl." The actors in that noisy scene are all silent now,
for the green sod them. The mutchkin-stoup and "tappit
hen" which did duty on the occasion have also doubtless vanished. It happened one day that there was
standing at this publican's door a puncheon of whisky,
which had just arrived from the distillery, and a friend
passing at the time, said to him, "I wonder hoo mony
oaths an' curses are in that cask, John?"

DUNCAN SHULEBRED'S STRANGE VISION.

THE following extraordinary but authentic incident may
yet be in the recollection of some of the older citizens of
the town. I have heard it repeated in my young days
over and over again, and it is very well told in the *Tales
of the Borders*. With the authority of the publishers of
that work, it is here recorded, but in a condensed form,
and freed from much that may be considered extraneous.
It has the merit of being at least a perfectly true narrative.

Duncan Shulebred was a hand-loom weaver in Dunfermline, and he also did a little in the manufacturing
way. He was considered by all who had dealings with
him to be over-reaching, hard, mean, and even dishonest in
his ways. He was very fond of a dram, and took every
opportunity of getting drunk at some other person's
expense. He would meet with a crony or two of an
evening in some public-house, drink with them, and before
the lawin' came to be settled, would quietly slip out of
the room on some pretence or other, and say he would be
back again, thus leaving his friends to pay the publican's

bill. This mean trick was long ago familiarly called "singing the cobbler."

Like many others in Dunfermline at that period, he was at his loom during the one-half of the year, and the other half he was engaged hawking his cloth through the country. He often sold a good portion of his cloth in Edinburgh and the neighbourhood. One day he sold some linen to one there named Andrew Gavin, a small pettifogging lawyer. He had received his money, and as usual afterwards got plenty of drink at his customer's expense. The two went to a public-house, called the "John Barleycorn," in the Grassmarket, and soon were very jolly together.

Gavin.—" There's a great difference between the Edinburgh folk an' you folk o' Dumfarlin."

Duncan.—" Oo ay, very great; but I winna say on what side the advantage lies; we're at least a' honest on oor side o' the watter."

Gavin.—" You're mair than honest in Dumfarlin, you're prudent. Your maxim I understand is, '*Flee laigh, an' ye'll no fa' far,*' an' the consequence is, that ilka weaver is almost as sure to become a laird as he is to dee. When did ye ever hear o' an Edinburgh lawyer like me buyin' a sma' estate ? The maist o' our property consists of a braw front door, an' a weel polished brass plate on the front o 't."

The two sat thus conversing, laughing, and drinking for hours, but the time came for Duncan, muddled as he was, to adopt his usual tactics. He accordingly left the room on some pretext or other, the lawyer was left in the lurch, and ultimately was asked to pay the heavy bill for the night's drink. Duncan reached the street and staggered on, the open air taking effect upon him. Thus wandering on for a long time, not knowing where he was going, he at last reached the glass-works at Leith. He made for the door or open gate of one of the large buildings there, and then staggered in, and threw himself down in a dark corner near a furnace where all was still and quiet, and for some hours was in a deep sleep. In the early morning the workmen came to begin the labours of the day. The large furnace was soon lighted, and blown into a fierce glaring red heat. Large flames quickly shot forth with fiery glare, and at every blow of the roaring bellows vivid light flashed at intervals through the large dark space all around. The workmen were now busy, running backwards and forwards continuously between the fiery furnace and the reservoirs, with redhot glaring masses of molten glass at the ends of the tubes, crossing and recrossing, so that they looked from the dark, like demons flitting about, engaged in some mysterious and diabolic operations.

During all this time Duncan Shulebred had been as much unnoticed by the workmen as they had been by him. He, however, began to show some signs of returning consciousness, and to roll backwards and forwards, as if in a dreadful nightmare. And so he was, for some frightful dreams had filled his heart with terror. A keen recollection came into his mind of all his misdeeds, his mean dishonesty and wickedness, and of those he had defrauded by his short ellwand, his damaged linen, and "singing the cobbler." Conscience whispered deserved and terrible punishment, accompanied by the horrors of fire and brimstone. Thus he tossed about, while half sleeping, with painful, racking, maddened brain. The terrible noise soon awoke him to the consciousness that he was in the abode of the damned. He heard the roaring of the bellows, then he saw the fiery red brick walls rising as it were into the skies; his eyes beheld with horror the terrific furnace vomiting forth its blazing flames; while the half-naked bearers of the burning globes hurried hither and thither, to and fro, past him and around him, plunging their fiery weapons into hidden receptacles. The horrible spectacle rivetted his eager gaze, and filled him with unspeakable terror. Now and again he thought that he even felt the choking fumes of brimstone coming over his heart. "Mercy on my puir soul!" he exclaimed, but not so loud as to let the devils hear him—"Am I here at last?" When I was in the body how often did I think and dream of the bottomless pit. Can it be that I am in it noo? I fear it's owre true! What hae I, a puir wicked dishonest cratur, to expect frae thae awfu' fiends for a' the sins dune i' the body? But whan did I dee? I dinna recollect the circumstance o' my death! It micht be apoplexy though. Ay, ay! I was aye feared for that. But oh! michty me, death's a sma' affair compared to this! What an awfu' fiery furnace for a puir sinner! See the black deevils hoo they rin and dance constantly aboot, backwards an' forwards, to an' fro, wi' their burnin' brands, fork, forkin' them into thae dark pits, whar nae doot lie puir craturs as bad as mysel. But hoo do they no come an' tak me? Is it because my turn hasna come yet? Ah! the furnace is for me; mercy on me! I see Satan himsel at the bellows, blaw, blawin' wi' a' his micht, an' it's no for ilka common sinner he would work like that! It's for me, wha cheated an' robbed the folk wi' my short ellwand, wha drank, leed, deceived, an' committed sins as red as crimson. It's for me, wha deed in the very act o' cheatin' Andrew Gavin, by selling him short measure an' damaged claith, an' then leavin' him, puir fallow, to pay the lawin' at the Barleycorn Public-house."

This soliloquy was accompanied by deep groans, and the words caught the ears of a workman named David Leishman, who, looking over, saw lying behind a reservoir the unhappy Duncan. This man instantly understood the situation, and saw that the man, in a drunken, muddled state, had wandered into the glass-works, and that the awful terrors of remorse had now come. He communicated the intelligence to some of his fellow-workers, and also to the son of the proprietor of the works; so they determined to have some amusement at the weaver's expense. The proprietor's son, who was rather tall, and also a particularly clever young fellow, was deputed to act the part of Prince Beelzebub, and the others were to be his ministers and subordinate devils, each holding in his hand a glass tube, with a glowing ball of molten glass at the end of it.

The Prince held up his hand and cried with a voice of authority—" Where is the weaver that cheated the public at the rate of 36 inches per day, and died in the very act of cheating our special friend Andrew Gavin, the writer (for every writer is our special friend, and must be protected by us), by selling damaged linen to him, and also leaving him to pay the tavern bill? Where is the scarlet villain, that we may roast him by the infernal flames of our ever-burning fiery furnace?"

A loud and prolonged yell was the only reply by the attendant devils, and it pierced the very heart of the trembling wretch. The Prince now approached him as he lay trembling on his back, and the legion, with their flaming brands, also came near, dancing, hooting, and yelling with all their might.

"What is thy name, sinner?" asked the Prince.

"Mercy me! I'm in for 't noo!" whispered poor Duncan to himself. "Please your glorious Honour and Majesty," he said, in a voice quivering with terror, "I am Duncan Shulebred, wha in the upper world was a puir weaver in the toun o' Dumfarlin. I did your Honour some sma' service, and houp ye winna be sae hard upon me as ye threaten. Oh, keep they awfu' deevils frae me, and I'll confess to ye a' my crimes! Oh, be mercifu' to a puir sinner!"

"What service didst thou ever do to me?" said Satan.

"I did a' that was in my power to get the craturs i' the upper world to drink wi' me, till they were sae blind drunk that ye micht hae run awa wi' them as easy as ye did wi' Dr. Faustus or the Exciseman. Oh, think o' that, sir, and save me frae that awfu' furnace!"

"Confess, sinner, that thou not only gave false measure, but also wert dishonest with thy tavern bills!"

"Ou ay, true, true! its owre true I did cheat Andrew Gavin by sellin' him a wab o' rotten linen, and also leavin' him, puir man, to pay the reckonin' at the John Barleycorn public-house, a name your Royal Majesty kens weel."

"I think I should," replied Satan, "seeing that it is my own grain, wherewith I work greater wonders than ever came out of the mustard seed. This place of ours is fed with Barleycorns. The very man who sang the praises of the grain, and spoke of it and of 'barley bree' so lovingly, took our bait himself, but a redeeming angel touched him on the stomach, and made him at last throw it all out, and heaven at last got him for a prize."

"Miserable as I am, I'm real glad to hear that," said Duncan. "I wouldna hae liket to hae seen our darlin' poet in sic an awfu' place as this is."

"Impudent varlet!" said the devil. "In with him into the hottest furnace! Yet stay! How much money didst thou cheat our friend Gavin out of?"

"I needna try to conceal it," muttered Duncan to himself, "for he kens everything." So at last he said that he would willingly give Satan all the money he had on him if he would not consign him to the terrible furnace. "I ken," said Duncan, "that it was the love o' gold that brocht me here. O cursed dross! what am I to suffer for you?"

"Dost thou malign our staple and best commodity? Away with him to the fiery furnace; scorch him at once!"

Duncan screamed for mercy, while the minor devils laid hold of him and proceeded to carry him to the furnace, which was blown to a fierce red heat; while now and again some of them would come with their flaming globes and dance round him frantically. Having held him in this position for some time, Satan cried out—

"Ahithophel, get the red-hot pincers! he hath not confessed all. Lay him down close to the furnace, and bring a pair of hot pincers for each leg and arm."

The victim was laid before the furnace, screaming at the top of his voice. The pincers were brought forth and put into the fire, while the roaring bellows blew out a dreadful blast. The confusion caused by the hideous figures dancing around him and the roaring furnace grew worse and worse, but the loud screaming of Duncan and the high tone of Satan's word of command were heard above it all. But all at once Duncan's cries ceased; fear seemed now to have lost all its power over him, and he appeared as if he were going to faint, so the Prince gave the legion the signal to stop their revelries. They then lifted him up from the furnace, and some whisky which had been bought with Duncan's own money was poured into his mouth, which appeared to revive him, and he sat up.

As he thus sat, pale, haggard, and trembling in every limb, and looking about him with a terrified aspect, the chief actor filled up a glass of the spirits and offered it to him. He seemed irresolute as to what he should do, and his most extraordinary appearance forced the Prince to smile, which at once relieved Duncan, and helped him to regain some small degree of courage and hope.

"I didna think there was ony o' this liquor here. I expected naething but melted brimstone. But is 't real whisky? It's surely impossible!"

"It is already known on earth that whisky was first brewed in Pandemonium," said the Prince. "The nectar belongs to heaven, the wine to earth, and the whisky to our infernal regions. We distil it here. The only poet who has let out the secret of whisky being distilled here was a person named M'Neil, who sang—

> "Of a' the ills puir Caledonia
> E'er yet pree'd, or e'er will taste,
> Brew'd in hell's dark Pandemonia,
> Whisky's ill has scaithed her maist."

Another poet hath said—

> "Puir Scotland's scaith is whisky rife,
> The very king o' curses."

But for all that, we give whisky here sometimes to our victims as a medicine, whereby we revive them, in order that they may afterwards be more able to stand their terrible torments. Now, sinner, *remember this, that the moment thou drinkest, these burning pincers will be applied to thee!*"

"Then I beg leave to decline the liquor," said Duncan, "I see nae use for fire baith outside and in; besides, I hae renounced the practice o' drinkin' at anither person's expense—a thing which I often did i' the upper world."

"Thou hast paid for this whisky with thine own money which thou gavest me," said the Prince.

"That's mair than I ever did on earth," said Duncan, with a leer he could not restrain, as he threw the whisky away from him. It now began to dawn upon Duncan that he was surely labouring under some strange delusion or other, and soon a loud and continuous peal of hearty laughter from all the surrounding demons convinced him that he had been made a scapegoat.

"Ye hae dune mair for me, gentlemen, than a' the sermons I ever heard preached in Scotland. I hae confessed a' my crimes to ye, an' I will try an' mak amends for the future. Frae this moment henceforth, please Heaven, I shall try to be an upright an' a sober man. I will try to benefit them that I hae cheated. My very first act will be to stap awa' up to Edinburgh, an' pay Andrew Gavin the price he gae me for the damaged linen, and likewise settle the bill at the Barleycorn."

The regenerated Duncan left that place a wiser man, and formed the determination to do what was right henceforth and for evermore.

He proceeded to Gavin's house, knocked at the door, and asked if he was in. Mrs. Gavin appeared, and said "he hadna been in a' nicht. The last time I saw him he was wi' you. What hae ye dune wi' him? What kind o' linen was that ye sauld him?"

"It was a piece o' damaged linen I sauld him," said Duncan, sternly. Mrs. Gavin looked in amazement, and thought the man mad. "Ay, ay," said Duncan, "your puir husband's dootless locked up i' the Barleycorn public-house, whar I left him yesterday. He couldna' pay the lawin' that I should hae paid, an' I ran awa' an' left him in the lurch. I hae cheated thousands besides, an' if I got my due I wad hae been hanged langsyne, or banished to Botany Bay."

"Are ye mad? or do you glory in your shame and wickedness?" said Mrs. Gavin.

"Nane o' the twa," said Duncan. "I am as wise as ye are, and in place o' gloryin' in my wickedness, I am noo as repentant as a deein' martyr."

"Repentance is naething withoot warks," said she.

"Warks!" ejaculated Duncan, "bring me the damaged linen."

The astonished woman brought him the linen.

"There's the siller," said Duncan, "I got frae your husband for that wab o' claith. It is a vile piece o' deception ;" and he added, "A rotten-hearted wab is just like a rotten-hearted man. Oh! how gratefu' I am to the glass-blawers, wha hae blawn awa' my crimes, opened my een, an' I houp made me a better an' wiser man."

"Od," said Mrs. Gavin, "I wish the glass-blawers, as ye ca' them, wad dae something for my man, and gie him a guid blast; it wad do him some service, I reckon."

Duncan then left the astonished woman, and he repaired to the John Barleycorn, at the door of which stood the landlord, who was about to seize and apprehend him, and take him also for a hostage. He explained everything to mine host; he paid the landlord handsomely, and soon released Andrew Gavin, who, poor man, had been locked up in one of the rooms as a prisoner till the big reckoning was paid. Duncan told Andrew where he had been, and what he had come through, and that he had now got "new licht on mony things;" that "he noo saw what a bad man he had hitherto been." He determined to be a better man, and to lead a better life. Above all things, he resolved never again to taste drink while he lived; also to break and throw away his short ellwand, and in what remained of his future life to be honest and just in all his transactions.

The Fratery.

APPENDIX.

❖

AN EPITOME OF THE HISTORY OF DUNFERMLINE,
A.D. 1064-1880.

THE portion of the following epitome of the history of Dunfermline, extending from A.D. 1064-1833, was published in the
form of a large chart in the year 1833 by Mr. Andrew Mercer,
one of the historians of the old city. Few copies of it will
now be in existence.

Some of the items embraced in his narration are here somewhat amplified, and some that were deemed of no public interest
have been excluded. There are also a number of additional
interesting incidents herein recorded, and the whole has been
brought down to the year 1880,—thus affording a bird's-eye
view, as it were, of the history of ancient and modern Dunfermline.

The writer is indebted to the works of the late Dr. E. Henderson, Rev. Dr. P. Chalmers, Dr. Robert Chambers, and others,
for much of the historical information herein recorded, especially
from the period A.D. 1834-1878. He has also to express his
thanks to Messrs. W. Clark & Son for kindly granting the use
of some of the plates required in the illustration of the book.

MALCOLM III. (Canmore) was born in 1024, and in 1057
ascended the Scottish throne, after the death of the
usurper Macbeth. He was the descendant of a race
which had given kings to Scotland for six hundred
years, and he introduced a comparatively enlightened
era into that kingdom.

1064   MALCOLM III., King, who was the contemporary of
          William the Conqueror, is supposed to have built
          the Tower in the Glen of Pittencrieff, Dunfermline.

1069   Arrival at Dunfermline of Prince Edgar Atheling, with
          his mother and sisters, Margaret and Christian, and
          their retinue,—their ship having been driven into the
          Firth of Forth, and nearly wrecked through stress of
          weather.   The refugees were hospitably welcomed by
          the King in Dunfermline Tower.

1070   MALCOLM III. marries at Dunfermline the above Prin-
          cess Margaret, daughter of Edward of Hungary,
          heir-apparent to the English throne.   Age of
          Malcolm forty-seven, and of Margaret twenty-four
          years.

1072   MALCOLM and MARGARET resolve to found the Church
          and Convent, it is supposed, about this period.

1074   The Church, partly completed, is dedicated to
          the "Holy Trinity," and ordained to be the
          future sepulchre of the Scottish Kings.
          The Consort of Malcolm afterwards enriched the Abbey
          with jewels and vessels of gold and silver, and gave
          it a magnificent black cross, set in diamonds.

1075   Foundation Charter of Dunfermline Church granted by
          Malcolm III.

1080   MATILDA, daughter of Malcolm and Margaret, supposed
          to have been born this year in the Tower, which
          stood on the Tower Hill.
          The Signet of the Church, &c. at this period had for its
          motto—" *Sigill. Capit'i Ecclesiæ Trinitatis de Dun-
          ferelin.*"

1081   DAVID, afterwards David I., the youngest of Malcolm
          and Margaret's six sons, was born about this year.

1086   MARGARET and MALCOLM bequeath to the Church of the
          Holy Trinity, for ever, the lands of "Petnurcha,
          Petticorthin, Pethbalechin, Lavar, Bolgin, Shiram de
          Kircaladinet, Inveresk Minor, and the whole of
          Forthriff.

          QUEEN MARGARET, being of a deeply pious dis-
          position, is said to have frequently repaired,
          for devotional purposes and for solitude, to
          the Oratory Cave in the Glen, now known as
          St. Margaret's Cave.   According to Turgot, her

Confessor, the Queen "fell a victim to her long vigils, fastings, and mortifications."

While she was in favour of a certain amount of Court parade and splendour, and insisted on the King being served at table on gold and silver plate, she at the same time made it her daily duty to prepare food for nine indigent orphans. "On her bended knees she fed them. With her own hands she ministered at table to crowds of poor persons, and washed the feet of some poor children every evening. She was revered and loved by all who approached her."

1090 ETHELRED, second son of Malcolm and Margaret, bequeathed to the Church of the Holy Trinity the farm of Hailes.

1093 MALCOLM III. founded the new Cathedral at Durham in August of this year.

MALCOLM III. and his eldest son, Prince Edward, were slain at the siege of Alnwick Castle, 13th November. Edward was interred at Dunfermline, and Malcolm at Tynemouth. (Alexander I. afterwards exhumed his father's body, and re-interred it at Dunfermline.)

MARGARET, Queen of Malcolm, died from grief and long vigils in the "Castrum Puellarum" (Edinburgh Castle), 16th November. She was interred at Dunfermline, in the Church of the Holy Trinity, close by Edward, her son.

1094 DUNCAN I., son of Malcolm III., bequeaths to the Church of the Holy Trinity, for ever, the Villas of Luschar (Luscar).

1097 DONALD VII. is supposed to have died this year, and to have been interred at Dunfermline.

1098 The Convent supposed to have been dedicated to the Order of St. Benedict.

EDGAR, fourth son of Malcolm III., succeeded to the throne.

EDGAR (King) bequeathes to the Church for ever the farm of Galald, and beautifies the Church by his alterations and improvements.

1104 An individual named Peter was now Prior of the Convent.

1107 EDGAR (King) died at Dundee, January. His remains were interred in the Church at Dunfermline.

ALEXANDER I., fifth son of Malcolm III., ascended the throne.

1109 *St. Eustace de Morvell,* "Grate Constable of Scotland," was witness to a donation given by Alexander I. to the Monastery of Dunfermline.

1112 ALEXANDER I. confers on the Monastery of Dunfermline the privilege of holding its Courts in the "fullest manner," and to give judgment by "combat, by iron, or by water."

1115 SIBILLA, Queen of Alexander I., bequeaths to the Church of the Holy Trinity, for ever, the farm or mansion of Beeth.

1118 ALEXANDER I. completes the Church of Dunfermline, and bequeaths to it for ever the "farms of Gatemile, Petton-muachin, Balchevie, Duninbernin, and Keeth."*

1120 "*Waldeve*" gives the church of Inverkeithing to the Monastery, for "the love of God and St. Margaret."

1123 SIBILLA (Queen) died, and is supposed to have been interred at Dunfermline.

1124 ALEXANDER I. died at Stirling, April, and was interred at Dunfermline, in the Church of the Holy Trinity."

DAVID I., his brother, succeeded him. He raises the Convent to the dignity of an Abbey, and translates to it thirteen Monks from Canterbury, and ordains that "an abbot, prior, and sub-prior shall be the principal ecclesiastics." The Monasteries of Kelso, Dryburgh, and Melrose were reared by him.

1125 DAVID I. transfers thirteen Benedictine Monks from Dunfermline Abbey to the Priory of Urquhart, Morayshire.

1126 DAVID I. gives to the Monks of Dunfermline 100 shillings of his rents in England.

1128 *Gosfrid,* or *Gaufrid,* ordained first Abbot of Dunfermline by Robert, Bishop of St. Andrews.

1130 *A Corn Mill* in or about Dunfermline at this period.

DAVID I. grants to the Monastery all the gold that should accrue to him in Fife and Fothrif.

1140 During this century the clergy "were the schoolmasters, the statesmen, the architects, the lawyers, the physicians, bankers, agriculturalists, &c. &c. of the age."

---

* Places which are now unknown.

It is decreed that if any of the men belonging to the Abbey should commit a crime, they shall be bound to answer for it nowhere but in the Court of the Holy Trinity and the Abbots of Dunfermline.

1146   *St. Jerome's Bible*, copy of, used in the church here as early as this period.

DAVID I. grants a "Charter of Confirmation to the Monastery of Dunfermline" about this period.

1150   DAVID I. grants another Charter to the Monastery.

1153   DAVID I. dies at Carlisle; his remains are brought here, and are interred in the Church of the Holy Trinity.

GOSFRID, or GAUFRID, Abbot of Dunfermline, dies, and is interred in the choir of the Church of the Holy Trinity.

GEODFRY ordained Abbot of Dunfermline by the Bishop of St. Andrews.

1160   MALCOLM IV. enjoins the protection of the Abbey, "where the body of his grandfather, King David, rests in God."

1163   *The Monks of the Abbey* are prohibited from forsaking the Abbey after their professions, without the Abbot's permission, unless entering into stricter orders.

MALCOLM IV. grants to the Monastery, by Charter, half the fat of the "crespies caught between Forth and Tay, for lights before the altar."

1165   MALCOLM IV. grants a Charter to the Monastery.

MALCOLM IV. died at Jedburgh; his remains are afterwards interred in the Church of the Holy Trinity in Dunfermline.

The men belonging to the Abbot and Monks of Dunfermline assist, of their own "good will," at the request of William (the King), to repair his castles in Ross.

WILLIAM THE LYON, grandson of King David, was the first monarch to adopt the badge of the Lion, which has figured in the Scottish Shield ever since.

1172   *Malcolm, Earl of Athole*, and his Countess, appointed the Monastery of Dunfermline to be the place of their interment.

Shortly after, they both died, and were interred in the place they had appointed.

1173   Perth and Stirling had schools at this period, wherein youthful candidates for ecclesiastical preferment were instructed in "Grammar and Logicke;" the Monks of Dunfermline were the directors.

1176 *Margaret de Ouyeth* gives to the Abbey certain lands, that a mass should be celebrated on her birthday for "her soul."

1180 WILLIAM (King) about this period states that xxiis. iiijd. was the specific sum of the tithe of the malt which the Monks drew from his lands at Fithkill.

1184 Dunkeld Cathedral Church becomes the property of the Abbey of Dunfermline.

1185 *Geodfry*, Abbot, dies, and is interred in the church choir. *Galfrid* ordained Abbot by the Bishop of St. Andrews.

1200 The Seal of the Abbey had for its legend "*Sigillum Sancti Trinitatis.*"

1202 *William de Malvoisin*, Bishop of St. Andrews, deprives the Abbey of the presentation of two churches, because the monks had neglected to provide him with a sufficient quantity of wine after supper. It appears the Bishop's own attendants had largely consumed it.

1214 WILLIAM THE LYON died, after reigning forty-eight years. ALEXANDER II. (son of William), succeeded him as king of Scotland.

1220 Galfrid, Abbot, died, and was interred in the Church of the Holy Trinity; Robert of Kaldeleth ordained Abbot by the Bishop of St. Andrews.

ALEXANDER II. is supposed to have built a regaling house at the King's Seat on the Hill.

1230 The Monks of Scone pleaded their rights with the Abbot and Monks of Dunfermline to the tithe of the mills on the Water of Amund.

1231 The Abbot and Monks notify to Pope Innocent IV. that their number had formerly been thirty, but in future was to consist of fifty.

The Abbey is, at great expense, enlarged and adorned with elegant structures.

1237 ALEXANDER II. bequeaths the forest of Dollar to the Monastery of Dunfermline.

1240 David, Bishop of St. Andrews, gives the Church of Kinghorn-the-Less to the Monastery, also the Church of Kirkcaldy, and orders the Abbot and Monks to present Vicars.

1244 Pope Innocent IV., at the request of the King, empowers the Abbot to assume the mitre, ring, and other pontifical ornaments, and the Monks to wear leather caps suitable to their order.

1245 Alexander II. solicits Pope Innocent IV. to have Queen Margaret enrolled in the catalogue of the Saints, as her body had exhibited "infinite miracles." The Pope issues a Bull to the Bishops of St. Andrews, Dunkeld, and Dunblane, commanding them to make strict enquiry into her life, merits, and miracles, to reduce what was proved to writing, attested by their seals, and to transmit it by a trusty messenger, that he might thence learn how far to indulge the King's request.

1246 The Bishops proceeded to investigate the matter; but neglected to record either the names or words of the witnesses, on which account the Pope refuses the King's request.

ALEXANDER II. died at Kerrera, near Oban, in the thirty-fifth year of his reign.

1249 ALEXANDER III. succeeded his father in 1249, at the age of eight years.

A Cardinal is charged with a new enquiry regarding the "*miracles of Queen Margaret,*" and corresponds with the Bishop of St. Andrews concerning it.

1250 The "miracles" attributed to Queen Margaret's relicts having been particularly enquired into, and the facts proved, she was canonized, and her remains removed to a situation contiguous to the high altar.

The Chartulary of the Abbey begins about this period.

1251 *Robert, Abbot of Dunfermline,* and Chancellor of the Kingdom, legitimizes the wife of Allan Durward (natural daughter of Alexander II.), and is accused of having "illegally furnished an heiress to the crown." He resigns his seal of office, assumes the habit of a monk, retires from the Abbey to Newbattle, where he soon afterwards died.

ALEXANDER III. at the age of ten, married the Princess Margaret, eldest daughter of Henry III. of England.

Radalphus ordained Abbot of Dunfermline.

1254   The Abbot and Monks found entitled to certain provision from the King and Queen's kitchen.

1274   MARGARET, Queen of Alexander III., dies, and is interred in the Church of the Holy Trinity at Dunfermline.

1275   *Radalphus, Abbot*, grants eight oars in the new passage boat at New Queensferry to seven persons, for the payment of eightpence yearly for each oar.

1280   DAVID, Prince (son of Alexander III.), dies at Stirling; his remains are interred at Dunfermline, in the Church of Holy Trinity.

      Radalphus, Abbot, dies about this period.

1283   ALEXANDER, Prince (third son of Alexander III.), dies at Lyndores; his remains are interred at Dunfermline in the Church of the Holy Trinity.

1285   ALEXANDER III. is killed by a fall from his horse, upon the sands between Easter and Wester Kinghorn. His remains are interred "as became a king" in the Church of the Holy Trinity, Dunfermline.

1290   At this period the burgh received from the Abbey a common moor.

1291   *William de Oberwill* grants a Charter to the Abbot and Monks, and gives them a coal mine on his estate of Pittencrieff.

      The untimely death of Alexander III. brought many calamities upon Scotland.

      EDWARD I., King of England, arrives at the Abbey on his way from Berwick to Perth. He here calls upon the people of Scotland to enrol themselves vassals of his kingdom.

1291   On the death of the Princess Margaret, John Baliol laid claim to the Scottish Crown.

1295   JOHN BALIOL, King of Scotland, is in Dunfermline, where the marriage of his son Edward is ratified, and receives the assent of the clergy, nobility, and burghs.

1296   EDWARD I. arrives again at the Abbey on Monday, 13th of August, and ruthlessly destroys its records, &c.

1298   *The Ports* of the burgh supposed to have been built.

1300   Dunfermline Abbey arrives at the zenith of its external splendour, and of the devotional fame of its Monks, and is declared to be capable of

giving ample accommodation to three distinguished Sovereigns, with their retinue of
attendants.

William de Lamberton, Bishop of St. Andrews, gives
the Monks the vicarage of a Church to render them
" still more fervent."

1303   SIR WILLIAM WALLACE and his mother in
the autumn of this year visited Dunfermline
in disguise. They travelled on foot from
Dundee, where "he had been in hiding."

EDWARD I. arrived in Dunfermline, 6th November, where he was joined by his Queen, and
a large retinue of his nobility ; here they spent
the winter.

About this period Edward seized the Coronation
Stone of Scotland, which had been brought
from Iona to Scone Monastery, and was of
great antiquity. It is now in Westminster
Abbey, and is the Coronation Stone of Great
Britain.

1304   The Abbey was burned on the 10th February by
order of Edward on his departure. This was
his fifth visit to Dunfermline.

SIR WILLIAM WALLACE was driven to the
"Foreste of Dunferlin" about the beginning
of the year, "a proscribed man." The country
was now groaning under English oppression,
and the mean-spiritedness and duplicity of
some of the Scottish nobility.

1305   Ralph ordained Abbot of Dunfermline by the Bishop
of St. Andrews.

1310   *The Abbey partly rebuilt,* and rendered sufficient for the
accommodation of the King and Queen, &c.

1314   *The Vicar of Inverkeithing* is found liable in eight
merks to the Monastery, for the non-payment of
which it is declared that he shall be excommunicated.

1315   *Robert de Carel* ordained Abbot of Dunfermline by
the Bishop of St. Andrews.

1316   A jury summoned to decide whether homage was due
by the Earls of Fife to the Abbot of Dunfermline.
Verdict in favour of the Abbot.

1318   Robert, Abbot, &c., grants a charter to the Convent in
favour of the burgesses of the burgh.

1322   ROBERT I. (King), intimates to his Great Chamberlain that the Monastery had a gift of "the great customs of wool, skins, and leather, arising from their own land, &c., and men's" throughout the Kingdom.

1323   DAVID (afterwards David II., son of King Robert Bruce), born at Dunfermline, 5th March.

  ROBERT I. "gives a Church to the Abbey, to maintain a burning and perpetual light in the choir, before the shrine of the blessed Margaret."

1326   The "*Church of Kynross* and Chapel of Urwell given to the Monastery by Robert I., in honour of his predecessors who were interred in it."

1327   ELIZABETH, Queen of Robert I., dies at Gordon Castle; her remains are interred in Dunfermline Church of the Holy Trinity, 26th October.

  Arnold Blair, a Monk of the Order of St. Benedict in Dunfermline, writes a history of Sir William Wallace. This monk had previously been chaplain to the great Scottish patriot.

1328   KING ROBERT BRUCE spent a portion of his time this year at Dunfermline, also at Scotland Well (*Fons Scotiæ*), near Lochleven, fifteen miles distant, where he took the benefit of the waters there for his complaints.

1329   ROBERT I. (Bruce) dies at Cardross (Dumbartonshire), 7th June, in his fifty-fifth year, and the twenty-third of his reign. His remains are (in accordance with his special desire) interred at Dunfermline in the Church of the Holy Trinity. They were interred with great pomp and ceremony, and amid the universal and heartfelt lamentations of the Scottish nation.

  DAVID II. succeeded his father when only five years old.

1330   *John de Kinross*, perpetual Vicar of Inverkeithing, represents that his vicarage was much exhausted by exactions, &c.; the Monastery agrees to pay half the expense of repairing the choir, which had been going to decay.

1332   *Randolph* (one of the heroes at Bannockburn), Earl of Murray and Regent of Scotland, dies at Musselburgh, 20th July. His remains are interred in the Monastery of Dunfermline.

  Edward Baliol, with his army, takes possession of the

Abbey, and finds in it "five hundred excellent spears," and a quantity of provisions, &c. He afterwards was crowned king, but enjoyed that dignity for only three months.

1333 The gold mine in Fife which David I. granted to the Abbey in 1136 abandoned, as "it never turned out to much account."

1334 DAVID II. holds the Parliament in Dunfermline, at which the town of Kirkcaldy is made a Royal Burgh, and given to Dunfermline.

1335 A Parliament held at Dunfermline, in which Sir Andrew Murray is elected "Regent of Scotland" during the minority of David II.

Alexander ordained Abbot of Dunfermline about this period.

1337 EDWARD III. (of England) orders the town of Perth to be fortified at the joint expense of the Abbeys of Aberbrothock, Coupar, Lindores, Balmerinock, Dunfermline, and St. Andrews.

1342 *Alexander, Abbot,* repairs to South Queensferry to enquire into some misconduct of the "oar men."

1350 The present site of the Collier Row, called *Crow-hill*, was at this time the most populous part of the town.

1356 Christian de Bruce, sister of King Robert Bruce, died, and was interred in the Abbey.

Garvock House, near Dunfermline, supposed to have been built this year.

1358 *John* ordained Abbot of Dunfermline.

1363 DAVID II. grants a charter in favour of the Monastery.

1366 Matilda, daughter of King Robert Bruce, died, and was interred in the Abbey.

The Monastery obtains the patronage of the Church of St. Giles, Edinburgh, from the Bishop of Lindisfarne.

1370 *St. Leonard's Hospital* supposed to have been built.

1371 DAVID II. died, and his death terminated the Bruce dynasty.

ROBERT II. ascended the Scottish throne.

1375 William de Yetam was Clerk of the Abbey.

1382 Cupar-Fife constituted a Royal Burgh by King Robert II. at his court at Dunfermline.

1383 ROBERT II. orders the "trone and customs" to be arrested and brought into his hands. It is removed

1390   *John de Torrie*, Abbot, grants to William de Yetam,
       Clerk of the Monastery, funds for his support, as also
       a clerk, three boys, three horses, and a stable, &c.

1394   JAMES I. of Scotland was born at Dunfermline
       this year.

1400   *The houses of Dunfermline*, according to tradition, were
       composed chiefly of wood, with heather thatched roofs.
       Population of burgh about 500. Number of *Monks*
       in the Abbey, 45 ; others, 15—total, 60.

1403   ANNABELLA DRUMMOND, Queen of Robert II., died in a
       minor palace which she adopted at Inverkeithing.
       Her remains were interred in the Church of the Holy
       Trinity, Dunfermline.

1406   *Robert, Duke of Albany*, died, and was interred here.

1409   *John, Abbot*, grants to each of the Monks 40s. of the
       current money yearly, to purchase vestments with.

1413   JAMES I. (King), visits the Royal Tombs at Dun-
       fermline, after a long absence in England.
       When the tomb of his ancestor King David I.
       was pointed out, he remarked that "David
       was ane sair sanct for the Crown." This was
       said in reference to King David's lavish ex-
       penditure on monasteries, churches, &c.

1419   *Robert Stewart, Duke of Albany*, and Regent of Scotland,
       died, and was interred in Dunfermline.

1420   *Andrew* ordained Abbot about this period.

1436   Dunfermline, Perth, Stirling, and Scone declared unsafe
       for the residence of royalty, on account of the designs
       of the nobility. (Edinburgh then became the metro-
       polis of Scotland.)

1437   *The Scottish language* appears for the first time, in the
       Chartulary of the Abbey.

1439   *The general famine* of this year was severely felt in
       Dunfermline and neighbourhood.

1440   *The Monks of Dunfermline* protest against the town of
       Perth, that they did not relinquish special funeral
       emoluments, offerings of wax, &c. &c.

1441   *James Bruce*, parson of Kilmeny, consecrated "Bishop
       of Dunkeld" in the Church of the Holy Trinity,
       Dunfermline.

The text at the top:

by solicitation of the Abbot. The convent had been
encroaching on the customs due to the king.

James, Bishop of St. Andrews, grants a discharge to Andrew, Abbot of Dunfermline, for eighty merks Scots.

1444 Patrick Grahame, Archbishop of St. Andrews, imprisoned in the Monastery of Dunfermline for "heresy." He afterwards died in Lochleven Castle.

1448 Richard ordained Abbot of Dunfermline about this period.

John Wright, Provost. This is the earliest notice on record of a lay Provost.

1449 The Monastery exempted from attending courts of law.

1450 The Abbot and Convent of Dunfermline dispones to the "Bailies of Kirkaldy, and their successors for ever," their burgh, harbour, &c. given them by David II. in the year 1334.

1453 *Richard, Abbot, &c.* of Dunfermline, sent along with others to the King of England, to deliver a pacific mission.

1455 JAMES II. holds a Parliament at Edinburgh, in which he annexes to the Crown several lands belonging to the Monastery of Dunfermline.

1456 *Richard, Abbot of Dunfermline*, and others, represent the Barons in the administration of justice in the Sessions at Edinburgh, November 6.

John de Benaly, Prior of Pluscardine, in Moray, near Elgin, "resigns his office" in consequence of various disputes he had with the Abbey. The "Sacrist is appointed to fill the said Priory in his stead."

1457 *Richard, Abbot, &c.*, lets "the teind sheaves of the croft of St. Ryan's chapel, in liferent, to the minister of Calder, for one boll of meill and one boll of barley yearly."

The spiritual and temporal rights of the Abbey very extensive. The Abbot is superior of the property of others, and receives the resignation of his vassals, while they kneel before him.

1459 The Abbey of Dunfermline, along with St. Andrews, is allowed, by an edict from the Holy See, to use butter and other products from milk without any scruple.

1463 *Richard, Abbot of Dunfermline*, in consequence of past favours to Thomas de Bully, Canon of the Cathedrals of Glasgow and Dunkeld, is, "with the whole Convent, made free of expense of the table of the house of Canons whenever they shall choose to come hither."

1472   *Alexander Thominson* ordained Abbot of Dunfermline.

1478   *Alexander, Abbot, &c.,* is extruded from his place, and Henry Curichton, Abbot of Paisley, surrogated in his stead by the Pope at the King's intercession.

Robert Henryson of Fordel is witness to a Charter of Patrick, Baron of the lands of Spittlefield.

James ordained Abbot of Dunfermline.

1479   JAMES, Abbot, &c., grants the office of a chaplainry, newly founded at North Queensferry, to David Storrey, with a stipend of ten marks yearly from the coffers of the Monastery.

1488   Tradition states that about this period a stone cross pillar stood on a rising ground south of St. Leonard's Hospital. "Perhaps the '*Cross Head*' is derived from it."

1490   *Robert Henryson,* the poet, and preceptor of youth in the Monastery, died about this period, and was interred in the Church.

1491   The first notice regarding Dunfermline weavers appears this year.

1494   *James Henryson,* son of the poet, was chosen King's Advocate.

St. Margaret's Altar.—Schir Andrew Peirson, Chaplain ; Schir Steven Stirling, Chaplain of the Morning Service.

1499   Preparations going on for repairing and beautifying the palace and the church.

1500   JAMES IV. finishes his repairs on the palace, &c.

1509   JAMES IV., through the Pope, gets Alexander, his natural son, ordained Abbot of Dunfermline, to which abbacy the priory of Coldingham is annexed.

1511   The Palace of Dunfermline at this period was the chief place of residence of James IV. and his consort Margaret, daughter of Henry VII. of England.

1513   KING JAMES IV., and Alexander his son, Abbot, slain at the battle of Flodden.

1515   *The "Postulate"* of Dunfermline, a legal functionary, attends the Court at Edinburgh.

1522   *Andrew Forman* ordained Abbot of Dunfermline.

1526   *Andrew, Abbot*, slain in battle near Linlithgow.

       Dunfermline Abbey pillaged by Angus after the battle.

1529   *James Beaton* ordained Abbot of Dunfermline.

1530   *James Beaton, Abbot of Dunfermline,* died.

       Baldris and Gallo-reg have gallows for the execution of the feudal law.

       George Dury ordained Abbot of Dunfermline.

1539   Adam Blackwood, the historian, born at Dunfermline.

1540   The lands of Buckhaven given to the Abbey in exchange for Western Kinghorn.

       The Palace of Dunfermline repaired and much enlarged at this period.

1542   *George Dury, Abbot*, appointed one of the council of the Earl of Arran, the guardian of Mary during her nonage.

1549   *George Dury*, grants a Charter to the burgh, 2d August.

1550   Dunfermline, &c. signet legend—" *S. Georgii Abbatis de Dumfermling Ard. St. Andr.*"

1551   James V. builds cellars, &c. at Limekilns, near the town.

1557   *George Dury, Abbot*, issues a decree to prevent the inhabitants of Kirkcaldy from building wind, water, or horse mills.

1558   *George Dury, Abbot, &c.*, gives his voice against Walter Mill, empannelled at St. Andrews for heresy. He was burnt, in conformity to his sentence. George Dury, Abbot, &c., brings to trial John Dury, his cousin, for "the crimes of heresy." He is found guilty, and condemned to be built up between two walls until he died. Through the influence of the Earl of Arran he is set at liberty.

1560   **The Church and Abbey completely destroyed by the "Reformers," 28th March, and the royal tombs and monuments were all thrown down.**

       Robert Pitcairn appointed Commendator of Dunfermline Abbey.

       David Ferguson inducted minister of Dunfermline Reformed Church.

1561   James VI. much engaged at golf over lands now called Golfdrum, *i.e.*, Golfridge.

MARY QUEEN OF SCOTS visited Dunfermline, and thence went on to Dysart and St. Andrews, 3d March.

1562   Dunfermline Church partly repaired from the destruction of 28th March 1560, and fitted up as a Protestant place of worship.

1563   MARY QUEEN OF SCOTS again visited Dunfermline, February 14th.

1566   *Robert Pitcairn,* Commendator of Dunfermline, &c., repairs to Stirling to the coronation of the Prince.

1567   *Robert Pitcairn* attends a meeting of Parliament held at Edinburgh.

1568   MARY QUEEN OF SCOTS, in her flight from Lochleven Castle, passed through the parish of Dunfermline.

1569   Robert Pitcairn is sent by Regent Murray to the English Court regarding Queen Mary.

1570   Robert Pitcairn appointed Secretary of State for Scotland, November.

1571   *David Ferguson,* minister, of Dunfermline, preaches a sermon at Leith before the Regent and nobility of Scotland.

1572   *George Dury, Abbot of Dunfermline* and Archdeacon of St. Andrews, died, and was interred in the Western Church of Dunfermline.

1576   The Assembly of the Church refuses to give "libertie to the bailie of Dunfermling to play upon the Sunday afternoon in the Church a play not founded upon the Canonical parts of Scripture."

1581   Andrew Steuart sentenced to be "burnt on the richt shoulder with the common markin yron of Dunfermling."

1584   *Robert Pitcairn, Commendator of Dunfermline Abbey,* Archdeacon of St. Andrews, and Secretary of State for Scotland, died, and was interred in the western division of the Church. He lived for some time in Limekilns for his health.

1585   "The Master of Gray," appointed Commendator. A Parliament appointed to be held at Dunfermline by order of King James VI., to consider the propriety of recalling the banished Lords and Ministers, there being no other toun so convenient on account of "ye pest." The ports of the town are shut in by order of the Laird of Petfirren to prevent "said meeting."

1586　*David Ferguson*, minister of Dunfermline, appointed by the General Assembly one of the assessors to assist the Bishop of St. Andrews in the trial of persons presented to benefices in the county of Fife.

1587　Hew Watt is condemned by the Court of Regality to be "hangit to the death on Baldris gallows, or elles drownit, at will of the judges," for stealing cattle, &c.

　　The temporality of the Church of Dunfermline, with some exceptions, is annexed to the Crown.

　　"The Master of Gray" extruded from his office by an Act of Parliament held at Edinburgh 29th July.

　　Henry Pitcairn appointed Commendator of Dunfermline Monastery, with consent of the whole Convent.

1588　JAMES VI. constitutes Dunfermline a Royal Burgh, and grants it a Charter of Confirmation.

1589　*The Abbey* is erected into a temporal lordship.

1590　ANNA, QUEEN OF SCOTLAND, infeft in the Lordship of Dunfermline 17th May.

　　The Annexation of the "Abbey of Dunfermling," ratified by Parliament 21st July.

　　An Act of Parliament confers on the Queen "a richt to the third of Dunfermling."

1593　The Queen, in a Charter dated 15th February, appoints Alexander Seaton Heritable Bailie of the Lordship of Dunfermline.

　　The Monks of the Abbey of Dunfermline give in portion to the Queen the eighth part of the first-fruits or fifth penny of any benefice which belonged to them.

1596　Elizabeth, daughter of James VI., born in the Palace of Dunfermline, 19th August. Through her, in an unbroken line, has descended Her Majesty Queen Victoria.

　　The Provincial Synod of Fife held at Dunfermline 12th May, for the purpose of amending and renewing the Covenant.

　　A Convention of the Estates held at Dunfermline, by James VI., regarding the Popish Lords and Ministers.

　　"2d November, the princes cam out of Dunfermline to the Abbey of Holy-ruid-hous."

1598　JAMES VI. makes considerable alterations and repairs on the western division of the Church. Is said to have built the steeple and laid out the bowling-green. Steeple 156 feet 8 inches high.

David Ferguson, minister of Dunfermline, dies, aged sixty-five years ; he was thirty-eight years minister of Dunfermline ; is interred in the eastern church.

1599   Andro Foster inducted minister of Dunfermline.

1600   Dunfermline contains about 480 males and 500 females. Total, about 1000 inhabitants.

   CHARLES I., son of James VI., born in Dunfermline Palace 19th November 1600, afterwards baptised by the Bishop of Ross, 23d December.

1602   William Shaw, architect to King James VI., died in April.

   RORERT, son of James VI., supposed to have been born at Dunfermline, was baptised in Dunfermline Church by various titles 2d May, died 27th May, and was interred at Dunfermline.

1605   Alexander Seaton, Lord Urquhart, &c. &c., created Earl of Dunfermline 4th March.

1610   Queen Anna, Lady Dunfermline, consort of James VI., mortifies into the hands of the Town-Council the sum of £2000 Scots, for the support of the masters of the grammar and singing school.

1612   Henry Wardlaw of Balmule, afterwards Sir Henry Wardlaw of Pitreavie, appointed by Queen Anna Chamberlain of her rents at Dunfermline.

1615   John Moray inducted minister of Dunfermline.

1616   Queen Anna bequeathes to Sir Henry Wardlaw, her Chamberlain, &c., a burying vault attached to the south side of the church.

1617   KING JAMES VI. visits Dunfermline, the first visit since his accession to the English throne in 1603. Is " received with tumultuous joy."

1622   John Moray, minister, deposed by sentence of the High Commission for refusing to conform to the five articles of Perth, &c.

   Harrie Makgill inducted minister of Dunfermline.

1624   Dunfermline burnt 25th May ; 220 houses totally consumed; occupied by 287 families, and their whole plenishing, consisting of 500 bolls of grain in barns. The town consists of 700 adults and 320 children under six years of age.

The burgesses having a right to the Wood of Garvock, near the town, completely denuded it of its old trees for the purpose of rebuilding the town ; the proprietor in consequence removes his residence to Pitliver.

1625   The Burgh (High) School built ; perhaps the school to which the Queen granted £2000 Scots was burnt at the fire.

1627   The west of Fife, especially Dunfermline and Torryburn, infested with witches and warlocks.

1633   CHARLES I. (King) revokes in an Act of Parliament the former disposition belonging to the Abbey.

1638   Charles Seaton, Earl of Dunfermline, affixes his seal to the National League and Covenant.

1640   Pat Mayne held the office of hangman and witch burner.

1641   CHARLES I. grants to the Earl of Dunfermline a lease of the feu-duties and teinds of the Lordship of Dunfermline for fifty-seven years, commencing with 1639.

1642   The Scots proverbs of David Ferguson published at Edinburgh by " Andro Hart."

Harrie Makgill, minister of Dunfermline, died, and was interred in the church.

1643   Six women burnt for witchcraft at the Witch Knowe or Loan, north-east of the burgh. Other two who were accused of that crime died in prison, viz. —

Janet Fentoun, the witch who died miserably, and was afterwards brought to the Witch Knowe, " being trailed and carted yrto, and castin into a hole there without a kist (coffin)," 20th June. " Isobel Mair, witch, hangs herself in the laich thieves hole." The " Witch Dub," north-east of the town, was the place where witches were drowned. Witchcraft very prevalent between this period and 1650 all over Europe, and was regarded everywhere with deep-seated dread.

1645   The plague rages in the town and parish.

Dunfermline Church becomes " Collegiate," the population having greatly increased in town and parish ; it is provided with two ministers, viz., Robert Kay and William Oliphant.

1648   Margaret Nicholson, spouse of Alexander Dempster the
fiddler, ordained to stand with the branks in her
mouth for two hours on the market-day for scolding
and drunkenness, and as a public example.

William Crichton, the warlock, who confessed he had
" made a paction with the devil," was publicly burnt.

1649   CHARLES II. succeeds his father, who was decapitated
January 1649.

1650   CHARLES II. spends a good part of August in the
Palace of Dunfermline, and subscribes to the
National League and Covenant.

1651   The Battle of Pitreavie fought in July this year. About
10,000 warriors were engaged in this most sanguinary
conflict. Tradition records that the little stream
traversing the neighbourhood " ran with blood for
several days."

Cromwell's army arrives in Dunfermline after the battle,
and remains there for many weeks.

They demolish the boards and seats of the session-
house, &c., and plunder the church box.

1652   In the parochial register of births, the 23d of March
this year is named " *Mirk Monday.*" The great
mid-day darkness was occasioned by an eclipse of
the sun.

The spouse of W. Scotland, summoned for cursing and
swearing, " was sharplie admonished, " and if again
found guiltye, " she shall stand at the tron wi' the
branks in her mouth."

1665   John, Earl (afterwards Marquis) of Tweeddale, in consequence of a debt due to him by the Earl of Dunfermline, obtains a right to the Lordship, Heritable
Bailie, &c.

1666   Robert Kay, minister, demitts his office 17th January.
William Pearson inducted minister of Dunfermline.
Thomas Kinymount inducted minister of Dunferm-
line 18th July.

1667   Dunfermline was assessed to the extent of £102 Scots,
in order to assist in liquidating the " voluntar offar
to his Majestie."

1668   Thomas Kinymount translated from Dunfermline to the
Church of Auchterderran.

1669   John, Marquis of Tweeddale, had his office of Heritable bailie, &c. constituted by a charter under the Great Seal, dated 12th February.

1672 " A house of correction for the reception of idle beggars and vagrants " ordered to be built.

1673 Alexander Monro inducted a minister of Dunfermline Church 7th April.

1675 Pitreavie Hospital (near Dunfermline), the most ancient charitable institution in the parish, founded by Sir H. Wardlaw in favour of four widows of " honest fame."

1676 William Peirson, minister, translated to the church of Stirling.

Alexander Dunbar inducted minister of Dunfermline 19th October.

Alexander Monro, minister, translated to the church of Kinglassie.

1678 Robert Norie inducted minister of Dunfermline 18th September.

1679 Witchcraft still prevails, notwithstanding all the burning and drowning of witches which has taken place.

" John Drysdaill in the Nether-toun mortifies 500 merks Scots to the kirk-session for the support of puir scholars."

1680 The Dunfermline " *Blue Blanket*," drawn up by the trades of the burgh. (This was a design for the centre-piece of the Convener's flag, which was blue, and contained emblems of the incorporated trades.)

1686 Robert Norie, minister, translated to the church of Dundee.

1690 Supposed population of Dunfermline about 800 males and 1000 females. Of the town and parish 3800. Number of houses 250.

1694 The debt of the burgh amounts to about 5573 merks Scots (mortification excepted).

1695 The title of the Earldom of Dunfermline becomes extinct, the Earl dying without issue.

The post-office supposed to have been established.

1698 Part of the roof of Rosythe Castle fell in this year.

1699 Dunfermline consists of a few straggling houses about the ports and the purlieus of the Abbey ; houses covered chiefly with thatch ; winding stairs to the middle of the streets, &c.

1700   John Bell elected to the office of town's piper.
        Dunfermline trade greatly depressed; only a little doing
            in brewing.
1701   Hugh Kempt inducted a minister of Dunfermline.
1705   Hugh Kempt translated to the church of Carnbee.
1706   **The Magistrates, Town-Council, and inhabitants
            of Dunfermline protest and petition against
            the Union of Scotland and England. Sir Peter
            Halket is Provost.***
1708   Dunfermline Palace having been long neglected and
            deserted, the roof falls.
1710   James Grame, minister, dies, and leaves 600 merks
            Scots for the use of the poor.
        Thomas Buchanan translated from Tulliallan, and in-
            ducted a minister of Dunfermline.
1711   **Ralph Erskine inducted into the second charge
            of Dunfermline Church 7th August.**
1713   The parishioners, according to a census, number 5000.
        About this period Lassodie and Meiklebeath were dis-
            joined from the parish of Dunfermline and annexed
            to the parish of Beath.
1714   George I. proclaimed king by the Magistrates and Town-
            Council at the Pillory, Cross, and East Port.
1715   Thomas Buchanan, minister, died 10th April.
        A Jacobite detachment takes quarters in the Abbey, but
            are dispersed by Colonel Cathcart, &c.
1716   Ralph Erskine, minister of the second charge, is inducted
            minister of the first charge of Dunfermline Church,
            1st May.
        The Society of Gardeners instituted.
1718   Weaving: James Blake, John Beveridge, and John
            Gilmour establish a small manufactory of table linen
            in the Abbey.
        James Wardlaw inducted into the second charge of the
            Church of Dunfermline.
1719   James Blake, table linen manufacturer in the Abbey,
            manufactures a curiously wrought napkin, which
            is greatly admired.

        * Thirty-three Scottish burghs voted for the *Union*, and
            twenty-nine against it. While Sir Peter presented this
            petition and protest, he voted *for the Union!*

1720	Dunfermline Church and bells repaired.
1722	Daniel Defoe, author of *Robinson Crusoe*, visits Dunfermline.
1726	The ruins of the Abbey inhabited by various mechanics, &c.
1727	*Elizabeth Halket*, spouse of Sir Henry Wardlaw of Pitreavie, the celebrated authoress of the heroic Poem entitled "Hardyknute," in commemoration of the battle of Largs, died, and is interred in the vault of the Wardlaw family. Of this ballad Sir Walter Scott said it "was the first I ever learned, the last that I shall forget."
	George II. proclaimed king by the Magistrates and Council, at the Pillory, the Cross, and the East Port.
1728	*The church and steeple* repaired, and the bells re-founded.
1730	Grass growing along the eastern part of the High Street; the cadgers' horses feed upon it during the time that the owners are disposing of their wares.
1733	*Ralph Erskine* and others differ with the Established Church. They constitute themselves into an ecclesiastical court under the name of the "Associate Presbytery." This secession from the Established Church, which was nursed in Dunfermline, may therefore be regarded as the acorn of the Secession and the United Presbyterian Church.
1734	James Young, merchant, tried before the Court of Regality for bruising, &c. Henry Wardlaw, son of Lieutenant Wardlaw, and is acquitted.
1736	*Weaving.*—David Mackie carries on the manufacture of damask weaving; has three looms in that department; this is considered a heavy stock.
1740	A church built for the congregation of Ralph Erskine, near the Burgh School, October.
	Society of Weavers constituted.
	Severe frost continues 107 days. (Tradition.)
1741	George Whitfield, the celebrated Methodist divine, preaches from the pulpit of Ralph Erskine, and also in a public park, to many thousands of persons.
1742	Francis Paterson teaches in the "Queen's House."
	Rev. James Wardlaw, minister, died 2d May.
1743	James Thomson inducted into the Established Church.
	James Hay and William Gordon imprisoned for horse-stealing. Gordon hangs himself.

1744 Rev. Thomas Fernie inducted minister of the Established Church.

1745 *Town cess* demanded by the agents of the Pretender. £80 is collected with some difficulty, and tendered.

1746 *Lord Charles Hay,* Provost of the town, nearly shot by one of Prince Charles' men, a highland spy; a part of his peruke shot off.

Distaff spinning discontinued; the spinning wheel introduced.

1748 The heritable jurisdiction of monasteries being generally abolished, compensations are given to proprietors. The regality of Dunfermline is valued at £2672 : 7s., and the office of clerk at £500.

1749 *The "British Linen Company"* employs a great number of looms in the weaving of table linen.

1750 Arthur Martin teaches in the Queen's House the common rudiments of learning.

The fashionable parts of the town at this period were the Maygate, Kirkgate, and St. Catherine's Wynd.

1751 *Weaving.*—It was customary for weavers to work during the winter season at ticks and checks, and in the summer at table linen.

The large lantern tower of the Eastern Church fell, and started a great many coffins in the churchyard—May (Sunday).

1752 Twelve lamps are ordered from Edinburgh by the Town Council to light "the corners" of the principal streets—October.

Thomas Gillespie, minister of Carnock, deposed; opens a relief meeting-house in the town.

Dunfermline Market Cross, Pillory, the East and Cross Wynd Ports removed by command of the Town Council. Guildhall Street opened.

Weaving.—"Back harness" introduced.

Ralph Erskine, minister of the Secession Church, died 6th November.

1753 A new pillory erected.

The ancient Constabulary House, near the Monastery, removed at this period.

1754 *The Collier Row* port removed by order of the Town Council.

1755 The church at Cairneyhill founded this year. Population of the parish of Dunfermline, 8552.

The Rev. James Burt ordained minister of Cairneyhill.

1756 Mr. Moir teaches in the "Queen's House."

1757 *Dunfermline gallows* disappears; is some years afterwards converted by a weaver into a loom.

Weaving.—An invention by a weaver supersedes the necessity of a cord drawer.

1760 *Agriculture.*—George Chalmers, Esq. of Pittencrieff, introduces a new system of agriculture in the parish.

Chicken-Pie Club constituted.

Weaving.—David Campbell comes to Dunfermline, opens an extensive manufactury of table linen. Some time afterwards he retires to Edinburgh with a fortune of £7000.

1762 *One printing press* in the town at this time.

The Abbey Park and Garden advertised for feuing.

Mason Lodge, Mill Port, built.

GEORGE III. proclaimed at the site of the Pillory, at the Cross, and Port by the Magistrates.

1763 *Price of butter* at the Tron Market 6d. per lb. of 22 oz.

Table linens sent to London for sale for the first time.

1764 *Water, great scarcity.* The Guildry, &c. resolve to have water brought to the town from St. Margaret's well in leaden pipes. Reservoir built.

1765 The inhabitants are supplied with water from St. Margaret's well.

1766 *Great scarcity of water* still continues to be felt, especially in time of drought.

1767 *The bridge* over the "Tower Burn" founded by George Chalmers, Esq. of Pittencrieff.

1768 *Nuptial bed of Queen Anne,* which she brought with her from Denmark to Dunfermline, decorates an alehouse in the town. It was afterwards presented to the Earl of Elgin.

(Queen Anne's almry is at Logie, a seat of J. Hunt, Esq).

1769 *The Tolbooth* or Town-house founded, in consequence of the old Tolbooth being incommodious.

1770 *Bridge over the "Tower Burn"* finished, and a new road opened in a line with the High Street.

Bad harvest and meal mobs this year.

1771   *The Tolbooth* or Town-House finished.   Height of steeple 98 feet 7 inches.

The *Canon* fixed in its present position.

1772   *Weaving.*—The rate of wages of a good weaver and his cord drawer is about £30 per annum.

1774   *Thomas Gillespie,* minister of the Relief Church, died.

Adam Smith, the celebrated writer on political economy, and author of the "Wealth of Nations," who lived at Kirkcaldy, paid a visit to Dunfermline one Sabbath morning. He had walked from Kirkcaldy, and appeared in a reverie of deep thought. He wandered through the streets *en deshabille,* having nothing on him but "his small clothes, a morning gown and cap." His appearance caused great astonishment amongst the church-goers. The ringing of the church bells " roused him out of his reverie," and he was as much amazed as the bystanders at the strange predicament he was in.

Roman urns found on Carneill Hill, near Carnock.

Only three teachers in the town.

1775   A clock fitted up in the Tolbooth steeple, with four dial plates, by James Simpson, clock-maker.

Unseemly fracas in the Established Church. The minister, the Rev. Mr. Thomson (who had formerly been a military chaplain), having charged Mr. Scotland from the pulpit with accepting bribes at a parliamentary election, the latter shouted out, " Thou art a liar, thou old military blunderbuss, in the place of verity where thou standeth ! "

Relief meeting-house founded.

1776   Mr Stark erected *beetling mills* and other appliances at Brucefield, near Dunfermline.

1777   Weaving.—At this period the shuttle was thrown alternately by two men.

1778   Weaving.—Mr. John Wilson, of this burgh, invents the fly shuttle, and thus supersedes the services of two men. The freedom of the city was afterwards conferred on him for his valuable invention.

The " Queen's House " partly inhabited.

1779   *A Chapel of Ease* founded.

1779   *Church of the Reformed Presbyterians, or Cameronians,* established—Rev. Walter Grieve, minister.

1780   The last grant to the Tweeddale family of the feu-duties, &c. of the "Lordship of Dunfermline," expires. The Earl of Elgin, the Countess of Rothes, &c., obtain a lease for nineteen years.

     A Baptist congregation formed.

     The northern pend of the Abbey removed.

1781   A branch of the Bank of Scotland established.

     Knabbie and Moodie Streets formed.

1782   Funeral intimations by the "*dead bell*" discontinued.

     The last "Dunfermline hangman" died—September.

     A *distillery* erected in St. Margaret Street (commonly called Distillery Brae), by Messrs. Fairley and Scotland.

     Weaving.— About 900 looms employed in the town and neighbourhood.

     Debt of the burgh about £3000 sterling.

1783   *Printing* first introduced by Mr. Crerar, bookseller, High Street.

1784   *A curling club* formed.

     The old thorn-tree in the church-yard blown down ; the present tree a branch from the old one.

1785   Town Moor planted with firs.

     Umbrellas first introduced into Dunfermline. They caused great wonder.

     Great snow-storm, January 7th, followed by severe frost, which continued for 123 days.

1786   The ruins of Garvock House removed.

     The flesh-market built.

1787   ROBERT BURNS, poet, visits Dunfermline, 20th October.

1788   *Rev. Thomas Fernie,* of the Established Church, died.

1789   *Rev. John Fernie* inducted to second charge, Established Church.

     Public rejoicings in consequence of the King's (George III.) restoration to health.

     The Dunfermline Library established.

     Weaving.—Patterns or devices of flowers, birds, &c. introduced generally.

1790   *Rev. H. Fergus* inducted minister of Relief Church.

1790   A party secedes from the Burgher Meeting-house, organizes a congregation, and builds an Anti-Burgher Church in Chalmers Street.

Post-Office revenue about £300 per annum.

Rev. James Thomson, minister of the Established Church, died October 19th, and bequeathed £100 to the poor of the church.

1791   *Census.*— Population of the town, and suburbs of Pitten-crieff, 5192 souls.

Present thorn-tree planted in the churchyard over the spot where, according to tradition, the mother of Sir William Wallace was buried. (See 1784.)

Weaving.—About 1200 looms in the town.

Rev. Allan M'Lean, of the Chapel of Ease, Dunfermline, inducted to the first charge of the Established Church.

1792   *Town-House.*—In consequence of this building being found too small, two additional stories were added to it, the clock removed from the steeple, and placed in a turret of the new building.

J. Moodie, Esquire, elected Provost, which office he held for fifteen years.

Brucefield Spinning Mill built.

About forty-nine poor on the roll of the kirk-session.

1793   The Society of Weavers becomes a "Friendly Society."

Much political agitation about "Reform."

Great snow-storm; snow in several places from twelve to twenty feet deep in the town.

1795   The Society of Gardeners becomes a "Friendly Society."

1796   The meeting-house of the Burghers is considered incommodious; a new one is ordered to be built.

The press-gang visits Dunfermline and neighbourhood, and carries off some weavers and sailors with them.

Post-Office revenue about £350.

1797   *Water.*—*Great scarcity.* Water brought from the Cairn-cubie springs in wooden pipes 3 inches in diameter.

The "Queen's House" removed. A human skeleton found built up in one of the walls.

1798   The new Burgher Church in Queen Anne Street built.

Debt of the burgh £5000.

1799   *Dunfermline Volunteers* raised.

1799   A tannage begun in Clay Acres by Mr. Forfar.
1800   The congregation of " Original Burghers " formed ; they
          build a small chapel in Canmore Street.
       Great dearth of meal, &c., locally called the "black
          dearth." Indian corn meal introduced.
       Great destitution and sickness abounding. Meal 3s. 9d.
          per peck.
       Post-Office revenue £500.
       Distillery in St. Margaret's Street discontinued.
1801   *Census.*—First Government census. Population, town
          and suburbs, 5484.
       The famous violinist Neil Gow, and his son, visit
          Dunfermline.
1802   A congregation of Independents formed. They soon
          dissolve, and the greater part join the Baptists.
       Two severe shocks of earthquake felt.
1803   Baldridge Burn bridge carried away by a flood.
       Post-Office revenue £550. Stamp office £654 : 10s.
       Weaving.—Mr. D. Bonnar obtains a patent for an
          improvement in loom mounting. The trade pur-
          chases it from him for £600.
1804   A brick-work established at the " Footpath."
       Dunfermline Volunteers enrolled themselves in great
          numbers, as an "invasion" by Bonaparte was con-
          sidered "imminent." Drilling was carried on in the
          Bowling-green daily, amidst much enthusiasm.
       The British Linen Company establish a branch of their
          bank in the town.
       Marriages this year 77, baptisms 314, deaths 200.
1805   *Water.*—Private pipes introduced into some of the houses.
       Dunfermline illuminated for the victory gained by
          Lord Nelson at Trafalgar, October. A towns-
          man illuminates his windows with white and
          black candles—the white ones for the victory,
          the black ones for the death of Nelson !
1806   *Weaving.*—John Philp makes various improvements on
          those of David Bonnar (see year 1803).
       Spinning Mill, the first in the town, by Mr. G. Rontree,
          in Knabbie Street, intended to spin yarn for the
          home manufacturers.
       Tambouring, a species of embroidering, extensively
          carried on by a large number of the females of the
          town.

1807   *Guildhall* founded 29th July. Masonic procession. The steeple 131 feet 9 inches high.

The Royal Tombs searched by J. G. Dalyell, Esq. Nothing found of any consequence.

The Town-Council ordered 34 new lamps for the town, which made the number 106.

A proposition was made to make a tunnel under the Firth of Forth, betwixt the north and south sides, near Rossyth.

The town legally assessed for the support of the poor.

An old ruinous tower, on the south-west corner of the Established Church, falls and kills five horses.

1808   *Debt* of the burgh, £10,450.

Weaving.—Henry Meldrum weaves a man's shirt without seams, and finishes it without the assistance of a needle.

The water conduit at "the Goat" rebuilt.

1809   In burgh records at this period the designations "the City," the "Lord Provost," are frequently met with.

Chartulary of the Abbey analysed, and a few extracts of it published by J. G. Dalyell, Esq.

Public rejoicings at the jubilee of His Majesty, he having entered on the fiftieth year of his reign—October.

1810   *Water.*—Filtering pits for the water furnished. The quantity of water discharged per hour found to average 900 gallons.

Fire engines procured from London.

1811   *Census.*—Population of the parish 11,649 ; of the town 6492 ; inhabited houses in the town 874.

The manufacture of tailors' thread introduced by Mr. Finlayson.

Police Bill for the improvement of the burgh, and for a set of watchmen, passed in Parliament—May.

1812   *Dunfermline Burns Club* instituted—January.

The Commercial Banking Company of Scotland establish a branch of their bank in the town.

The ruins of the Abbey and Palace undergo repair ; the date 1100, in cypher, discovered in one of the high windows of the Palace.

Railway between Dunfermline and Charlestown, for the conveyance of coal to the latter place, finished ; also one between Venterfair and Knabbie Row.

1812   *The Shoemakers' Society* formed.

      Election of Commissioners of districts commenced, 12th May, under Police Act.

1813   *Dunfermline Corn Market* established—January.

      Severe frost, lasted thirty-five days.

      Weaving.—Average value of table linen annually manufactured in the town, &c., about £100,000. About 1000 looms employed.

      Income tax of the parish £2680 : 6 : 11. Assessed taxes £2072 : 16 : 9.

      Weaving.—Henry Meldrum, who in 1808 wrought the seamless shirt, again displays his ingenuity by producing a more elaborate shirt without seam, and with no assistance from the needle except sewing on the buttons.

      Revenue of the burgh £1500.

      Revenue of the post-office £1050. Stamps £1515.

1814   Typhus fever rages with great severity in the town.

      Coals.—Average quantity annually wrought in the parish, 120,000 tons.

1815   Great rejoicings on the downfall of Paris and the result of the Battle of Waterloo, 18th June—the town illuminated.

      Weavers in the town number about 1100 ; scholars in the different schools 1194; street lamps supplied with oil 115 ; houses in the town, &c. 1024.

      Lancasterian School established in Priory Lane.

      Rev. Mr. Dalziel inducted minister in the Original Burgher Church.

      Campbell's Foundry removed from the Maygate to Clay Acres.

      Methodist Meeting-House, Maygate, erected.

      The Savings Bank established.

      Fernie's History of the town and parish published by John Millar.

      Voluntary Association for the support of the Poor instituted.

      New Burgh High School founded—February.

1816   *The Commercial Academy* founded. A masonic procession on the occasion.

      An old house called the "Sanctuary," in Maygate, rebuilt. It belonged to Mr. Meldrum.

1816   *John Reid*, teacher, dies, aged seventy years. He was
for nearly fifty years teacher in the town, and was
greatly respected.

1817   A Radical meeting held on the Anti-Burgher Brae, behind
the Chalmers Street Church.

Rev. George Bell Brand inducted minister of the Chapel
of Ease.

Rev. Peter Chalmers inducted to the second charge of the
Abbey Church.

A new coinage of George III. arrived at the Bank of
Scotland's office, under military escort—April.

"*The Gardener's Land*" feued for buildings.

The remains of William Buchanan, late merchant in the
town, discovered in the "Magazine," under the ruins
of the Abbey.

Provost Low, "the bone-setter," died, aged eighty-four.

The eastern part of the ancient church originally founded
by Canmore considered incommodious; a new one
to be built.

Old Burgh School removed.

Hairy Braes Spinning Mill begun.

1818   Dispute between the Magistrates and the ministers of
the "old Kirk respecting the power of ringing the
church bells. Decided by the Court of Session to
be invested with the ministers of the Abbey Church,
as being connected with ecclesiastical affairs."

Guildhall sold, and converted into a hotel.

Tomb of King Robert Bruce.—While proceeding with
the clearing away of the ground for the foundation of the new East Church, the workmen
came accidentally upon a vault, which was
found to be the tomb of King Robert Bruce,
the hero of Bannockburn and deliverer of
Scotland, whose remains had lain there for
489 years.

At the time of the general wreck of the
Abbey in 1560, a costly marble tomb or
monument, which had been erected over the
remains of the Scottish King, and which was
said to have been designed in Paris, was, along
with other magnificent tombs, entirely destroyed. Some fragments of this gilded marble
tomb were found.

1818 Great public demonstration and masonic procession at the laying of the foundation stone of the New Church, 10th March.

1819 *Re-entombment of King Robert Bruce.*—His remains were re-entombed 5th November, when the walls of the New Church were about seven feet high. Intense interest was manifested throughout the entire kingdom on the occasion.

Debt of the burgh £20,401 : 4 : 10.

Eastern Church, the last remnant of, removed.

Revenue of the Post Office £1017 : 17 : 5.

The *"Whipmen and Gardeners'"* procession discontinued.

1820 GEORGE IV. proclaimed king by the Magistrates, &c. at the Canon, Cross, and site of the Eastern Port, February.

Rev. Mr. Barlas inducted to Chalmers Street Church.

Three pitmen publicly whipped for assault upon a woman. A troop of dragoons attended, as a general rising was feared.

Reid's Park feued for building.

Illumination of the town in consequence of the "Bill of Pains and Penalties" against Queen Caroline having been thrown out of the House of Commons.

1821 *Census.*—Population of the parish, 13,690; of the town, 8041.

Female Beneficent Society instituted.

Rev. James Husband, D.D., died 14th May. He was minister of the first charge in Queen Anne Street Church, died in the forty-sixth year of his ministry, and was buried beside Ralph Erskine's grave.

The choosing of a successor to Dr. Husband occasioned violent disturbances for about six years, during which about 200 candidates preached to the congregation (*vide* 1825).

Abbey Church finished ; opened for Divine Service 30th September.

Rev. Dr. Black, D.D., minister of Chalmers Street Church, died.

1822 A new highway to Grange Farm in progress of formation.

Provost Major Wilson died; he was fourteen years in office.

Post-Office revenue £1009 : 2 : 1.

Grand Crispin Procession,—about 10,000 spectators.

The Old Kirk seatings, &c. disposed of by public auction. "King's loft" now at Abbotsford.

William Cant invented a machine for "walking on the water."

Great snow-storm. Snow in some parts of the town drifted to the height of 15 feet.

1823   "*Bowling-green*" added to the churchyard.

The west angle of the "Old Kirkyard," facing St. Catherine's Wynd, removed, &c.

Rev. J. M'Farlane, second charge of Secession Church, Queen Anne Street, died.

A life insurance society established.

A regular survey of the town and suburbs published by Mr. Wood, Canaan, Edinburgh.

Weaving in great depression,—wages consequently low; numbers out of work.

1824   *Four ale and porter breweries* in town. Excise duty, &c., £6000, including licenses of all kinds.

Post-Office revenue £1867 : 19 : 3½.

The old barley mill at Millport erected.

The Western District of Fife Bible Society established.

A coach called the "Antiquary" established to run between Dunfermline and Edinburgh—October.

Farmers' meeting for the exhibition of live stock revived, 22d November.

New weights and measures, according to Act of Parliament, brought to the town.

1825   Two young men condemned to be executed at Dunfermline for housebreaking, receive the King's pardon, and are transported for life. The Edinburgh gallows was brought to the town for the intended execution.

Pilmuir feued for building.

Dunfermline Ladies' Society in aid of Female Education in India established.

About 900 of the Queen Anne Street Congregation obtain a separation, who establish another Secession Church in Dunfermline. They meet *pro tem.* in the *Maygate Chapel,* and the following year they founded St. Margaret's Church.

A Mechanics' Institution established, 20th September.

1825 *Brucefield Spinning Mill* (the "East Mill") greatly damaged by fire—November.

Weaving.—The Jacquard weaving machine first introduced into Dunfermline by Mr. Alexander Robertson and Messrs. R. & J. Kerr. They came into general use about 1830.

Pollok's *Course of Time.* A considerable portion of this famous poem was written in Dunfermline, while the author was staying here for a change of air, he being in delicate health.

1826 *Philosophical Society* established by four young men of the town ; it continued for three years.

A coach called the "Aurora" commences running from Kirkcaldy to Glasgow, *via* Dunfermline, 5th June.

St. Margaret's Church, East Port Street, founded July.

Dunfermline Drawing Academy instituted for pattern designing 17th July ; ceases in 1831.

A new road formed to the north, through Broomhead old quarry.

A "*Society of Friends*" established.

Bridge Street Buildings finished.

1827 One hundred and seventeen licensed taverns in the town and suburbs.

Rev. A. Fisher inducted minister of Secession Church, Queen Anne Street ; died 1829, September.

Inglis' Park laid out into new streets.

Great snow-storm, Saturday, 2d March ; a number of the churches unopened. Snow about four feet deep all over the town.

Dunfermline Florist Society established—May.

Dunfermline Friendly Institution established.

One manufacturer of tobacco in town worked up during the past year 60,000 lbs. of the raw material

The soap manufacturer makes 216,282 lbs. of hard soap.

The *Dunfermline Register* first published by Mr. Millar.

The *Clay Acres Spinning Mill* erected.

1828 *Dunfermline Missionary Prayer Meeting* formed, 14th Jan.

Phrenological Society instituted.

Rev. R. Brown, minister of St. Margaret's Chapel, died.

History of Dunfermline, by Mr. Andrew Mercer, published by Mr. J. Millar.

1828   *Rev. J. Law* inducted to St. Margaret's Church.

About 1700 looms employed in the town and neighbourhood.

Milton Green Spinning Mill erected.

Sunday Schools connected with and in the town amount to 19 ; scholars about 500.

Part of the burgh lands sold to R. Downie, Esq. of Appin.

Dunfermline Gas-Light Company established, with a capital of £6000.

Mr. Kirkland's spinning mill founded.

Meteorology.—From January 1, 1828, to December 31, 1828, there were 157 rainy days, 51 of which were days of incessant rain. The number of days which the wind blew from W. and S.W. 216, from S. 39, easterly 51, and northerly 59.

1829   An old house in "the Horse-market," the last representative of "Grey Dunfermling," removed—May.

Great thunderstorm, 3d August.

Dumfermline lighted with gas, 24th October.

Marriages this year 150 ; deaths about 320.

Post-Office revenue about £1300.

1830   A *Temperance Society* established 15th February.

An *Infant School* instituted, 9th March.

WILLIAM IV. proclaimed king, by the Magistrates, &c. at the Canon, the Cross, and the East Port—July.

The Town Green shut up.

Golfdrum Spinning Mill begun.

Douglas Street opened.

A *Total Abstinence Society* formed by Mr. John Davie and some other members of the Dunfermline Temperance Society, 21st September. The pledge was drawn up by Mr. Davie, and the Society was the first in Scotland.

1831   *Great snow-storm*, the town drummer lost in a snowdrift.

Rev. James Young inducted to Queen Anne Street Church.

Census.—Population of the town and parish 17,068 ; of the town and suburbs 10,626.

Mr. Green, the celebrated aëronaut, ascended in his balloon from St. Margaret Street bleaching-green.

1831 *Reform Bill.*—Great rejoicings in Dunfermline at the second reading in the House of Commons.

Great Reform Procession on 10th of August.

1832 The Dunfermline electors stated to be 493.

Dye-work for the use of the manufacturers established by J. M. Low.

Cholera morbus appears in the suburbs of the town, 2d September, Thursday.

11th October kept with great solemnity as a fast, on account of the rapid spread of the disease.

Mr. William Cobbett delivers a lecture in the Maygate Chapel, October 15.

Splendid Reform Procession, 8th May, 10,000 spectators. Hustings fell; several persons severely hurt.

Cholera morbus.—The number of cases since the commencement 371 ; deaths 141. Extinguished November 17.

1833 Halybluid Acres feued for building.

Mr. Barlas, formerly minister of the Chalmers Street Meeting-house, opens a congregation in Maygate Chapel.

The Rev. Robert Cuthbertson inducted to Chalmers Street Church.

Southern part of Collier Row rebuilt, and named Bruce Street.

New Chapel of Ease finished, June 20th ; opened 23d.

Elgin Railway to Charlestown opened for passengers.

Centenary of the Secession Church held 11th December.

Census, &c.—Population of the parish, 31st December, about 19,000 ; of the town and suburbs, 12,000.

Places of worship in the town, 12. Streets, &c., 43.

Circumference of the town about $2\frac{1}{8}$ miles.

The Dunfermline Drawing Academy, which was established by some of the manufacturers in 1826, abandoned for want of public support.

1834 The houses, which until this period were only partially numbered, were now ordered to be numbered all over the town.

A branch from the Charlestown Railway, worked by horse-power, was brought into the west side of the Nether-town, for the conveyance of goods and passengers to Charlestown.

1834 *A new Baptist Church* built in East Queen Anne Street.

The Dunfermline Horticultural Society instituted this year.

The Dunfermline Scientific Association was instituted 28th November—David Lawrie, Esq., Preses.

1835 *St. Andrew's Church*, North Chapel Street, was made a *Quoad Sacra* Church.

A new Bleaching Machine was invented by William Cant.

The Town-house clock-dials were illuminated by gas.

Relief or Gillespie Church.—The Rev. Neil M'Michael, A.M., was ordained assistant and successor to the Rev. Henry Fergus, 11th August.

Debt of the burgh this year, £13,421 : 12 : 9½.

Weaving.—Flax to the value of £58,350 was purchased this year by the manufacturers of Dunfermline.

A course of twelve lectures on Physiology was delivered by the Rev. Mr. Barlas in Maygate Church.

1836 *The great annular eclipse of the sun* took place 15th May, on a Sunday afternoon. Great interest and some apprehension were manifested in connection with the unusual spectacle.

The Rev. Allan M'Lean, minister of the first charge in the Abbey Church, died 3d June.

Seven Spinning Mills in operation in the town.

Rev. Peter Chalmers inducted into the first charge in the Abbey Church.

The harvest of this year very late, and far below the average.

1837 *The Dunfermline Harmonists' Society* instituted by Mr. James Rankine, "Master of the Song."

The Rev. John Todd Brown ordained to the second charge, Dunfermline Abbey Church.

Rev. Henry Fergus, Relief Church, died.

Rev. George Barlas died in Viewfield House, 29th July.

Great stagnation in trade, and prevalence of typhus fever.

1838 *The Dunfermline burgh coal workings* were let on lease to a company. The burgh had previously worked its own coal at Townhill.

Rev. George Bell Brand, of St. Andrew's Church, died in the fifty-second year of his age.

1838 *The Dunfermline Savings Bank* was connected with the National Security Savings Bank. The business afterwards rapidly increased.

The Baldridge Works, built by Mr. R. Robertson, manufacturer, of Dunfermline and London, were unsuccessful, and were afterwards sold in 1855 to the Government for military barracks.

A course of Geological Lectures given by Mr. Rose, Geologist and Mineralogist, of Edinburgh.

1839 *Legal Assessment for the Poor* introduced early this year.

A course of Astronomical Lectures (with apparatus, &c.) was delivered by E. Henderson, LL.D., to large audiences in the Maygate and St. Margaret's churches.

The Rev. Andrew Sutherland ordained minister of St. Andrew's Church.

The Right Honourable James Abercrombie, M.P., Speaker of the House of Commons, called to the House of Peers under the title of Lord Dunfermline.

1840 Penny postage introduced. This boon was hailed with much satisfaction all over the country.

The North Church (Golfdrum) opened for public worship in November. Cost of the building £1673.

Premium of £10 offered for the best yarn beaming machine. The reward was equally divided between Robert Lawson, weaver, and James Robertson, wright.

1841 *Rev. James Gibson* ordained minister of the Maygate Church.

The Dunfermline Ornithological Society instituted.

" *Robert the Bruce* " *Tent of Rechabites* formed.

Rev. Charles Marshall inducted minister of the North Chapel, Golfdrum.

The Scottish Baptist Church, James' Street, originally formed in 1805, divided, and was formed into two congregations, one in James' Street, the other in North Inglis Street.

The municipal boundary of the burgh was this year extended to suit the increasing population.

The Rev. Neil M'Michael appointed Professor of Systematic Theology and Church History by the Relief Synod.

1842 *Congregational Chapel.*—This church was opened in

1842   Canmore Street for public worship—the Rev. George
          Thomson pastor.

Mr. Andrew Mercer, one of the historians and poets of
          Dunfermline, died July 12th.

The number of licensed houses (including grocers' shops)
          where spirits, ales, &c. are sold, is 140.

In the autumn of this year there was a great strike
          amongst the Dunfermline weavers for a increase of
          wages, which caused much loss and suffering.

The Trinity Episcopal Church in Queen Anne Place
          was opened for public worship 25th October.

Number of schools in the parish in 1842, 33 ; of scholars,
          2200.

1843   *The Poor's-house*, built on the site of the Old Town Green,
          was finished and occupied in July, having accom-
          modation for 130 persons.

Great excitement in the town and neighbourhood in
          connection with the *non-intrusion* question, and the
          subsequent building of new places of worship for
          the Free Church in town and country.

1844   *The Free Abbey Church* was finished, and opened for
          public worship in January. It was built on the
          site occupied by the " Auld Licht Kirk."

" Historical and Statistical Account of Dunfermline,"
          by the Rev. Peter Chalmers, was published.

Baths were established in Queen Anne Street this year
          by Mr. Edward Young, slater.

Episcopal or Trinity Church, Queen Anne's Place—the
          Rev. William Bruce ordained minister.

Chalmers Street Church.—The Rev. R. T. Walker of
          Comrie was ordained 16th November.

1845   *The New Prison* was finished and occupied early in
          January.

The Rev. James French, of St. Bernard's Church,
          Edinburgh, was inducted to the second charge of the
          Abbey Church, Dunfermline, 2d May.

The Burgh Tron and site of Fish Market removed to
          Black's Close, High Street.

1846   *The Western Bank of Scotland* opened a branch this
          year.

In consequence of the frequent want of water, *a new
          Water Company* was formed, with a share capital

1846 of £13,500. The water was to be brought from Craigluscar to the town.

A grand procession, public meeting, concert and soiree took place in Dunfermline, " in honour of the repeal of the Corn Laws, 3d July."

The East of Scotland Malleable Iron Company was formed.

An extraordinary flood caused much destruction on Sabbath evening, 5th July.

The Roman Catholic Congregation numbered 397 members, and a resident clergyman was appointed.

1847 *A public dinner* was given to the Earl of Elgin previous to his departure for Canada as Governor.

The Free Abbey Schools opened by Mr. Bruce on the 15th February.

The first turf of the Stirling and Dunfermline Railway was cut by James Anstruther, Esquire, in a field near Milesmark. A grand procession afterwards took place.

The union of the Secession and Relief Churches was accomplished, under the designation of the United Presbyterian Church, 13th May.

Free St. Andrew's Church, St. Margaret's Street, was opened for public worship, May 23. The services were conducted by the Rev. Dr. Candlish of Edinburgh.

The Rev. J. Middleton was inducted minister of St. Andrew's Church.

The construction of the Railway between Dunfermline and Thornton, in continuation of the Stirling and Dunfermline line, was commenced in October.

1848 *The Malleable Iron Company* commenced operations on the 2d day of August. It afterwards proved a failure.

1849 The clocks throughout the country altered to Greenwich time. The Dunfermline clock was put forward twelve and a half minutes.

Mr. James Rankine, " Master of the Song," and an accomplished vocalist, died in April, aged fifty-two years.

Mr. George Martin appointed parish clerk and "Master of the Song"—April.

A Statue was erected to the memory of the Rev. Ralph

1849   Erskine in front of Queen Anne Street Church,—the
sculptor, Mr. Handyside Ritchie of Edinburgh.

The Rev. Charles Rogers inducted minister of the
North Church, July 1849.

The *cholera* made great ravages this year, but it was not
so severe as in 1832.   There were prayer-meetings
held in Queen Anne Street Church.

The Rev. Mr. Craig was inducted minister of the Independent Church.

The Rev. James M'Kenzie from Annan was inducted
into the Free Church in Canmore Street.

Weaving by Steam Power.—After some unsuccessful attempts by Mr. Kirkland and others,
Messrs. Andrew and Henry Reid, manufacturers, were the first to succeed in introducing
steam power in damask weaving, which they
did in their factory in Pilmuir Street this
year.

Gillespie Church opened for Divine Service, November 4.

The railway between Dunfermline and Crossgates was
opened on the 14th December.

1850   *Craigluscar water* was introduced into the pipes of the
town on the evening of 15th May.

The Malleable Iron Works at Transey ceased working.

The first railway trip by the Edinburgh, Perth, and
Dundee Railway to Dunfermline was given on the
17th of July.

The *first trial railway trip* between Dunfermline and
Alloa took place, 8th August, on the Stirling and
Dunfermline Railway.

Archibald Haxton, rector of the Grammar School, died
in October, after a long and faithful service of forty
years.

Robert Gilfillan, poet, died 4th December.

A farewell soiree was given to the Rev. John Law on
his leaving for Innerleithen.

1851   The *well-known Geologist, Hugh Miller* delivered two
lectures on Geology in the Free Abbey Church, Canmore Street, to large audiences.

Population of town and parish in 1851, 21,234 ; town
and suburbs, within the parliamentary boundary,
13,861.

1851   *St. Leonard's Steam Power Factory*, erected by Messrs. Erskine Beveridge & Company, was opened for work in June. After this period hand-loom weaving was rapidly discontinued.

The Elgin Bleachfield, for boiling and bleaching linen yarn, was commenced by Mr. Ralph Walker.

The Rev. David Russell was ordained minister of St. Margaret's Church on 3d September.

1852   *A locomotive engine* was, for the first time, put on the Dunfermline and Charlestown Railway to facilitate passenger traffic.

The Dunfermline Bowling Club was established this year.

The Post-Office removed to the County Buildings at the Cross.

At a public meeting a presentation was made to the Rev. R. Cuthbertson, on his leaving Dunfermline for England.

Rev. Alex. M'Auslane ordained pastor of Canmore Street Independent Church.

The Music Hall, Guildhall Street, was opened, and a grand concert given on the occasion—Mr William Clark proprietor.

Public races and games took place in August this year.

1853   *Master of the Song, &c.*—Mr. John Locke appointed to this office. There was a large number of candidates.

Powder magazine built on Garvock Hill for the store of gunpowder.

1854   Stone pavements ordered by the Town-Council to be laid in all the streets.

The foundation stone of the new School of Arts was laid in March this year.

Scottish Baptist Church.—The Congregation of Scottish Baptists, established here in 1805, broke up as a congregation in 1854, when they joined the English Baptists. They sold their place of worship to the Catholic Apostolic Congregation, who worshipped in Maygate Chapel.

Cholera broke out with great violence in Limekilns and Charlestown.

The Electric Telegraph was first introduced into the Post-Office, Dunfermline, 4th October.

1854   *Great depression in trade* prevailed, 800 looms being idle,
and 500 men out of employment.

Mr. Louis opened the first photographic establishment in
Dunfermline.

1855   *The new Act for the Registration of Births, Marriages,
and Deaths* came into operation 1st January.

Evangelical Union.—This congregation assembled for
worship in the Masons' Hall, the Rev. J. Frame
pastor.

The Abbey Park Bowling Club Green was laid out this
year.

1856   *The Ordnance Map Department* intimated that they had
decided to designate Dunfermline a city.   This was
done at the instigation of Dr. Ebenezer Henderson.

M. Kossuth, of Hungary, visited Dunfermline, and the
freedom of the burgh was conferred upon him.

1857   *Post-Office pillar letter-boxes* first introduced, March 1.
The number of letters which passed through Dunferm-
line Post-Office between October 31, 1855, and
October 31, 1856, amounted to 320,000, or about
890 per day.

1858   *St. Andrew's Church.*—The Rev. James Rose inducted
minister in January.

The Western Bank of Scotland failed.   Many persons in
the town and all over Scotland suffered great loss.

The Rev. Thomas Smith was ordained minister of the
United Presbyterian Congregation in Maygate Chapel,
April 21.

Wilson's School, New Row, was opened on the 17th of
May for the free education of children in the town
and suburbs.   A preference was given to children of
the name of Wilson, whose parents belonged to the
Free Church.

Rev. Robert Walker, minister of Chalmers Street
Church, resigned his charge as minister.   He afterwards went to Ballarat, Australia.

1859   *Burns Centenary,* 25th January, was celebrated in Dunfermline with great enthusiasm.

The freedom of the burgh was conferred on Dr. E.
Henderson for his antiquarian researches, and in
recognition of his services in connection with the
restoration of the burgh to its ancient status as a

1859   city. A public dinner was given to him, at which Provost Robertson presided.

The Abbey Park and Dunfermline Bowling Green clubs were united.

The Dunfermline Press, weekly newspaper, was established this year.

The Rev. A. M. Jarvie was ordained minister of Chalmers Street Church, 7th September.

The Dunfermline Volunteer Corps originated 14th November.

1860   *St. Leonard's Schools*, in connection with St. Leonard's Factory, were erected.

The Abbey Gardens Steam Power Factory was erected by Messrs. Henry Reid & Son, and was opened in September.

Louis Blanc, the French Deputy, visited Dunfermline, and delivered a political lecture in the Music Hall.

1861   *The Dunfermline Co-operative Society* was inaugurated in January.

A public dinner and presentation was given to Ex-Provost Robertson for his faithful public services. Provost Whitelaw presided, and Erskine Beveridge, Esq., made the presentation.

The Volunteer Corps of Dunfermline created much excitement as it turned out in public for the first time, and paraded through the streets.

Population of town and parish, 20,952; town and suburbs, 13,504.

Chalmers Street Church (the old Anti-Burgher Kirk) was removed, and the foundation stone of a new and more commodious place of worship was laid in July.

1862   *Chalmers Street Church* finished and opened for public worship.

The Regality House, East Nethertown Street, was this year removed.

1863   *The Dunfermline Advertiser*, published for twenty-nine years by J. Millar, terminated its existence this year.

The New Cemetery was opened for interments on 31st July.

The Public Park, Hallbank, was opened in August. The Dunfermline and Charlestown Railway was discontinued.

1864   "Burgh Life in Dunfermline in the Olden Time," a

Lecture by the Rev. William Ross, Aberdour, was published this year.

1865 *The Bothwell Steam Power Weaving Factory* was erected in Elgin Street in June.

The Rev. James Mitchell Robbie was inducted minister of the Congregational Church, Canmore Street.

1866 *The "Malcolm Canmore" Lodge* was instituted in January.

Mr. Joseph Noel Paton, R.S.A., was this year appointed Her Majesty's Limner for Scotland.

The Dunfermline Co operative Society's New Buildings, at the top of Randolph Street, were commenced 4th June. There was a public procession on the occasion. The first year's transactions reached the sum of £6471 : 19 : 8.

The cone of the Town-House spire re-erected.

The Gymnasium of the Dunfermline Athletic Club was opened 13th of May. The Honorary President, John Whitelaw, Esq., Provost, in the chair, Mr. Andrew Blair Secretary.

Messrs. J. and T. Alexander's Power-Loom Factory in Damside Street was opened this year. It occupies the site of the old dam.

1868 *Castle Blair Steam Power Weaving Factory* was erected this year by Messrs. Inglis & Company.

The Old Market Cross was re-erected this year at the east corner of Guildhall Street and High Street.

The beautiful monument or altar tomb to the memory of General Bruce, a member of the Elgin family, who was sometime tutor to H.R.H. the Prince of Wales, was erected in the Abbey Church, south transept, in October 1868. It was executed by Foley, the eminent sculptor.

For the better despatch of business, four bailies are henceforth to be elected instead of two. The names of the first four who were elected were Messrs. Morrison, Duncanson, Balfour, and Walker.

Presentation to Ex-Provost Whitelaw.—A public soiree was held in the Music Hall on 1st December in honour of Ex-Provost Whitelaw, at which he was presented with a testimonial, consisting of a costly timepiece and upwards of £200 worth of silver plate, in recognition of his valuable services to the town.

1869   *The Rev. James Mackenzie*, of Canmore Street Free Abbey Church, died 10th June, aged fifty-one years.

The Rev. James Young, of Queen Anne Street Church, died suddenly in his manse, 5th December, in the sixty-sixth year of his age, and thirty-ninth of his ministry.

1870   *Messrs. Hay & Robertson's Steam Power Weaving Factory* was erected in Foundry Street this year.

The Rev. James M. Shiach was ordained minister of Canmore Street Free Abbey Church, 18th of May.

The Rev. Peter Chalmers, D.D., &c., historian of Dunfermline, died 11th April 1870, in the eightieth year of his age, and fifty-second of his ministry.

Great scarcity of water having been felt for some years past, the authorities resolved to increase the supply by bringing water from Loch Glow, distant six miles, but the scheme was so keenly opposed by the public that it was abandoned.

About this period Mr. George Lauder, a townsman, advocated with great spirit and persistency the "Devon Scheme."

The Rev. Robert French, M.A., was ordained minister of Queen Anne Street Church, 5th October. He resigned in 1872.

Evangelical Union Church.—The Rev. John Adam, pastor since 1869, demitted his charge.

The Rev. John Pitt was ordained minister of the second charge, Dunfermline Abbey Church, 22d September.

1871   *The "King Robert the Bruce" Lodge* of the Order of Foresters was instituted on the 21st January.

The "Bruce" Lodge, No. 280, of the Independent Order of Good Templars, was instituted at Dunfermline, 23d January.

Population.—Town and parish in April 1871, 23,116 ; population of the town within the new extended boundary, 14,958.

1872   *Evangelical Union Church.*—The Rev. James Foote inducted minister of this church.

Palace Ruins.—The proprietorship was settled in favour of the Crown, and against the claims of Mr. Hunt, by the House of Lords, 25th September, after twenty years' litigation.

1872   *Temperance Association.*—The "Queen Mary" Lodge, No. 8, was instituted in Dunfermline 8th December.

1873   *City of Glasgow Bank.*—A branch of this bank was established in Queen Anne Street in January.

The "Concord" Lodge of Good Templars instituted.

The Dunfermline Orchestral Society was instituted.

First School Board election took place in March.

The new Roman Catholic Chapel in Martyrs' Place was opened.   Bishop Strain of Edinburgh officiated.

Queen Anne Street Church.—The Rev. Robert Alexander, minister of Buckhaven, was inducted minister of this church, 1st October.

The Dunfermline Savings Bank, East Port Street, was built this year.

1874   *The Rev. Neil M'Michael, D.D.*, minister of Gillespie Church, Dunfermline, and Professor of Ecclesiastical History, &c. in the United Presbyterian Church, died 3d April.

Caledonian Steam Power Weaving Factory erected in Knabbie Street by Messrs. Steel & Company.

Joseph Paton, Esq., F.S.A., antiquarian and pattern designer, died 14th April.   He was unsurpassed as a pattern designer, and was much esteemed by his fellow-townsmen.   His private museum, containing rare and valuable antique furniture, &c. &c., was at all times generously thrown open to public inspection.

The Rev. Wm. Johnstone, D.D., of Limekilns U.P. Church, died 24th May, aged seventy-four years.   For fifty-one years he was minister there.

The Albany Steam Power Weaving Factory was erected in Gardeners' Street by Messrs. Walker, Reid, & Co.

1875   *The Rev. John M'Farlane, LL.D.*, died in London on 7th February.   He was a very popular preacher, and the author of numerous able works on Divinity, &c.

Part of the old Palace wall at the Pends was this year removed, and an iron railing substituted.

The Rev. J. W. Dunbar was inducted minister of Gillespie Church on 24th March.

Badges of office.—It was agreed that the Provost and the four Bailies should be provided with badges of distinction to wear while in office.

1875 *Mr. Lauder* and some others were the means of stirring up the public, and getting a very largely signed petition sent in to the Council, asking that body to " adopt the necessary means, by applying to Parliament, for obtaining for Dunfermline a supply of water from the River Devon."

The Council took action upon the receipt of that petition, and ultimately adopted Glensherup Burn (a tributary of the Devon), as the spot where an ample supply could be obtained.

Baptist Church, Maygate Street.—The Rev. J. T. Hagen was inducted minister of this Church—October.

The last meeting of Council was held in the old Town-House, prior to its being removed to make way for the new Town-House Buildings, December 13, 1875.

1876 *The Rev. William George* ordained minister of Chalmers Street Church, 28th March.

Victoria Steam Power Weaving Factory was erected at Grantsbank Street, by Messrs. Inglis and Company.

The Rev. David Imrie was inducted minister of St. Andrew's Free Church. (He succeeded the Rev. Andrew Brydie.)

St. Margaret's Hall.—The foundation stone was laid in June this year.

New Town-house.—The foundation stone was laid 11th October. A great masonic procession took place.

The Branch Bank of the British Linen Company in the High Street was built this year, and was opened on 18th September.

1877 *The number of employees at the factories in the town.*—There were 5930 operatives connected with the eleven factories. Many of them come daily from the neighbouring towns and villages.

Dunfermline Co-operative Society.—It was found that the transactions of this society during the sixteenth year of its existence amounted to £52,431 : 8 : 5.

Carnegie Baths opened.—Those splendid baths, the munificent gift of Andrew Carnegie, Esq., of New York, a native of Dunfermline, and which cost upwards of £5000, were publicly opened on the 12th of June by the donor himself, while on a visit to his native city.

1877   *The freedom of the city* was afterwards conferred on Mr. Carnegie.

New Water Scheme.—The first sod of the New Water Works was cut by Kenneth Mathieson, Esq., Provost of Dunfermline, at Glensherup, on the 29th of June.

The works for conveying the sewage of Dunfermline to Charlestown were completed in September, at a cost of £10,000.

Dunfermline and Edinburgh Railway was opened for traffic on 1st November.

1878   *St. Margaret's Hall Organ.*—A bazaar was held in this hall on April 23d, 24th, and 27th, to raise funds for an organ, which realised the handsome sum of £1851 : 7 : 8½.

The names of some of the streets were altered.

The Townhill Church was opened for Divine Service in May.

The Dunfermline Tan-Works destroyed by fire; loss amounted to about £14,000.

Glensherup water was first brought into the town direct on the 6th September. Since then a bountiful supply of excellent water has been obtained for every householder.

St. Margaret's Hall Organ was opened, and a grand concert given on the occasion, 1st October.

City of Glasgow Bank Branch in Dunfermline closed in consequence of the failure of the bank, which was regarded as almost a national calamity.

1879   *The New Factory Act.*—Mr. Cross' Factory Act came into operation, January 1st.

Honorary Degree.—The Senatus of the Aberdeen University conferred the degree of D.D. on the Rev. Alexander Mitchell, North Church.

1880   *Fast-Days.*—The United Presbyterian Churches in the town agreed to discontinue Fast-Day Services.

St. Margaret's Stone.—Funds were raised and steps taken to properly fix and preserve this ancient "resting-place" of Queen Margaret on the Queensferry Road. The work was completed in October 1879.

The number of voters for the burgh this year is 2283.

1880 *Death of Ebenezer Henderson, LL.D.*—On the 2d of November died Dr. E. Henderson. He was the author of several astronomical and other works, was an enthusiastic antiquarian, and the writer of the "Annals of Dunfermline." He was a true and loyal son of the old city he loved so well.

New Commercial School.—This fine seminary was opened in November.

The New Town-House was opened to the inspection of the public. To Provost Mathieson the credit is due of carrying out the New Town-house scheme.

Great Gale.—A strong gale swept over Dunfermline and did much damage to property. The same gale destroyed the Tay Bridge, which caused the loss of many lives.

Mr. Carnegie presented his native city with the handsome sum of £5000, which he afterwards increased to £8000, for a Free Public Library, to be placed under the "Libraries Act."

The Rev. James French of the Abbey Church died. The Rev. John Pitt appointed to the first charge in the Abbey Church.

Pitfirrane Estate.—This estate, which for nearly five hundred years had been in the possession of the Halket family, and which was purchased by Mr. L. Dalgleish in 1877, is again offered for sale.

Her Royal Highness Princess Mary, Duchess of Teck, accompanied by the Countess of Hopetoun, arrived at Dunfermline. They visited various places of interest in the city, such as the Abbey, St. Margaret's Tomb, the Palace ruins and Monastery, &c. &c.

Her Majesty's Surveyor of Works for Scotland, accompanied by the Chief Secretary of the Board of Works, visited the city, and inspected the Crown property, and gave instructions for the carrying out of much-needed improvements on the Abbey, the Palace ruins, &c., but more especially on St. Margaret's tomb, which had been suffering from neglect.

Note. – Those improvements have since been carried out, but still it is greatly to be regretted that neither stone nor slab exists to tell to visitors and strangers the spot around which are the royal tombs. Neither is there anything in the New Church to mark the exact spot where repose the remains of Scotland's great hero, King Robert Bruce.

LIST OF THE PROVOSTS OF DUNFERMLINE FOR THE LAST 150 YEARS.

According to Dr. E. HENDERSON, it appears that there were twenty-one Abbot-Provosts of Dunfermline, between the years 1128 and 1395, after which period Lay Aldermen—*Praepositi*—or Provosts were elected. The following is a list of the latter from the year 1734 to the present time :—

THE MARQUIS OF TWEEDDALE,	1734		GEORGE MELDRUM,	1830
LORD CHARLES HAY,	1739		JOHN KER,	1831
SIR PETER HALKET,	1752		HENRY RUSSELL,	1836
*ALEXANDER WEDDERBURN,	1755		GEORGE BIRRELL,	1836
MAJOR FRANCIS HALKET,	1758		JAMES MORRIS,	1838
DAVID TURNBULL,	1760		ERSKINE BEVERIDGE,	1842
JOHN WILSON,	1765		H. KIDD (interim),	1843
JOHN KIRK,	1774		JAMES S. RONALDSON,	1843
DAVID TURNBULL,	1778		WILLIAM KINNIS,	1849
JOHN WILSON,	1783		ERSKINE BEVERIDGE,	1853
ADAM LOW,	1787		ROBERT ROBERTSON,	1854
JOHN WILSON,	1789		JOHN WHITELAW,	1861
JAMES MOODIE,	1792		HENRY REID,	1868
JOHN WILSON,	1807		KENNETH MATHIESON,	1871
MAJOR DAVID WILSON,	1808		JAMES WALLS,	1877
JOHN SCOTLAND,	1822		ROBERT DONALD,	1883
JAMES BLACKWOOD,	1824			

Note.—The above Mr. WEDDERBURN went to London. He afterwards became Solicitor-General, then Attorney-General ; in 1780 he was created Lord Loughborough, and in January 1793 became Lord Chancellor of England. He was made Earl of Rosslyn in 1801, died in 1805, and was interred in St. Paul's Cathedral.

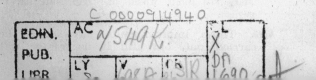